I0812878

IMAGES
of America

NEWTON

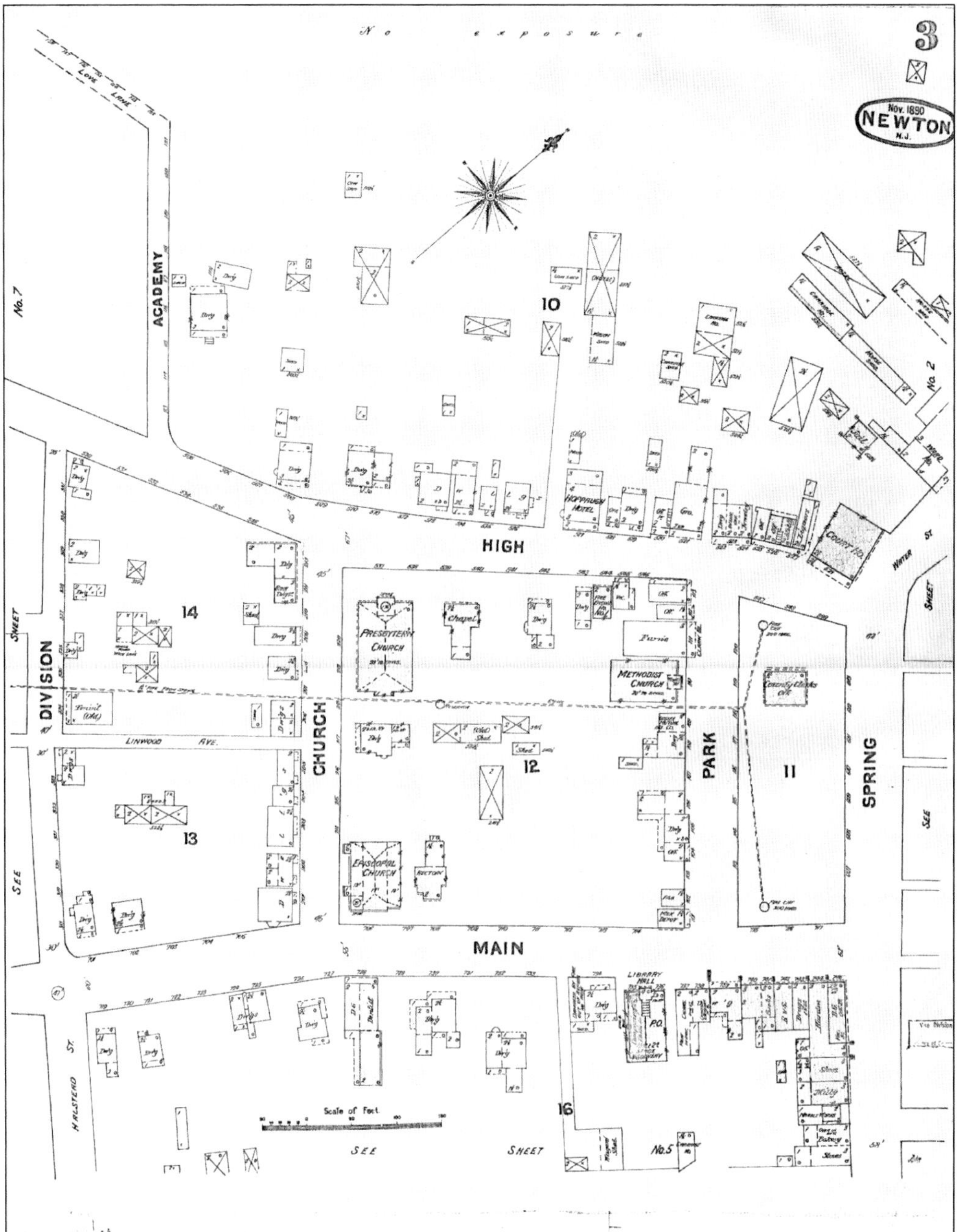

Newton is shown here in 1890, from the Sanborn Fire Insurance map.

IMAGES
of America

NEWTON

Kate Gordon
and Wayne T. McCabe

ARCADIA
PUBLISHING

ISBN 978-0-7385-4620-9

Published by Arcadia Publishing
Charleston, South Carolina

Printed in the United States of America

Library of Congress Catalog Card Number: 2006926834

For all general information contact Arcadia Publishing at:
Telephone 843-853-2070
Fax 843-853-0044
E-mail sales@arcadiapublishing.com
For customer service and orders:
Toll-Free 1-888-313-2665

Visit us on the Internet at www.arcadiapublishing.com

*The authors would like to dedicate
this book of memories to the memory of their fathers,
Donald Gordon and Thomas Joseph McCabe III,
and also to the memory of Oliver Watson Struble Jr.,
who welcomed an outlander into his Sussex County family
and introduced him to the intimate delights of local history.*

Contents

Acknowledgments

History is a cumulative science. Without the efforts of those who went before us, deliberately or unconsciously, to preserve our heritage, there would be no history. Therefore, the authors would first and foremost like to thank the unsung heroes of Sussex County history, the too-often anonymous writers, photographers, album compilers, and story-tellers who left us a record of their worlds and lives. In addition, we are grateful to the many friends and colleagues who have assisted in this project: Kevin Wright, Curator of the Steuben House in River Edge, who did much of the pioneering research on the history of Newton's buildings and businesses; Jan Gminder, of the Nostalgia Shop in Newton, the Merriam House, the *New Jersey Herald*, the Newton Fire Museum, and the Historical Society of Stillwater Township, all of whom generously loaned us photographs from their collections; the reference staff of the Sussex County Library, who were willing to answer all sorts of arcane questions; Louis Budd Jr. and Mary Goldsmith Struble, who shared their memories of early Newton; and perhaps most importantly, our spouses, Stephen W. Cox and Susan Struble McCabe, who have supported and encouraged all of our collaborations.

INTRODUCTION

The township of Newton was formed in 1750 as a precinct of Morris County, three years before the organization of Sussex County. Eleven years later, in 1761, the Royal Governor of New Jersey signed legislation establishing the Sussex County Courthouse and Jail on Jonathan Hampton's lands in Newton Township. From this quiet beginning as a county seat, Newton grew throughout the 19th century into a bustling commercial and industrial center.

In 1847, about ten years before the railroad came to Newton, Girard & Week opened the first photographic studio in town, using the recently developed Daguerrean process. As new photographic techniques were developed, more photographic "artists" opened their studios in Newton, and began taking pictures of not only people, but also of buildings, streets, and events. The advent of photographic negatives that could be used to produce multiple paper prints helped to assure that the images of Newton's past would be preserved for the future. By the time of the Civil War, I.G. Owen, J. Snyder, and A.C. Townley had each opened their own studios. They were followed by J.T. Jackson, M.F. Wintermute (Star Photographic Studio), and George Kintner, among others. These men, and their assistants, photographed the community during its greatest period of commercial, industrial, and residential growth.

In 1905, local merchants began commissioning these photographers to produce views showing town streets, buildings, the railroad yards, etc. The photographs were sent to local or overseas printing firms and transformed into picture postcards, which were sold for one or two cents each and mailed with a penny stamp. These prolific picture postcards, which were produced in mass quantities, provide us with many images of Newton from 1905 to the Second World War.

The authors have selected images of Newton from the earliest ones that are available (around the period of the Civil War) up to about 1920. The photographs in this book include original photographs from the studios mentioned, together with postcards produced for William C. Nicholls and other local merchants.

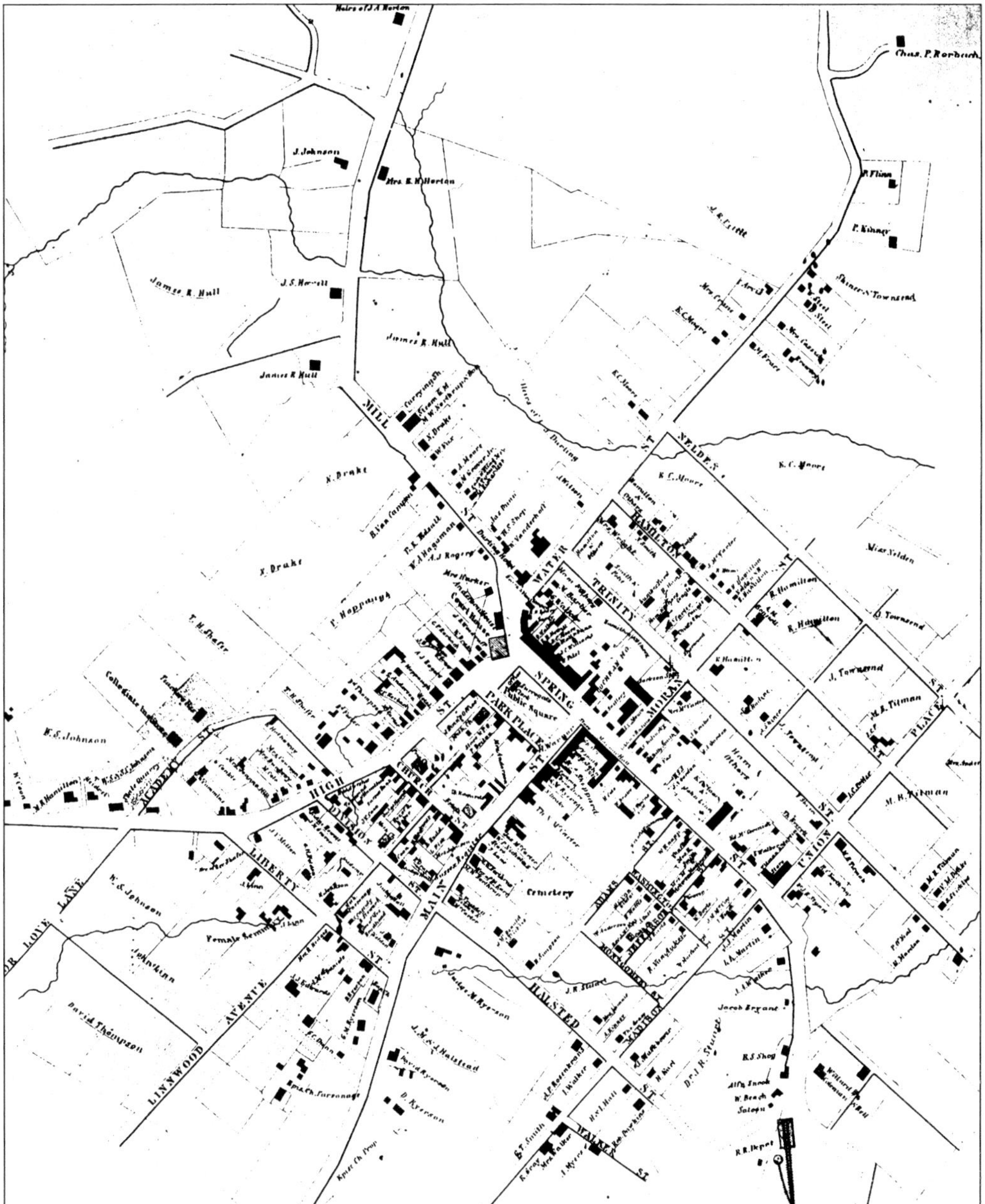

This detail of the town of Newton is from the 1860 Hopkins map of Sussex County.

One

Early Newton

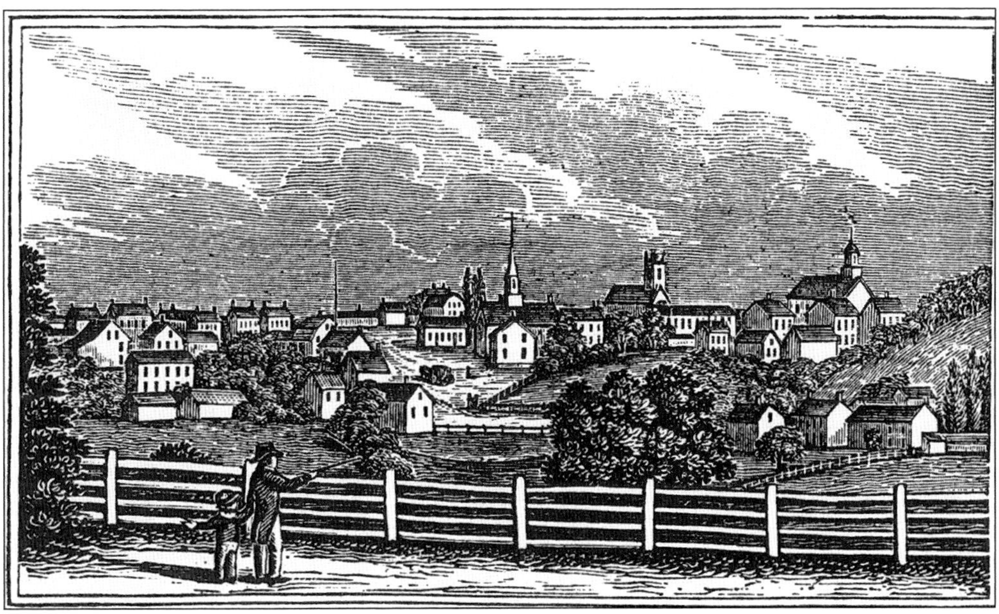

This 1854 woodcut of the town of Newton shows a quiet rural community. Looking south over the town from the Milford Road (now Smith Hill Road), one can see the county courthouse, as well as the spires of the Episcopal and Presbyterian churches. There is no sign of the industry that added to the bustle of the town at the turn of the century.

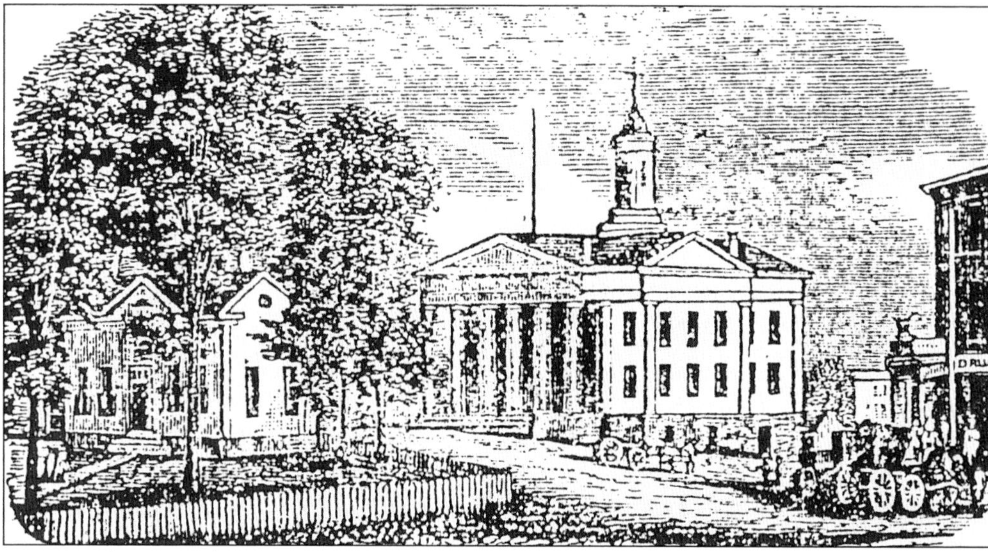

Newton's first courthouse was destroyed by fire on January 28, 1847. Before the year was out, a handsome new structure in the popular Greek Revival style was taking shape based on the plans of Newton's first architect, Amos A. Harrison. The new courthouse was dedicated on April 1, 1848, and Sheriff Osborne took command of his new office and jail in the basement.

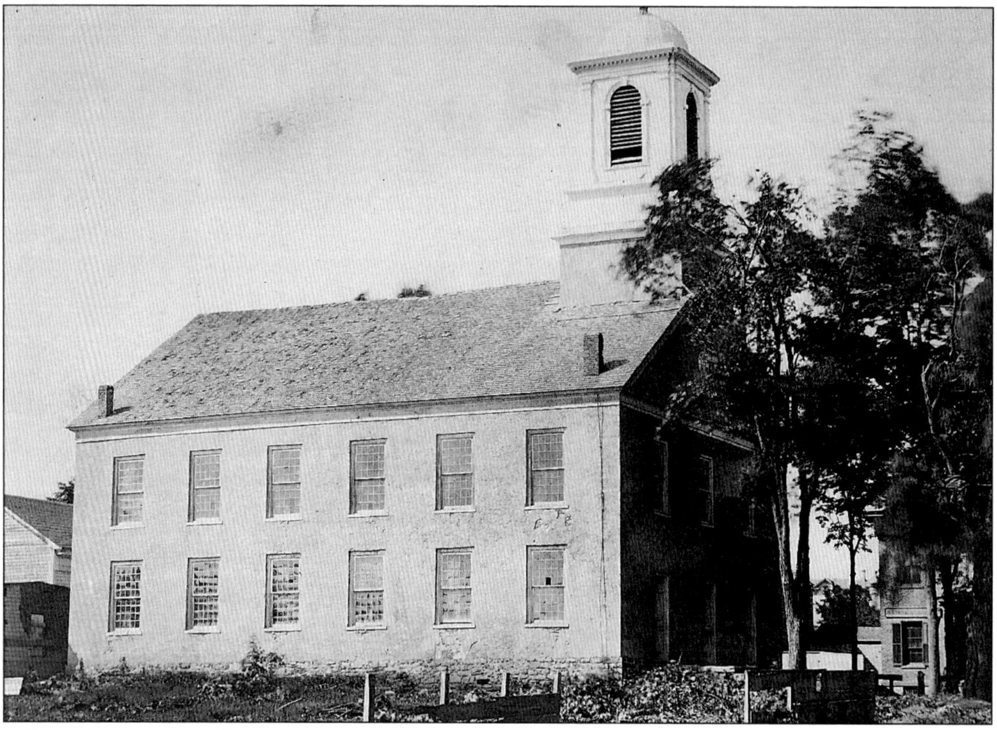

When Newton's Presbyterian congregation first formed in 1786, they began building a small sanctuary on Church Street, just east of High Street. Money was tight, so it took nearly 20 years to complete the first church. However, by 1827 the congregation was thriving and debt-free. They purchased the land between the original church lot and High Street, and in 1828 began construction of this impressive stone church facing High Street.

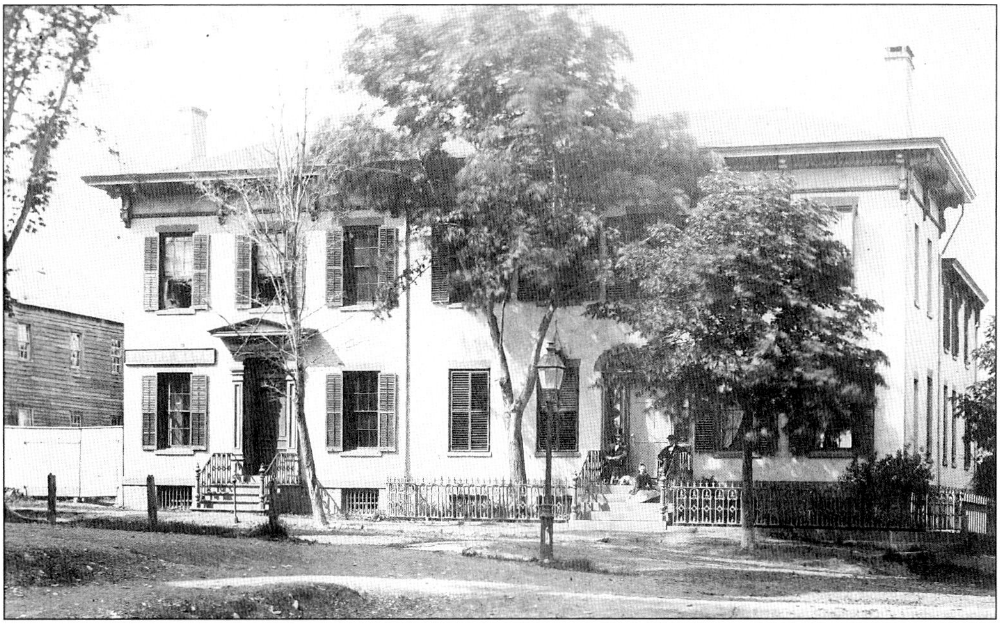

The Sussex Bank opened in 1818 on Main Street opposite the south corner of the square. At the time, it was the only bank in Sussex County, and remained so until 1865, to the benefit of Newton's commerce. In 1822, the bank built this new office at the intersection of High and Church Streets, seen here in an 1868 photograph. The right side of the building still stands.

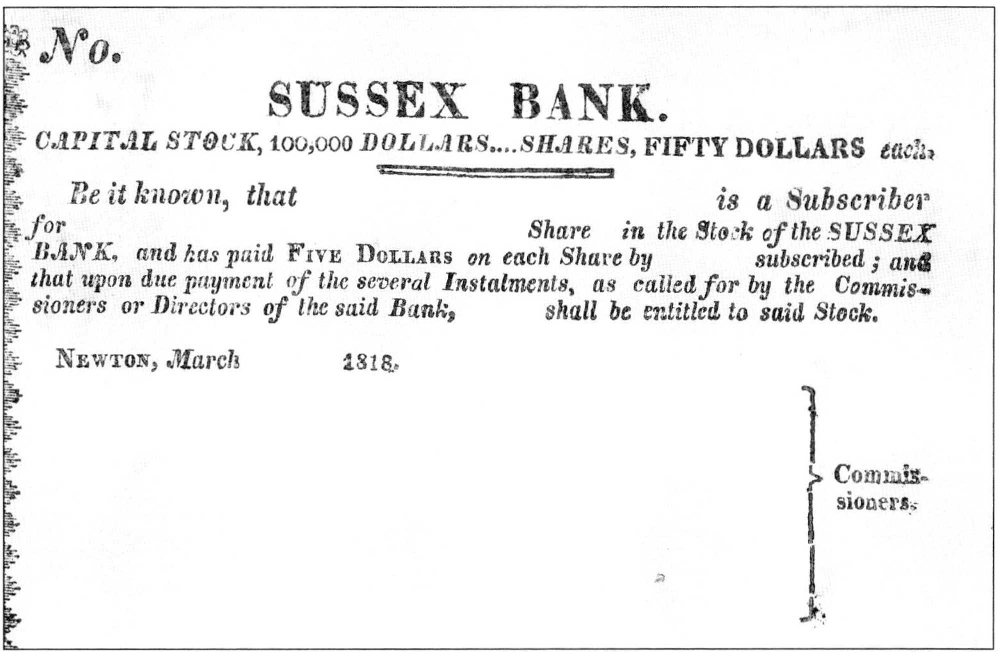

No.

SUSSEX BANK.

CAPITAL STOCK, 100,000 *DOLLARS....SHARES,* **FIFTY DOLLARS** *each,*

Be it known, that *is a Subscriber for* *Share in the Stock of the SUSSEX BANK, and has paid* FIVE DOLLARS *on each Share by* *subscribed; and that upon due payment of the several* ***Instalments,*** *as called for by the Commissioners or Directors of the said Bank,* ***shall be entitled to said Stock.***

NEWTON, *March* 1818.

Commissioners.

To raise capital for the Sussex Bank, the directors issued $100,000 in capital stock in March 1818. Potential investors could subscribe to the shares by making a down payment of $5 on each $50 share, and paying the balance in installments. The bank attributed its success to its policy of "extending loans to the many rather than accommodating a few individuals with large amounts."

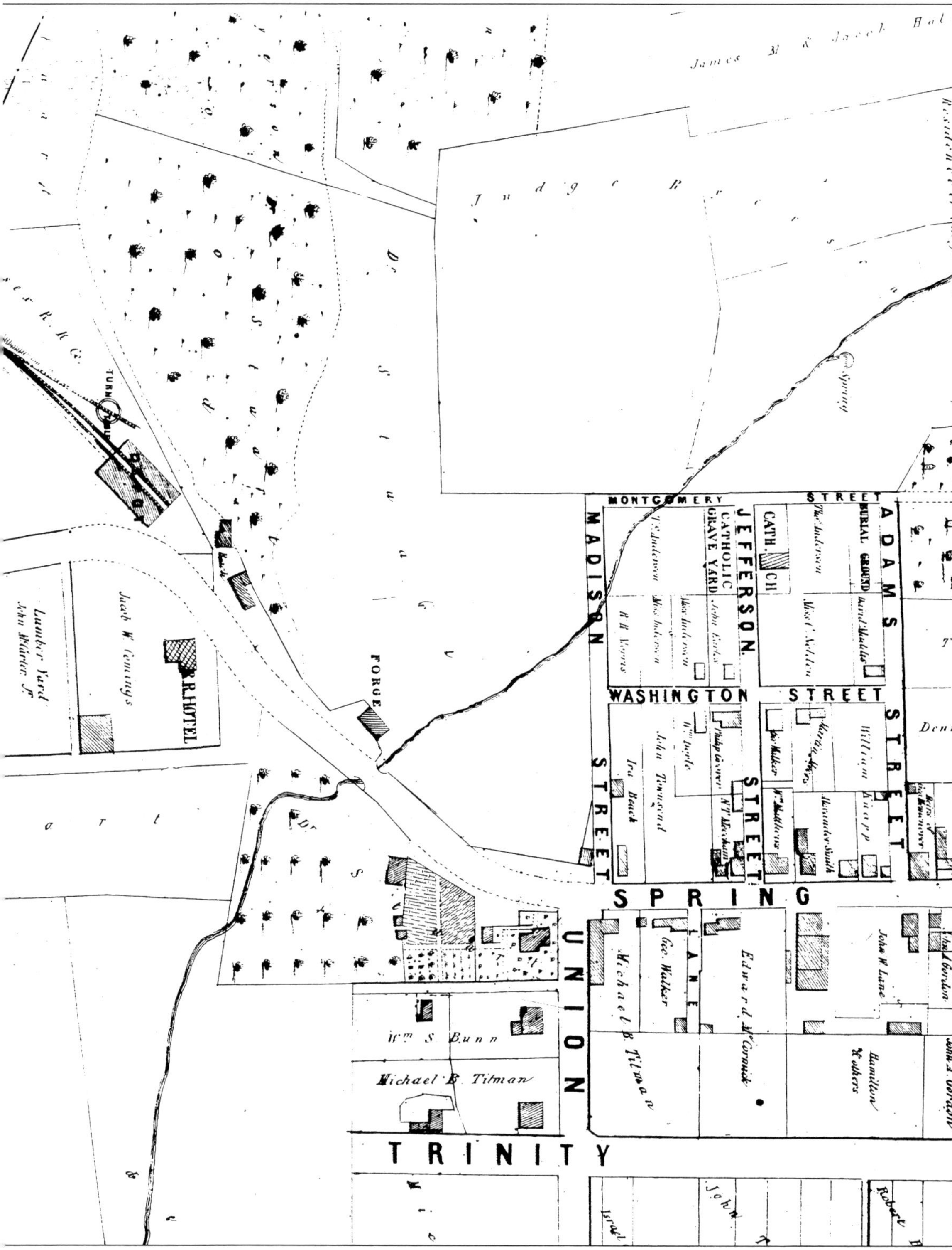

This is a portion of the *"Map of Newton, The Seat of Justice in Sussex County,"* published in 1856

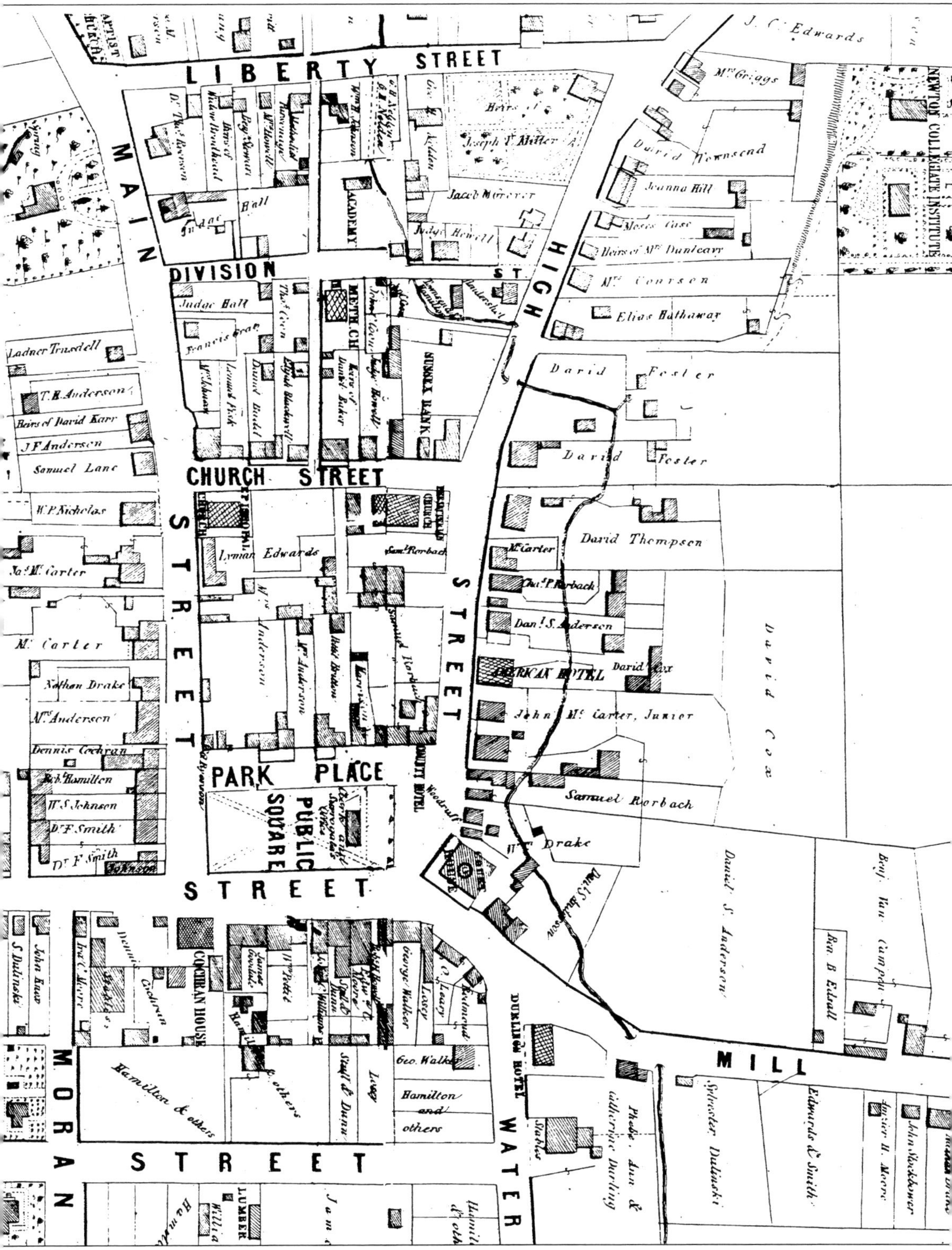

by Thomas Hughes, showing the area around the square.

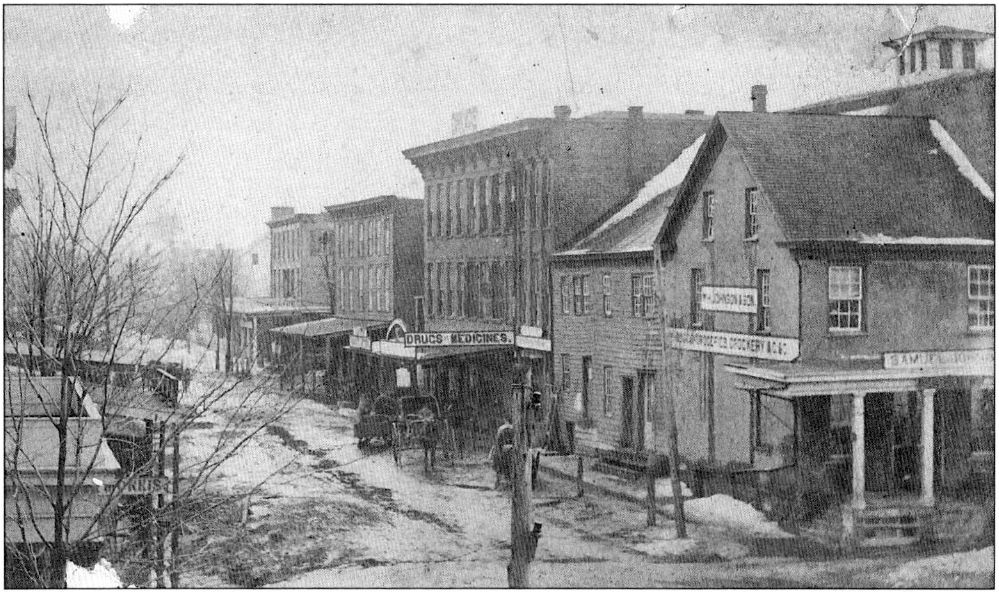

This is one of the earliest views of the corner of Main and Spring Streets. It was probably taken during the winter of 1870–71, after an early snowstorm and just before Samuel Johnson demolished the buildings on the corner to make way for his splendid new storehouse (see below). The dilapidated wooden building on Spring Street behind Johnson's storehouse was a rare survivor of the town's 18th-century commercial structures.

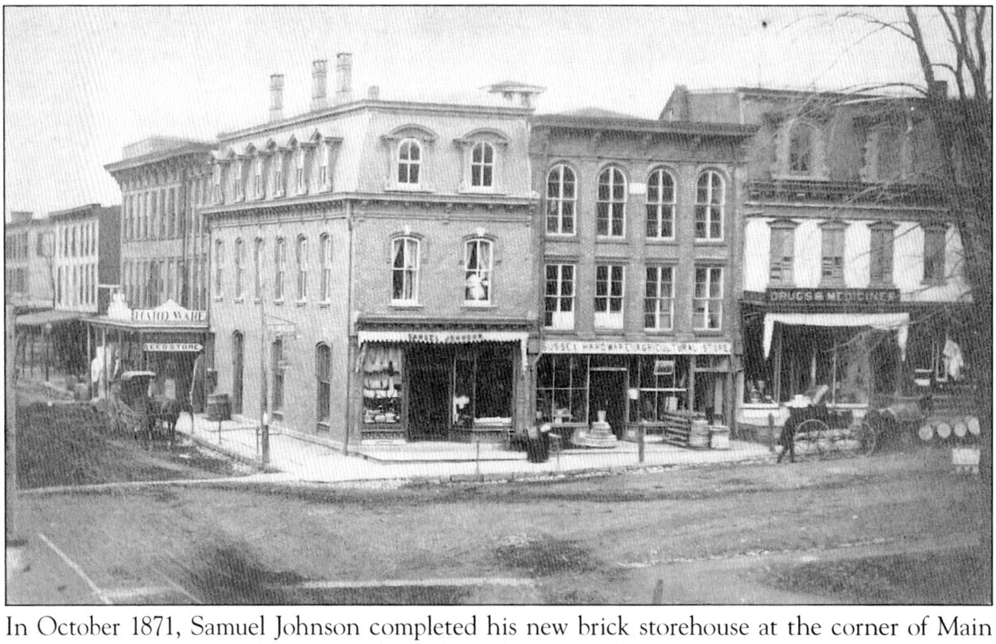

In October 1871, Samuel Johnson completed his new brick storehouse at the corner of Main and Spring Streets. He built it in the fashionable Second Empire style, with a mansard roof and fancy dormer windows. Johnson was a dry goods merchant, selling men's clothing, ladies' corsets, fabric, notions, china, carpets, lighting fixtures, and sundry housewares.

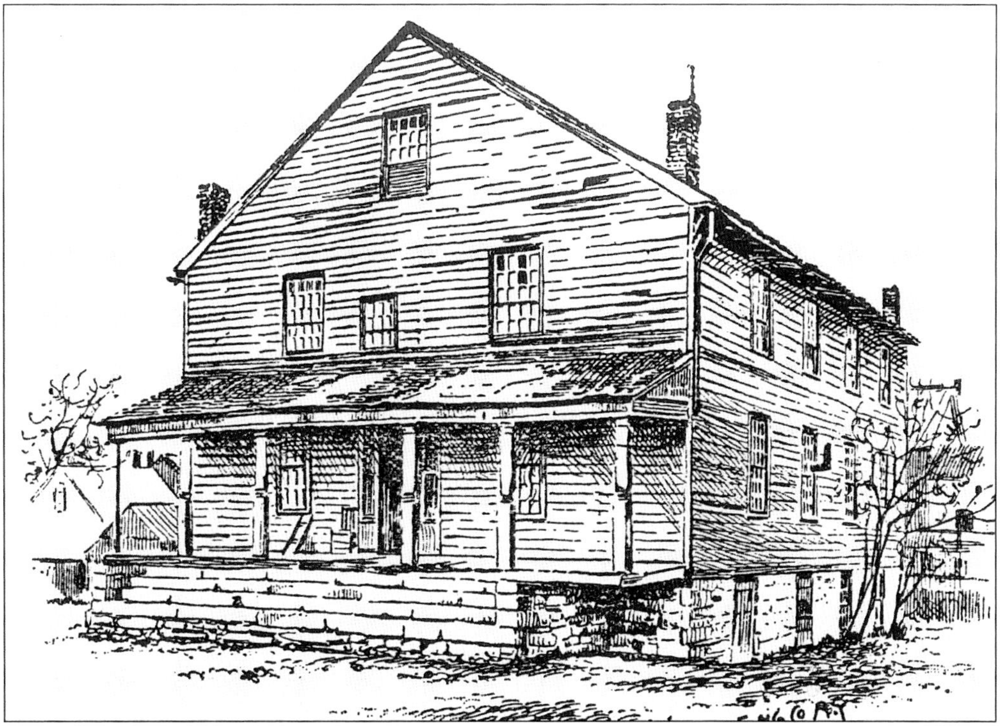

Newton's Methodist congregation built this meetinghouse in 1832 on Division Street. When the church sold it in 1859, it was converted into cheap apartments. When it was razed in 1896, the *Herald* commended "the removal of a structure that has afforded shelter to a class of residents who were not much credit to themselves and less to the town in which they lived."

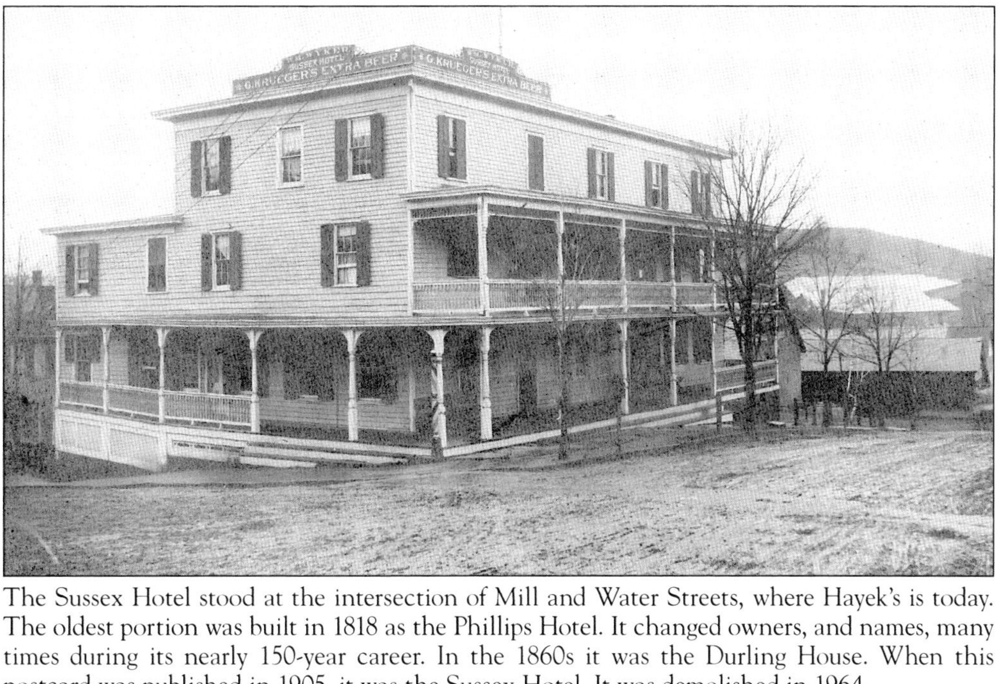

The Sussex Hotel stood at the intersection of Mill and Water Streets, where Hayek's is today. The oldest portion was built in 1818 as the Phillips Hotel. It changed owners, and names, many times during its nearly 150-year career. In the 1860s it was the Durling House. When this postcard was published in 1905, it was the Sussex Hotel. It was demolished in 1964.

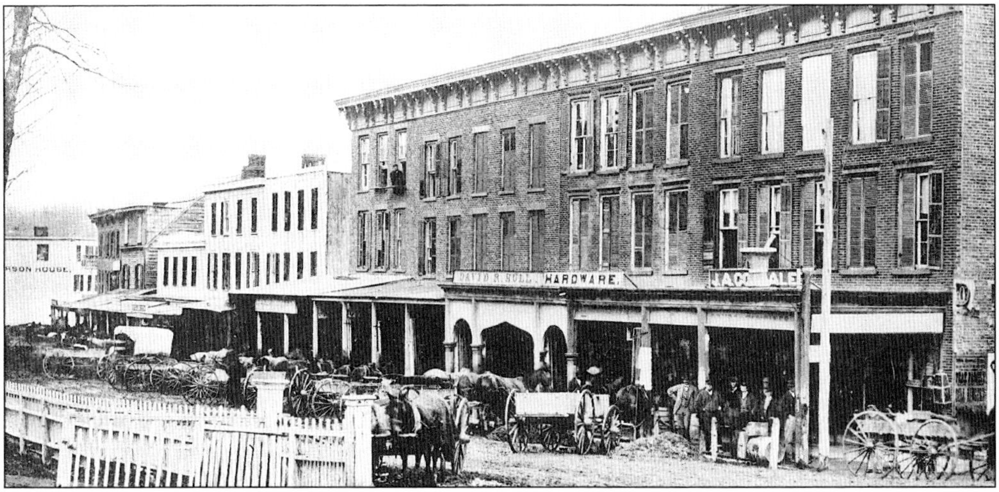

Taken in 1863, this is one of the earliest known photographs of the center of Newton. It shows the north side of Spring Street, facing the square. The brick buildings, which still stand, were built between 1856 and 1860. Unfortunately, the wooden awnings that covered the sidewalks were demolished about 1900, a victim of changing fashions in commercial storefronts. The fence enclosed the square from 1845 until 1871.

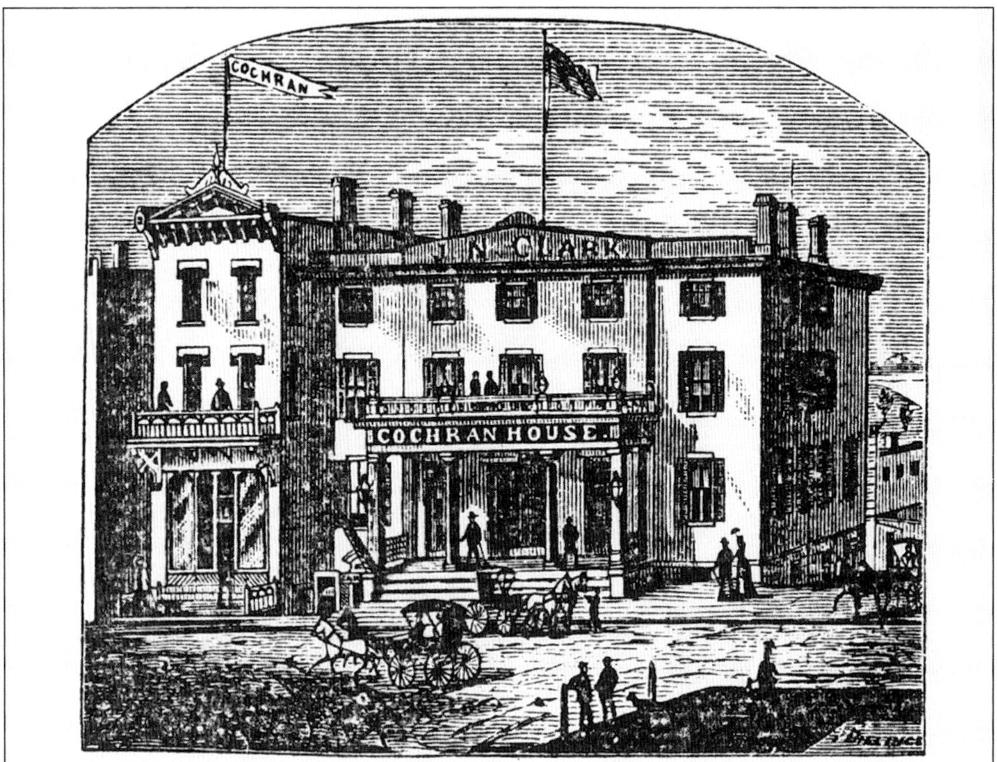

Newton's foremost hostelry was the Cochran House. It was built by Dennis Cochran in 1842 to serve the farmers, bankers, lawyers, businessmen, and traveling salesmen who came to Newton to transact their business. This 1844 woodcut shows its original, three-story appearance. Later it was raised to four stories.

Two

Around the Square

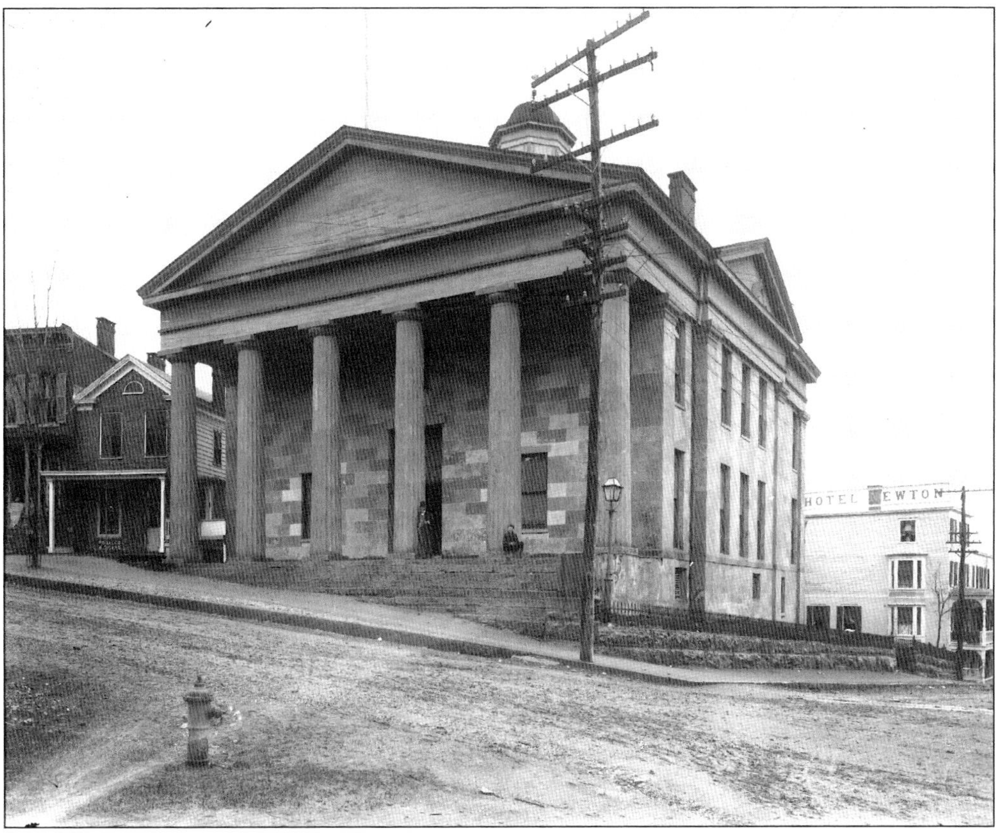

Newton's town square is anchored by the imposing Greek Revival courthouse. The building was constructed of rough stone. The walls were then stuccoed, scored, and painted to resemble elegant dressed stone blocks. Notice the birdhouse in the gable on the Spring Street side and the gas light at the corner. Behind the courthouse, lower down on Spring Street, stands the Hotel Newton, another of the town's many hostelries.

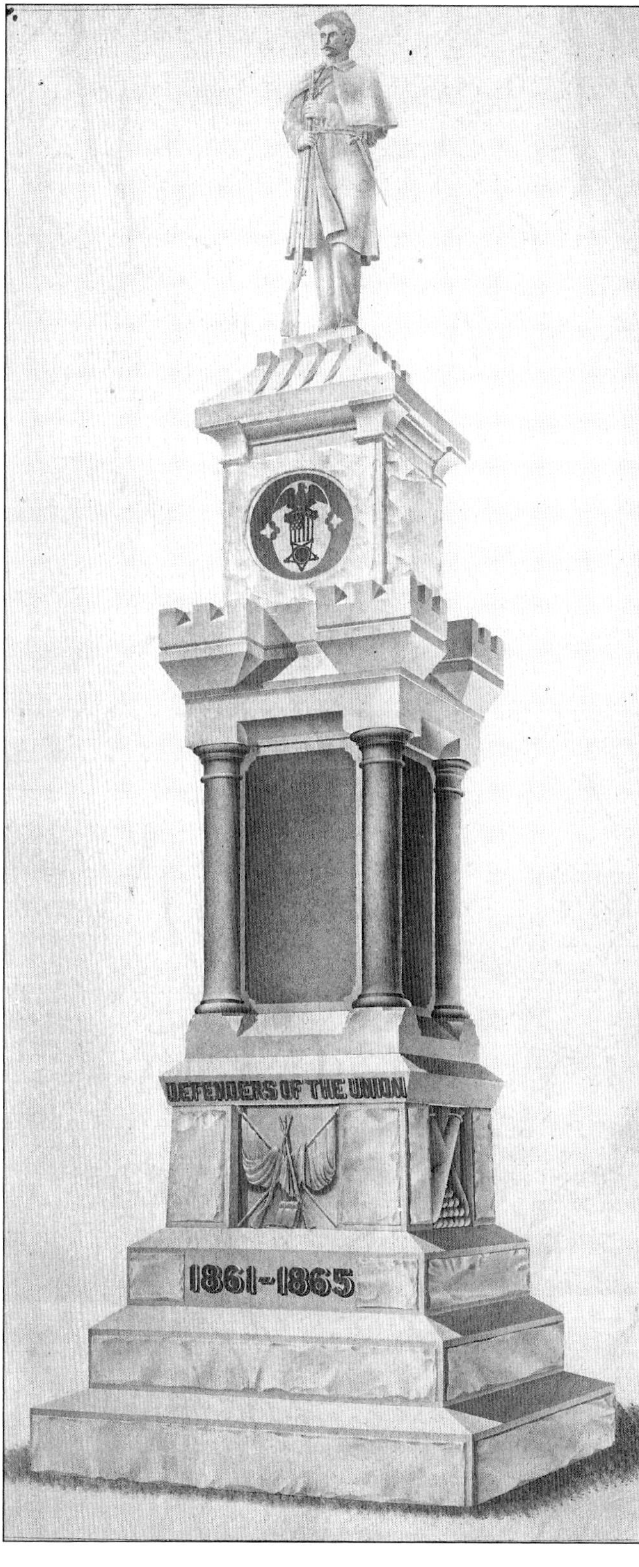

The Civil War ended in 1865, but it was not until the approach of the 30th anniversary of Lee's surrender at Appomattox that the residents of Sussex County agreed to erect a monument to the local men who gave their lives in that conflict. *The Defenders of the Union* was designed by A.F. O'Donnell, a resident of Newton. Copies of his rendering were distributed to publicize the proposed monument and raise funds for its construction. Local citizens contributed $2,000, while the county's board of chosen freeholders appropriated $4,000 to the project. The 33-foot-high monument was constructed from over 90 tons of granite. Panels on the sides bear artillery, cavalry, infantry, and navy insignia, and the names of the battles in which Sussex soldiers participated.

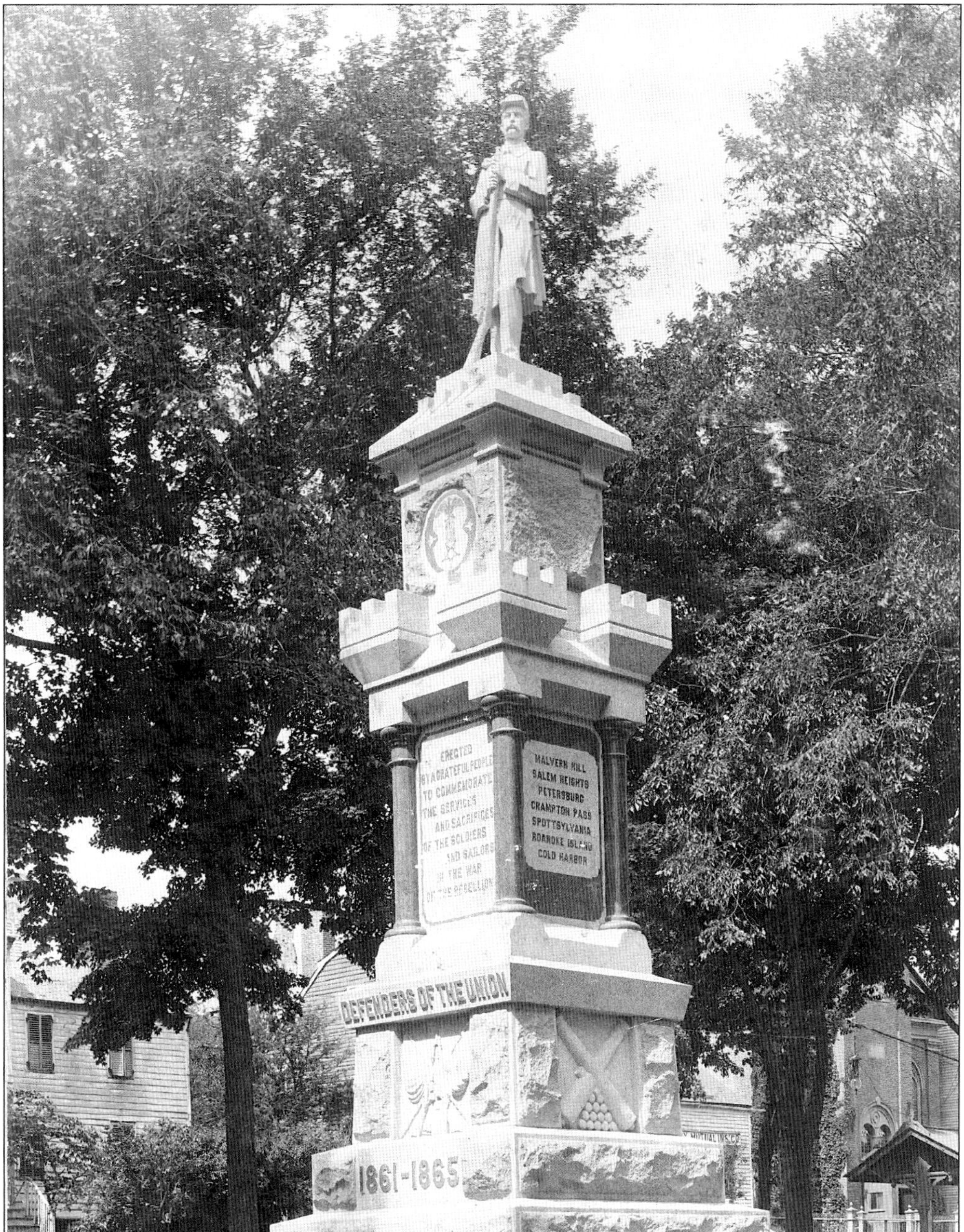

On September 5, 1895, approximately 8,000 county residents thronged the Newton green to witness the dedication of the Soldiers' and Sailors' Monument. A.C. Townley, a prominent Newton photographer, published these cabinet photographs of the newly erected monument, and most likely sold them as souvenirs at the dedication. In the lower right-hand corner of the picture you can see the gazebo that stood on the green from about 1880 to about 1900. It is also interesting to note the early wooden buildings standing on Park Place, facing the green. Both the houses and the Methodist church were subsequently demolished to make way for larger commercial structures. (Courtesy Jan Gminder.)

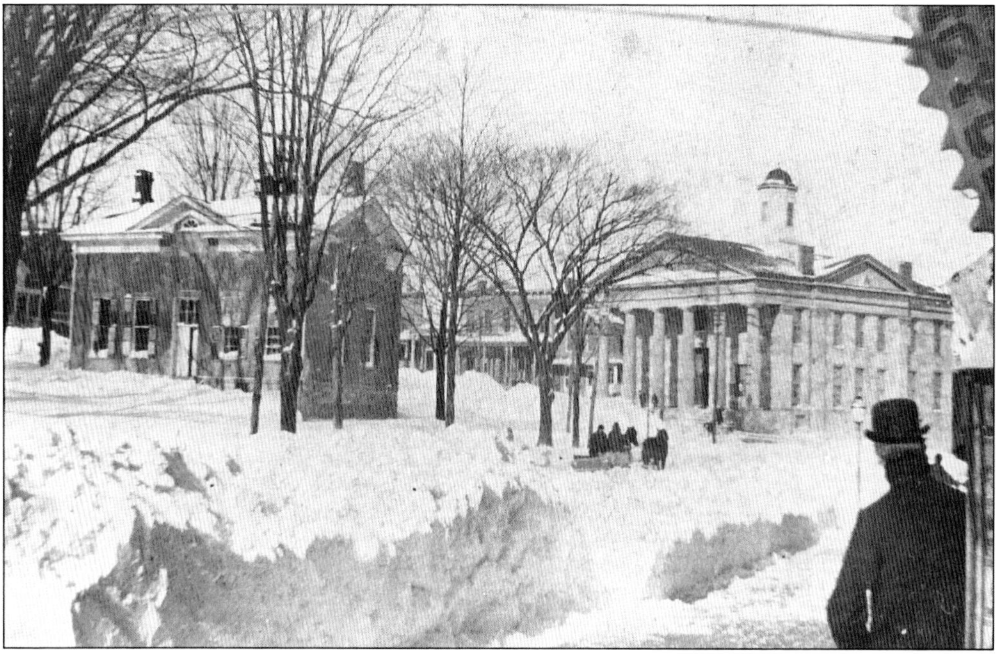

A blizzard buried the town of Newton in January 1905. The morning after the storm, shopkeepers carefully cleared their sidewalks so customers wouldn't slip, but the snow was left on the streets to accommodate horse-drawn sleighs. The one-story building in the square is the County Park building, which housed the offices of the county clerk and the surrogate.

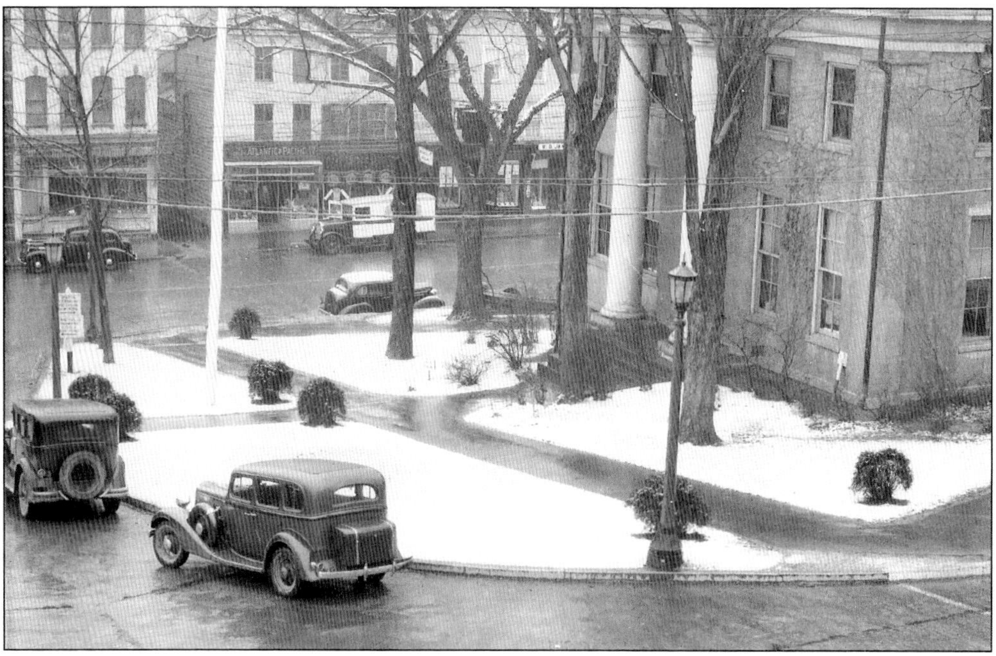

The first 25 years of this century brought rapid change to the center of Newton. The streets were paved in order to accommodate the rising population of automobiles, electric lights replaced the old gas lamps on street corners, and the County Park building was raised to two stories to house the county's expanding bureaucracy.

Members of the Sussex County Bar Association pose on the steps of the newly enlarged and remodeled County Park building in 1908. In addition to the county clerk and surrogate, the expanded building provided accommodations for the board of chosen freeholders and the county engineer.

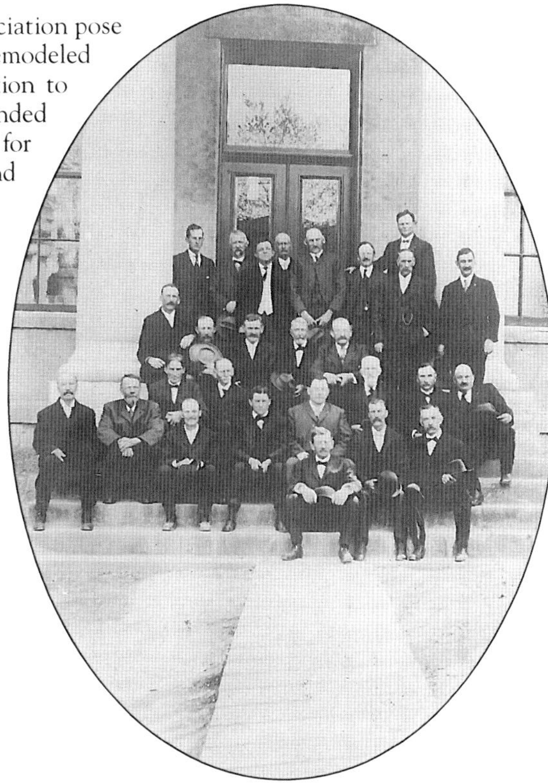

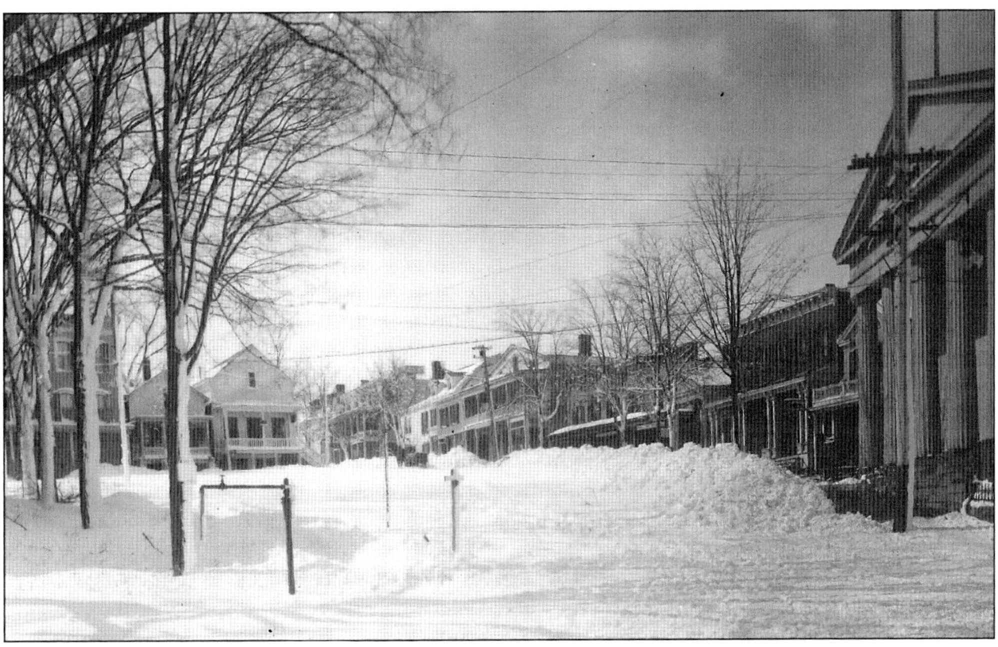

The blizzard of 1905 was popular with local photographers. This view looks past the courthouse toward High Street and the buildings on the south side of the square. Two frame houses stand an the corner of High Street and Park Place where the hall of records is today. The little one on the left was the law office of Judge Kays.

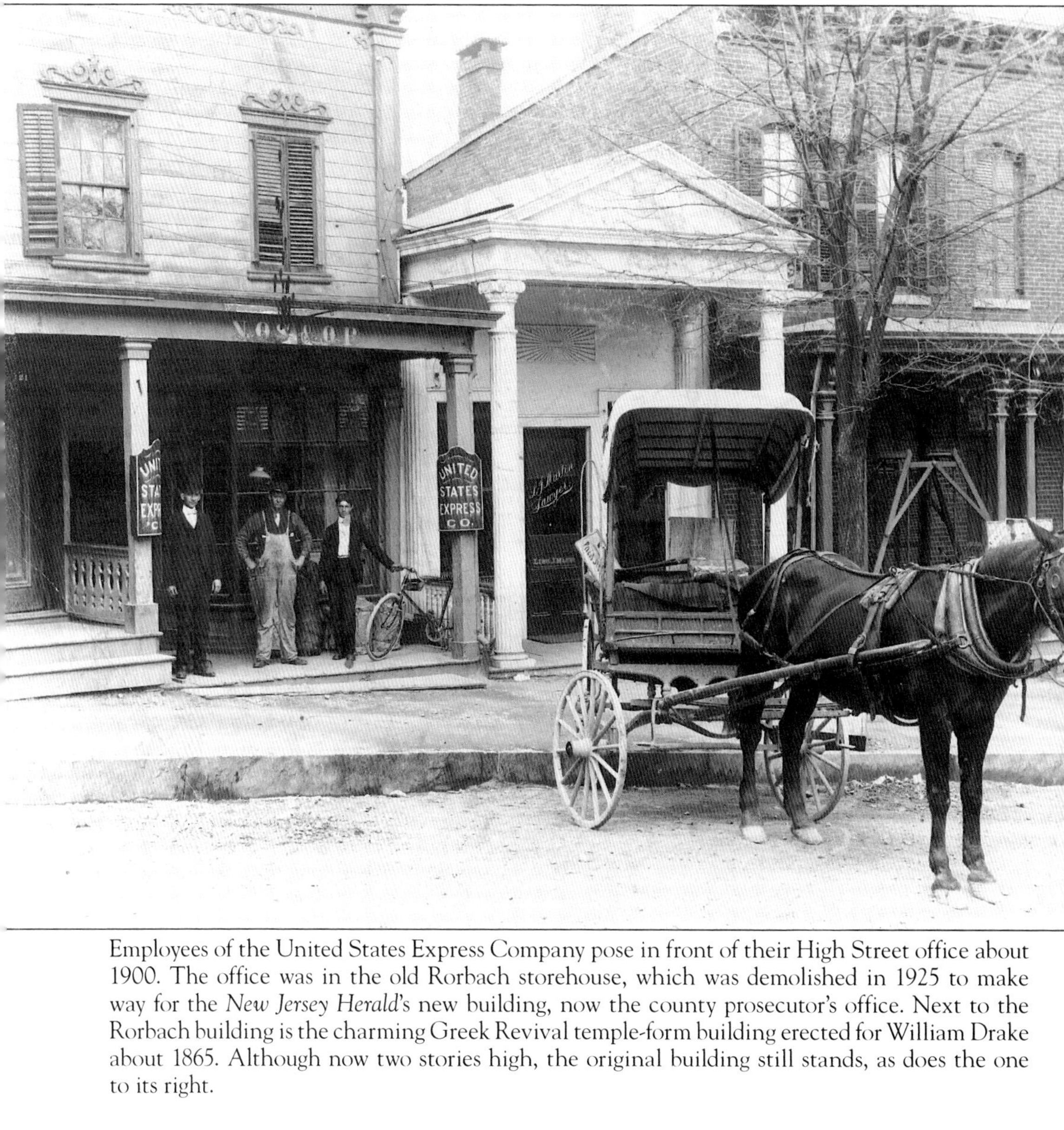

Employees of the United States Express Company pose in front of their High Street office about 1900. The office was in the old Rorbach storehouse, which was demolished in 1925 to make way for the *New Jersey Herald*'s new building, now the county prosecutor's office. Next to the Rorbach building is the charming Greek Revival temple-form building erected for William Drake about 1865. Although now two stories high, the original building still stands, as does the one to its right.

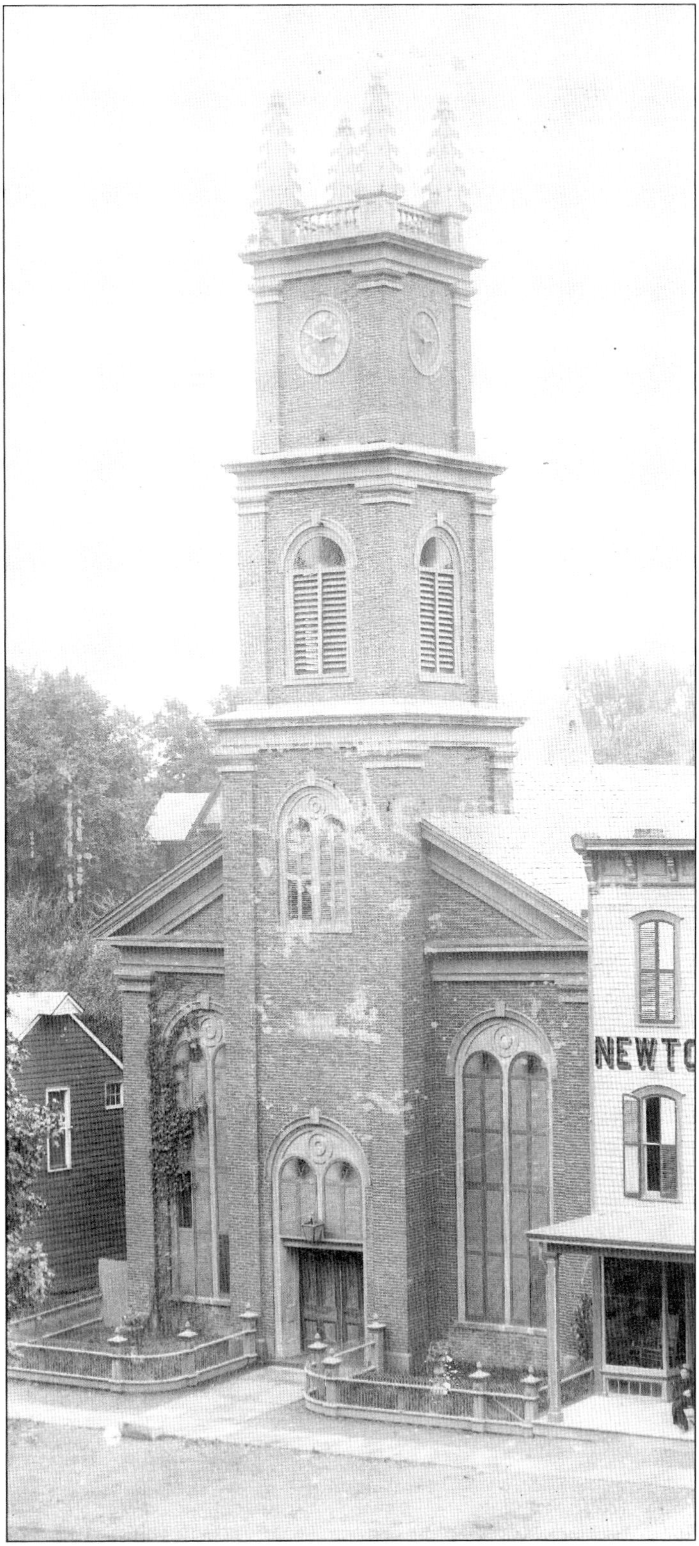

In 1856 the congregation of the Newton Methodist Church began to look for a site to build a substantial new sanctuary. Although they could have purchased a back-street lot for $100, they chose to buy a 50-foot-wide lot on Park Place in 1859. The lot was in the center of Newton, and they purchased it for $3,200 from E.C. Moore. That same year, construction began on their handsome new brick church. Work did not always go smoothly and there were difficulties with contractors. They even had to tear down and rebuild the brick walls due to poor workmanship. The dispute lasted over a year, and for a time the contractor stopped all work and refused to turn the building over to the congregation. The problems were ultimately resolved, and the church was formally dedicated on March 23, 1861.

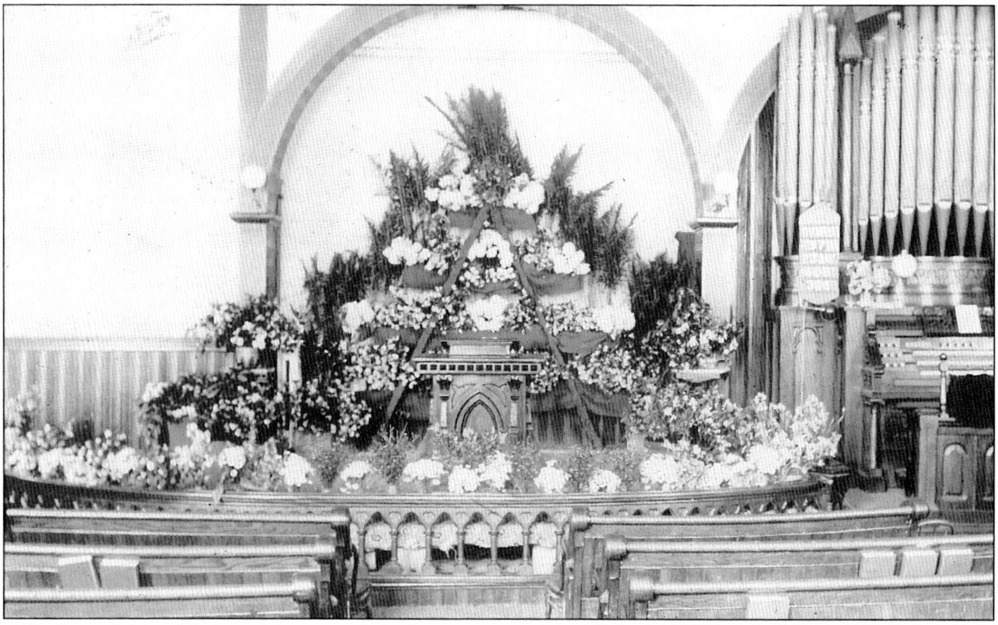

"This is our Children's day 'trim.' Ferns & Peonies in back, Buttercup & daisies & blue wild lilies [blue flag iris?] in front—Laurel at right & left in center of Pulpit. It was fine as ever." So wrote the Methodist parishioner who sent this postcard to a friend in Rutherford, New Jersey, in 1909. Children's Day was an annual event celebrated in mid-June by both the Methodists and the Presbyterians.

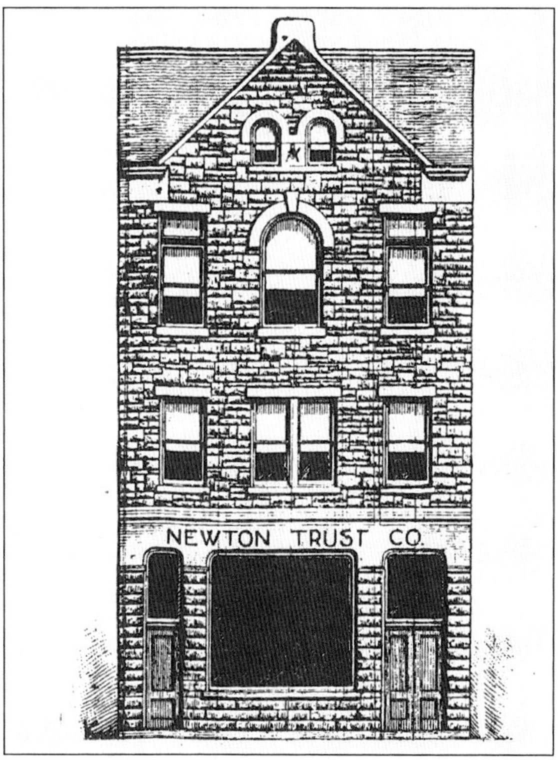

The recently incorporated Newton Trust Co. broke ground for a new bank building on Park Place on January 7, 1902. This woodcut was published while the building was still under construction. The tall stone structure was faced with granite, and boasted a 12-foot-square plate glass window in the facade. The bank opened early the following year.

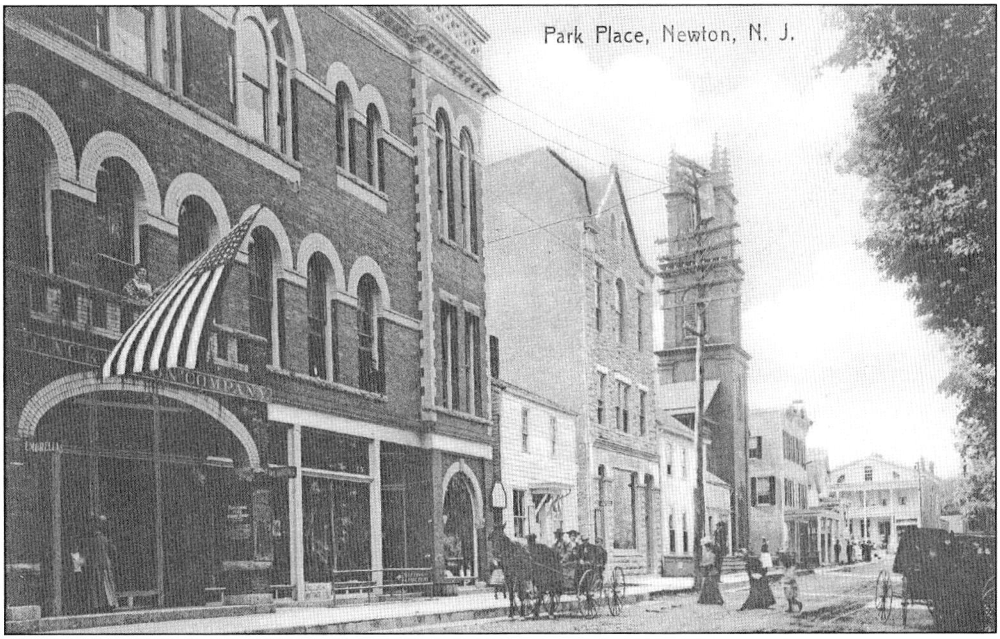

By the early years of the 20th century, Park Place was completely transformed from a quiet residential street facing the square to a bustling commercial thoroughfare. This 1908 view shows it in transition. From left to right, the Park Block building, the Newton Trust Company, the Methodist church, and the I & L Furniture Company's building tower over their older neighbors.

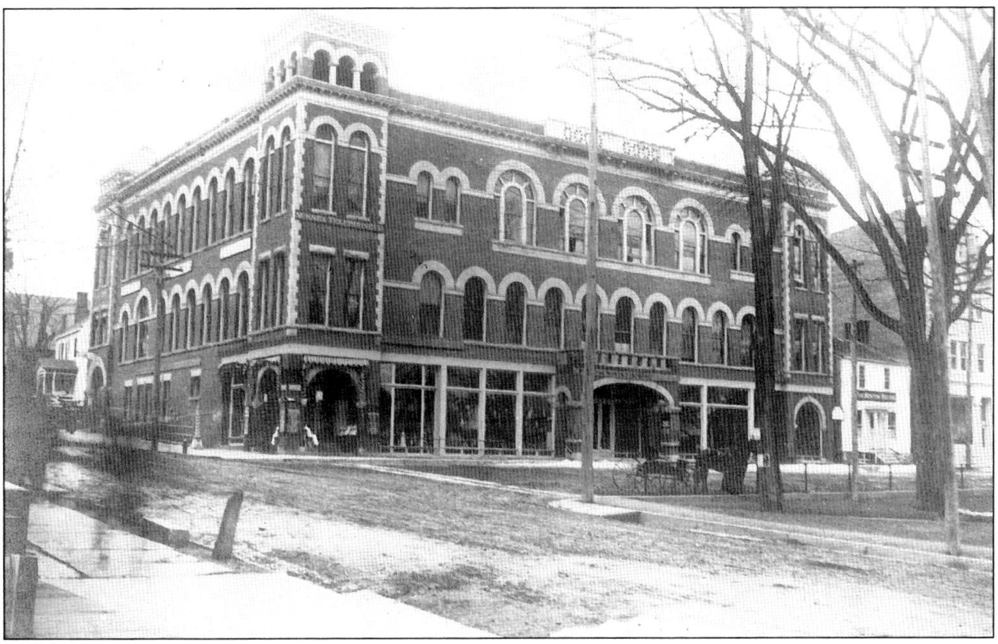

The Park Block building, constructed in 1896 for Messrs. Huston, VanBlarcom, and Ackerson, was the largest commercial building in Newton. The first floor was home to Ackerson's department store, the town's first store of this kind. The second floor was used for offices and boasted an opera house that seated 300 people. The building burned on December 3, 1940.

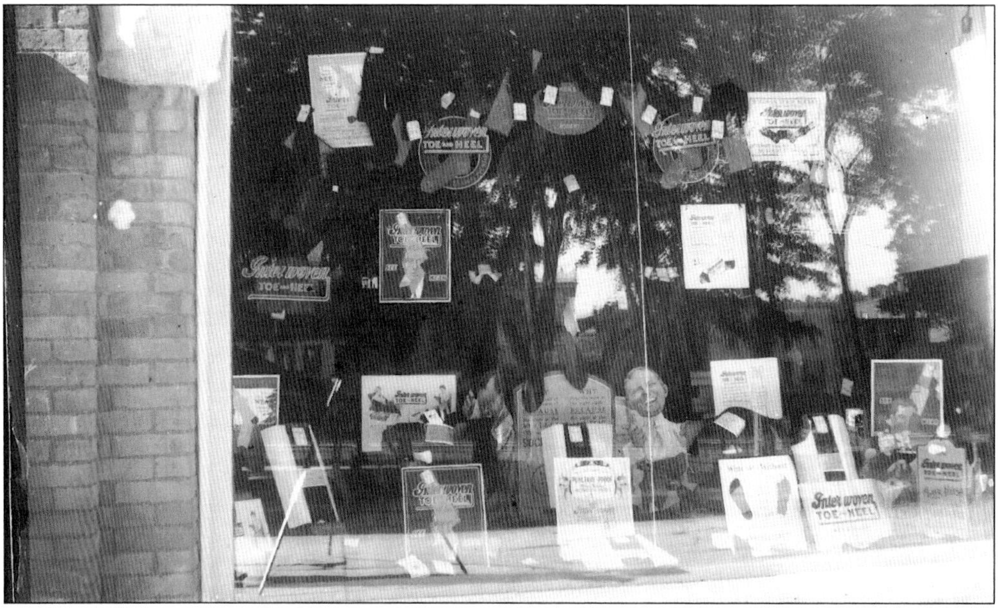

W.D. Ackerson Co.'s window in the Park Block displays an engaging array of hosiery for men and women. "Toe and Heel" socks are the featured brand.

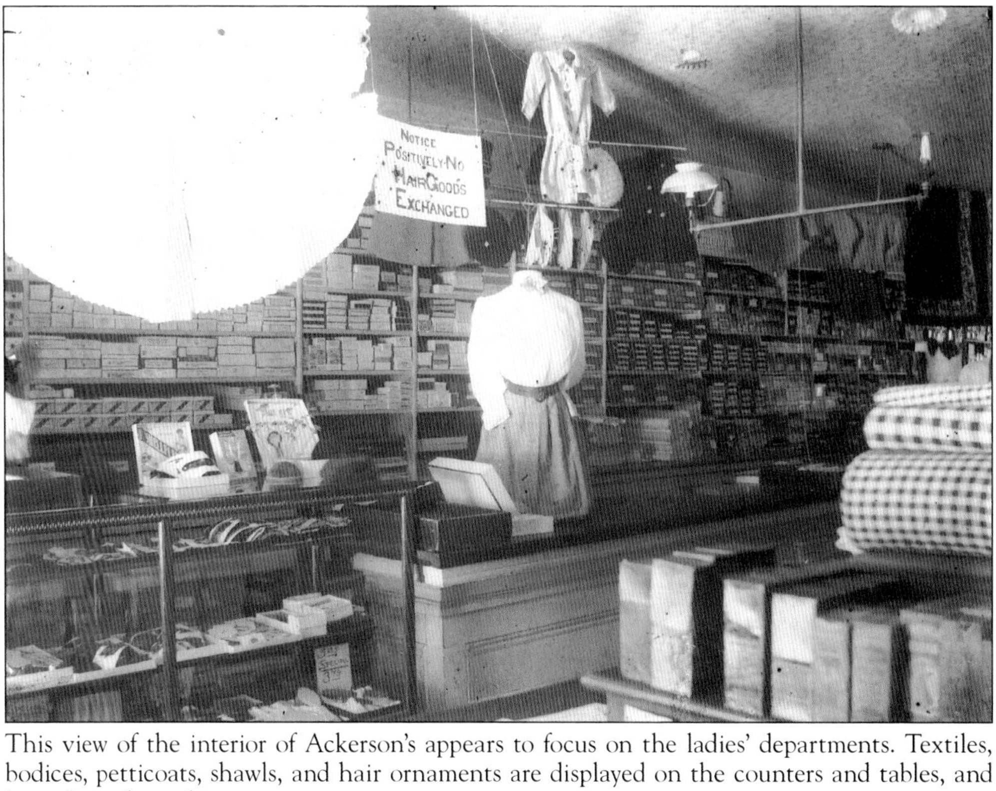

This view of the interior of Ackerson's appears to focus on the ladies' departments. Textiles, bodices, petticoats, shawls, and hair ornaments are displayed on the counters and tables, and hang from the ceiling.

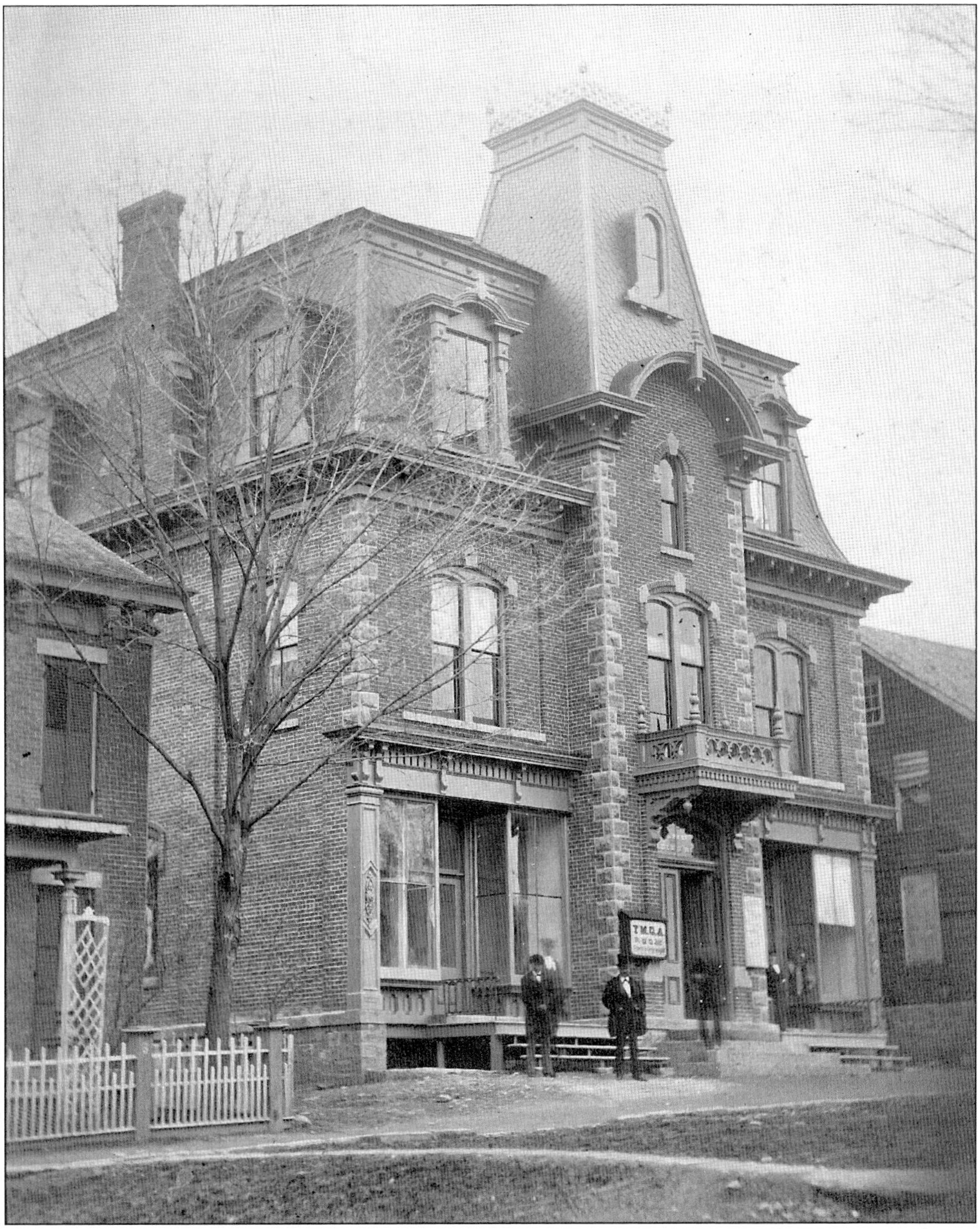

Alfred Dennis, a Newark bookseller and stationer, donated money to the Newton Library Association to build a library for the town. The association purchased George M. Ryerson's old drugstore where the post office stands today, and awarded a contract to Robert Baughn and Andrew M. Price to build this handsome mansard-roofed structure in 1871. When completed, the building housed several businesses, including the *New Jersey Herald*, in addition to the library. There was also a 500-seat auditorium on the third floor, which earned the building its popular name, "The Opera House."

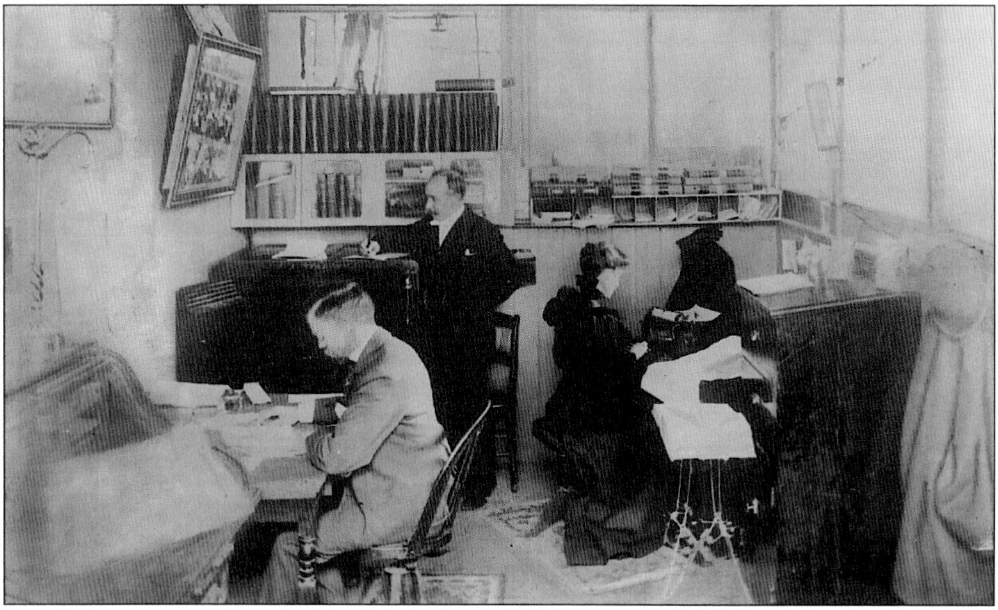

The *New Jersey Herald*, established in 1829, was the town's third newspaper. It was preceded by the *Farmers' Journal & Newton Advertiser* and the *Sussex Register*. This photograph shows the paper's editorial offices in the Opera House, about 1895. Jacob L. Bunnell, the paper's editor and publisher, is seated in the foreground. Behind him are Henry C. Bunnell, plant foreman and sometime writer, and Bessie Smith, the bookkeeper. (Courtesy of the *New Jersey Herald*.)

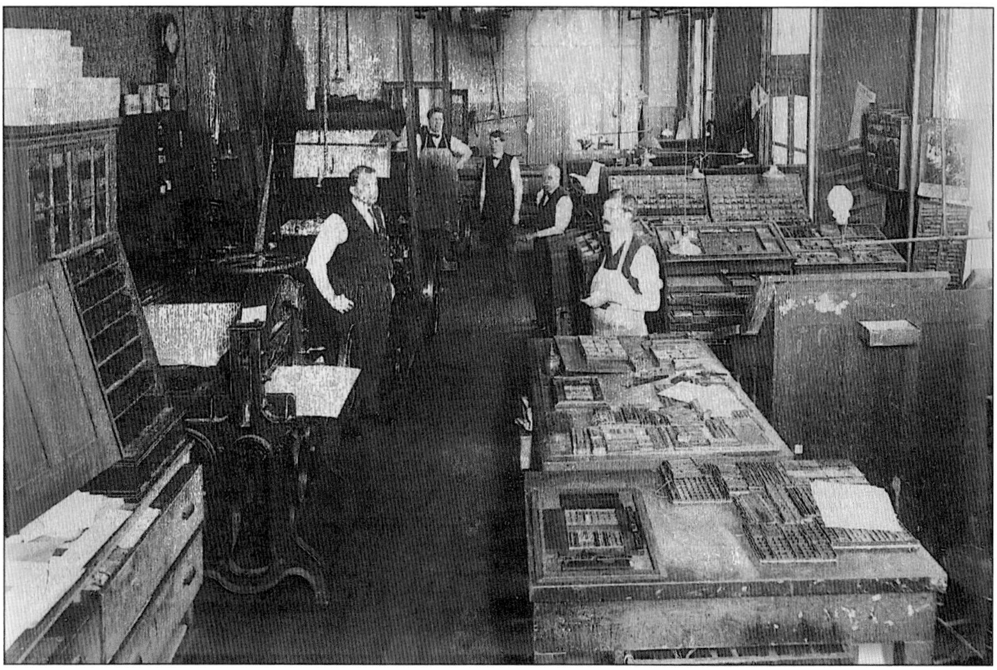

The *New Jersey Herald* moved its offices and presses into the Opera House in 1873. This photograph shows the composing room. The individual letters, or sorts, for each style and size of type were stored in special drawers, the famous California Job Cases. They were then compiled one letter at a time to create each line and column of text. (Courtesy of the *New Jersey Herald*.)

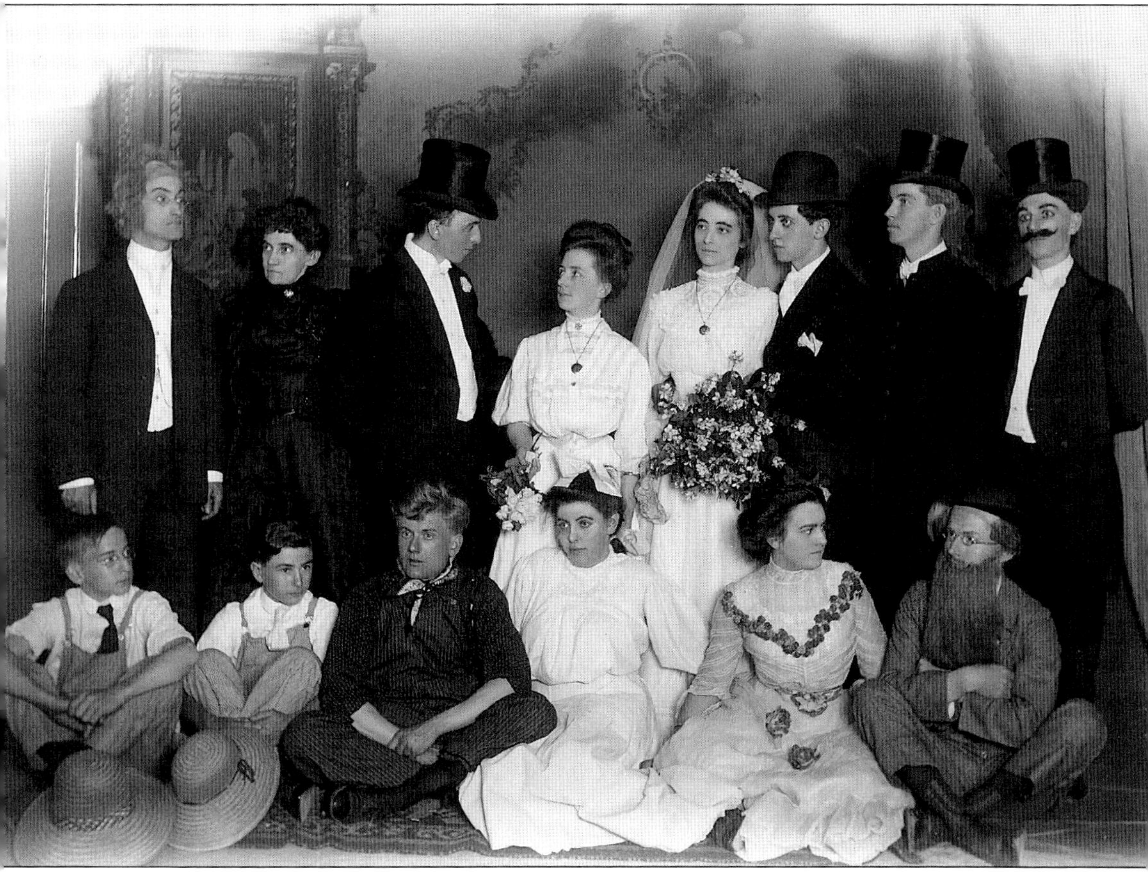

The Opera House was used for both professional and amateur performances. On May 28, 1908, the Epworth League of the Methodist church presented a production of the play *Willowgrove* to a sold-out house. The members of the cast posing here include the following, from left to right: (front row) Charles C. Iliff, Leon Stone, Jacob Fichter, Florence Steele, Grace Harris Morris, and William Morris; (back row) C. Arthur Boss, Miss Kate Taylor, Millard F. Goldsmith, Mary Predmore Wilson, Lulu Boss Stokes, F. Ernest Wallace, Floyd C. Devore, and Andrew L. Devore. In addition to the play, the evening's entertainment included a mixed quartet singing popular songs.

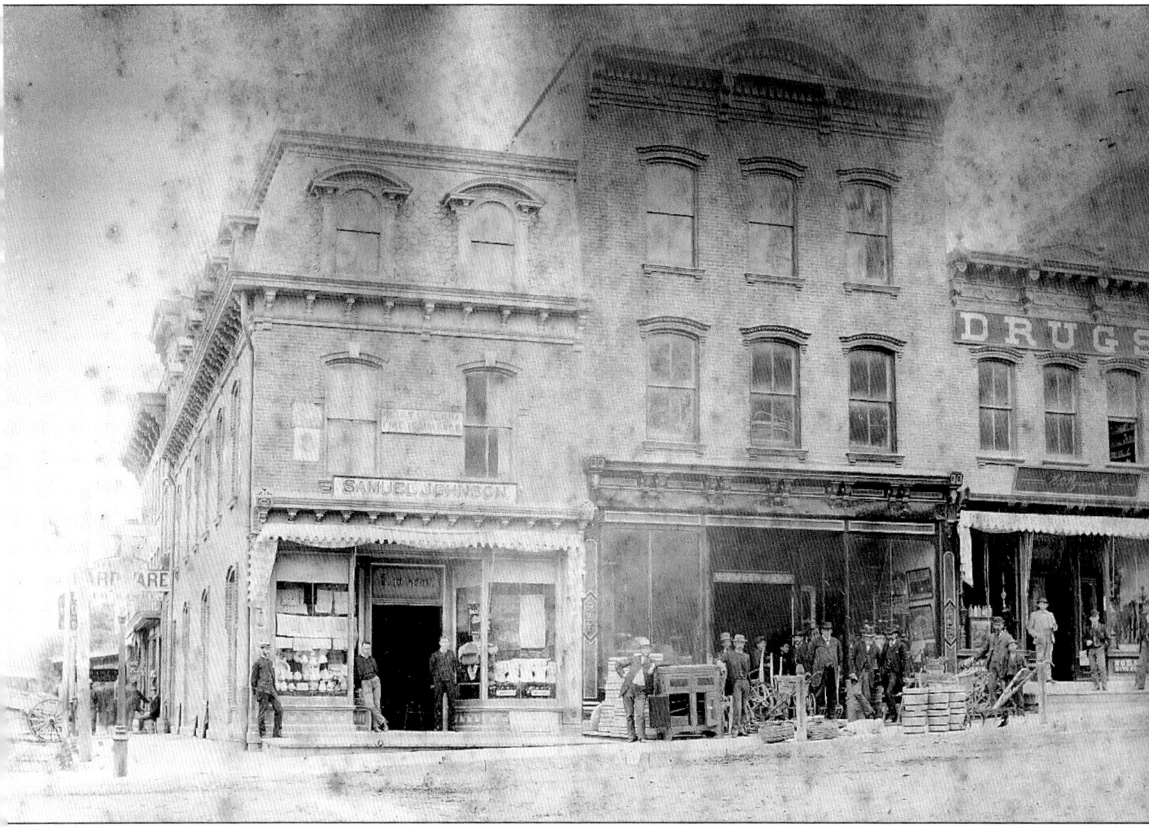

In the mid-1880s, the corner of Main and Spring Street was dominated by Samuel Johnson's dry goods store, William Woodward's hardware store, and Henry O. Ryerson's drug store. The second floor above Johnson's dry goods store was occupied by Hiram C. Clark, a fire insurance underwriter. Woodward, like many other Newton merchants, used the sidewalk as an extension of his shop floor and displayed items outside. Either the displays, or the presence of the photographer, brought a crowd of employees and shoppers to the entrances of the three shops. (Courtesy of the Historical Society of Stillwater Township.)

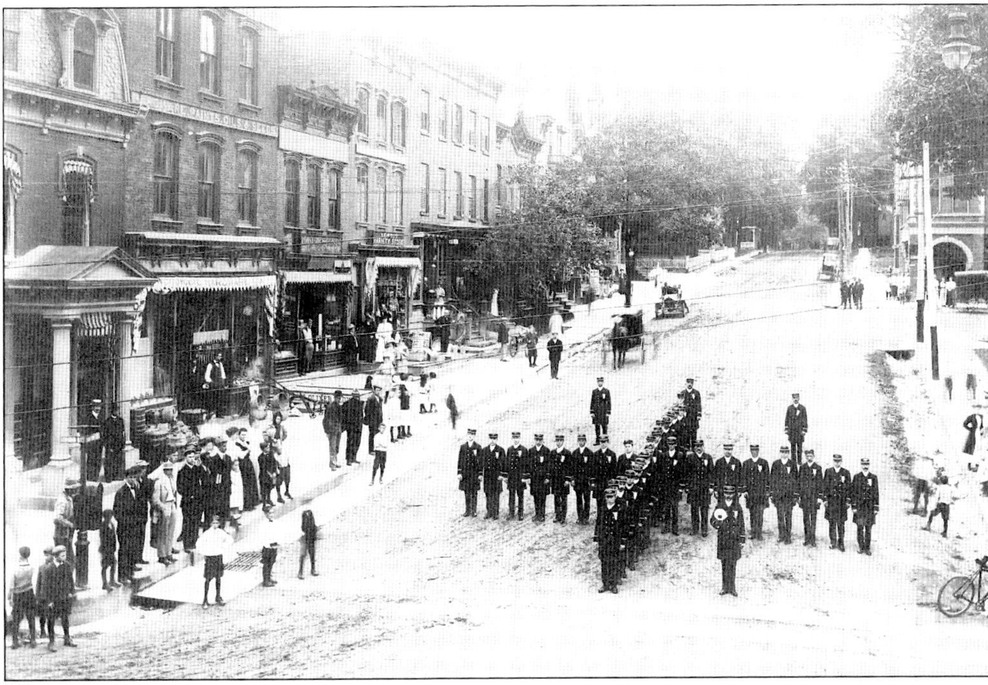

Thirty-seven members of the Kittatinny Hose Company stood in formation on Main Street facing Spring Street for this 1908 photograph. The Sussex National Bank occupied the mansard-roofed structure at the corner of Main and Spring. The bank purchased the building from Samuel Johnson (see p. 14) and moved their offices here in 1891, selling their original building on Church Street (shown on p. 11).

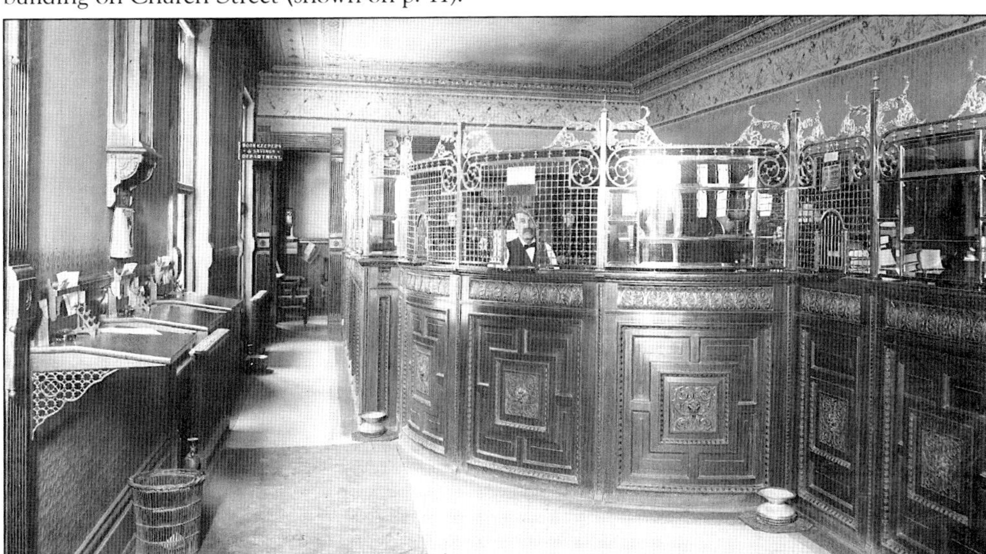

The Sussex National Bank completely renovated the interior of Samuel Johnson's storehouse at One Main Street, and ". . . neither pains nor expense were spared to make the new building attractive and convenient for the transaction of every branch of the banking business." The *Sussex Register* noted that "the banking room is the handsomest in the state." Charles S. Steele, assistant cashier, stands behind the teller's cage.

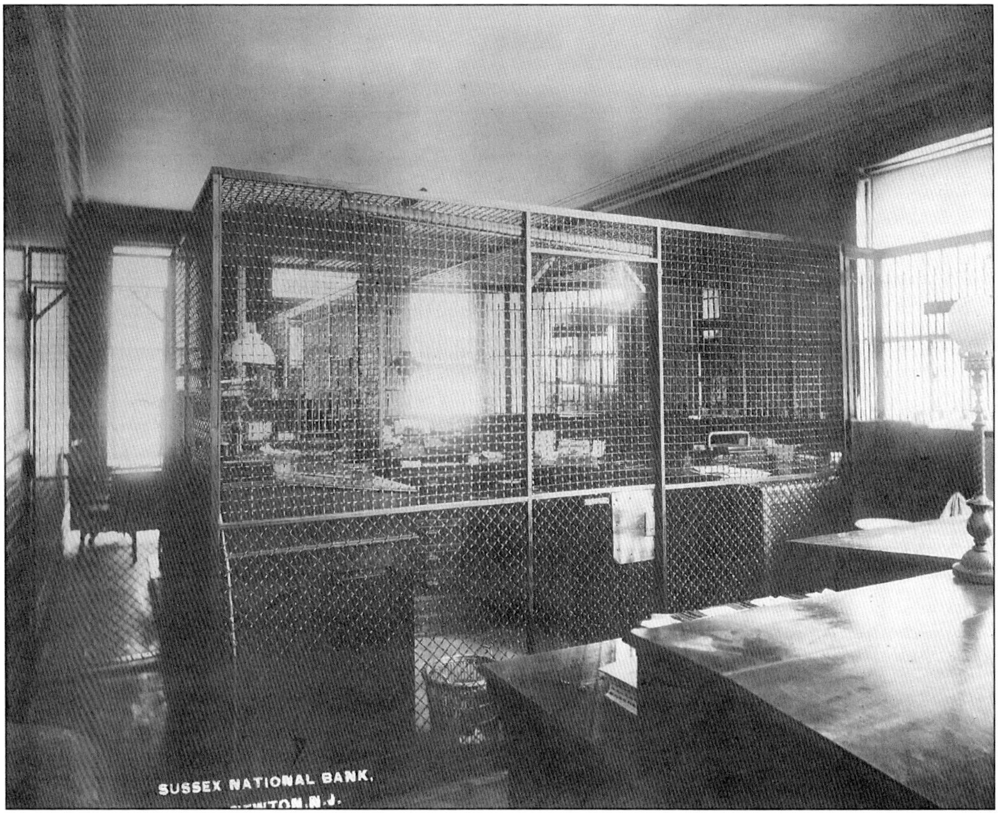

The Sussex National Bank took special precautions to ensure the security of its workers and funds. The accounting room on the second floor of their new Main Street office included a woven wire mesh cage for the bookkeepers to work in. Money and documents were passed through the slot to the right of the door.

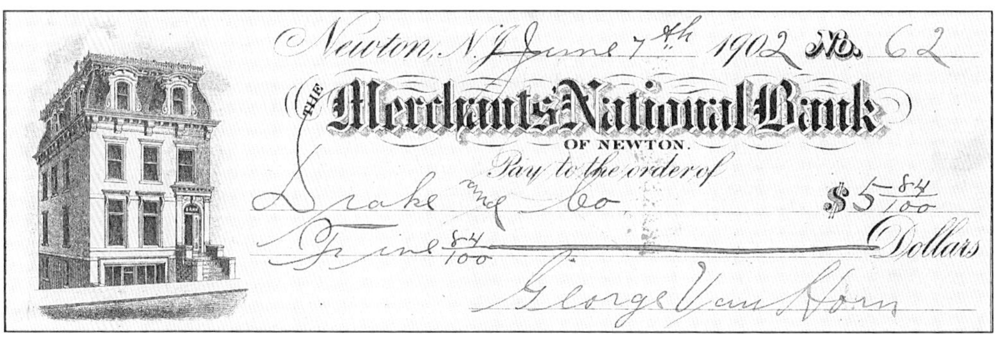

In 1866, the new Merchants' National Bank set up business in a prime location on Spring Street at the foot of Main Street, next door to the Cochran House hotel. The building is proudly emblazoned on their checks, including this one made out in 1902 by George VanHorn. The bank's success may have prompted the Sussex National Bank's 1891 move to Main Street, directly across from their competitors.

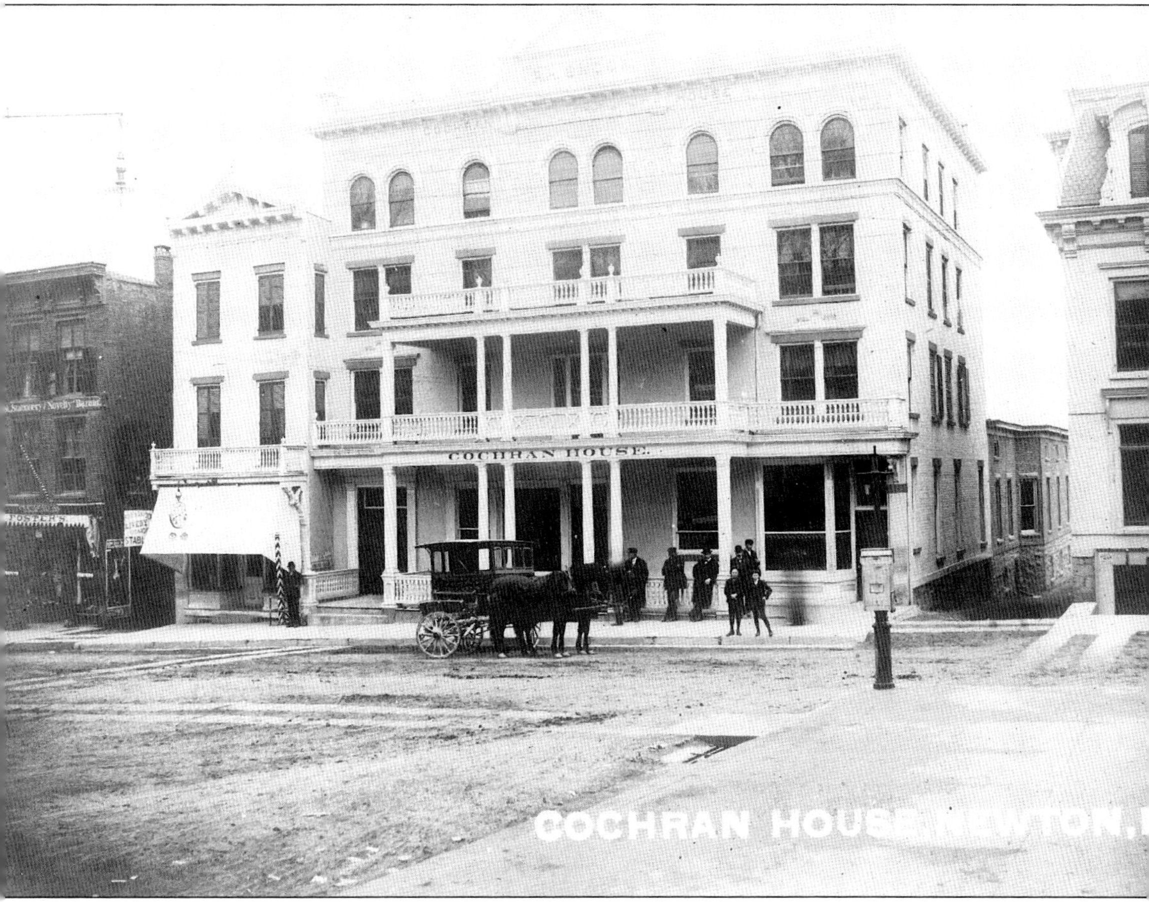

One of Newton's premier landmarks, the Cochran House hotel was built in 1842 and enlarged several times as the business prospered. In 1895, the new owner, R.H. Snook, remodeled and refurnished the hotel, which was now four stories tall and boasted 44 guest rooms with hot water, bathtubs, gas, and electric lighting. In 1897, Judge H. Huston noted that "the hotel is famous in the political annals of the county and State [sic]. Here, politicians, big and little, have met for years and concocted their plans." Politicians were not the only ones who gathered at the Cochran House. Many of the county's societies held regular meetings or annual banquets at the hotel, among them the Newton Rotary, which was first organized at the hotel in 1923 and continued to meet there weekly until the building was demolished in April 1961.

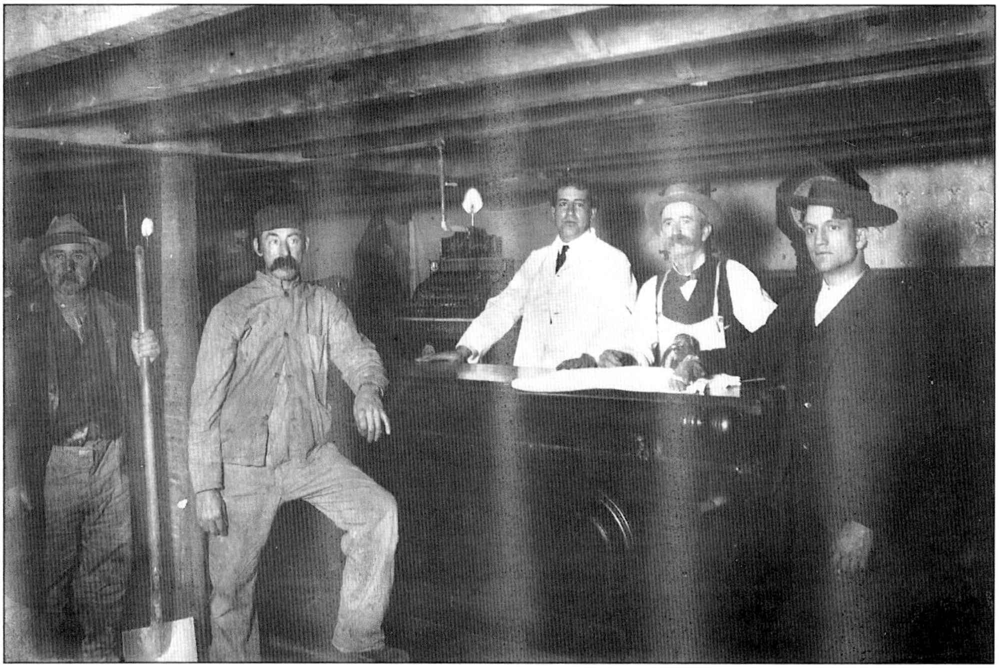

The flash of magnesium powder captured this scene on a glass negative: laborers drinking at the Cochran House's basement bar. The only fancy items here are the mahogany bar and brass cash register, perhaps moved downstairs when Snook remodeled the hotel. The room once had plaster walls and ceilings, as can be seen from the marks on the beams, but here the room is as rough as the workmen at the bar.

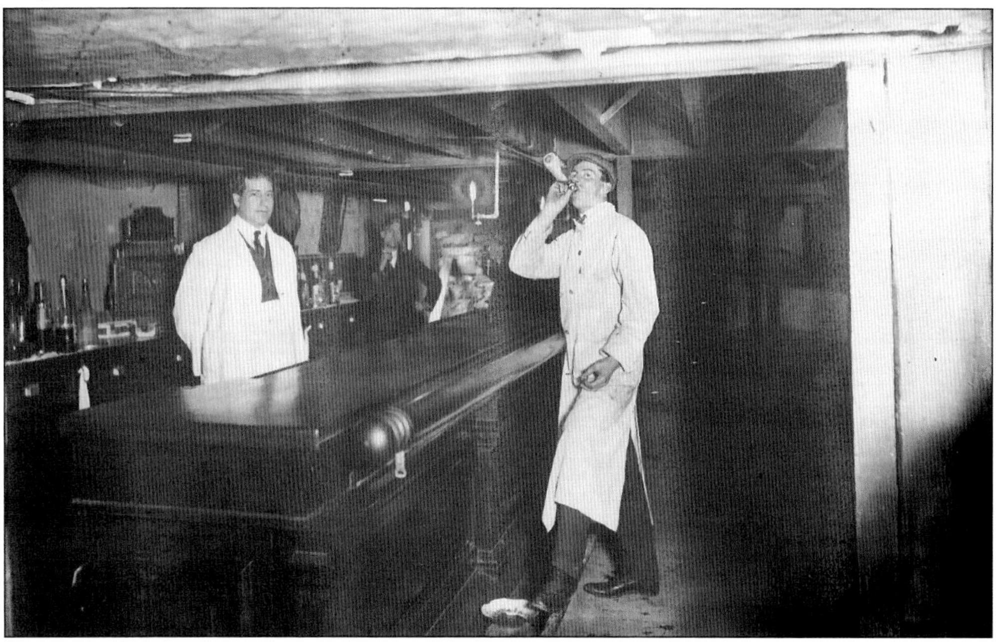

Shown here is another view of the "working man's" bar in the basement of the Cochran House. Common to bars of the period is the cuspidor or spittoon. Unfortunately, not all patrons were marksmen, as can be seen by the tobacco stains on the floor.

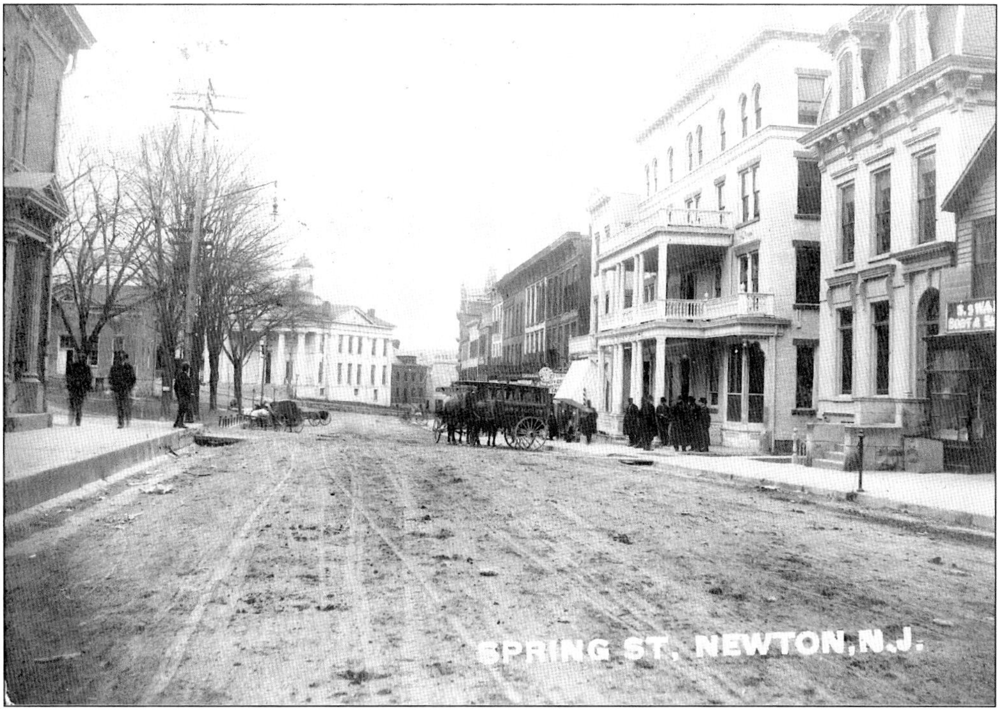

The Cochran House, like other Newton hotels, provided a wagon to ferry guests and their luggage to and from the railroad station. A group of men wait to board the "station wagon" in this 1906 postcard. The road is not yet paved, but one of the newly-installed electric street lights hangs from the telegraph pole on the left. The Merchant's National Bank is to the right of the hotel.

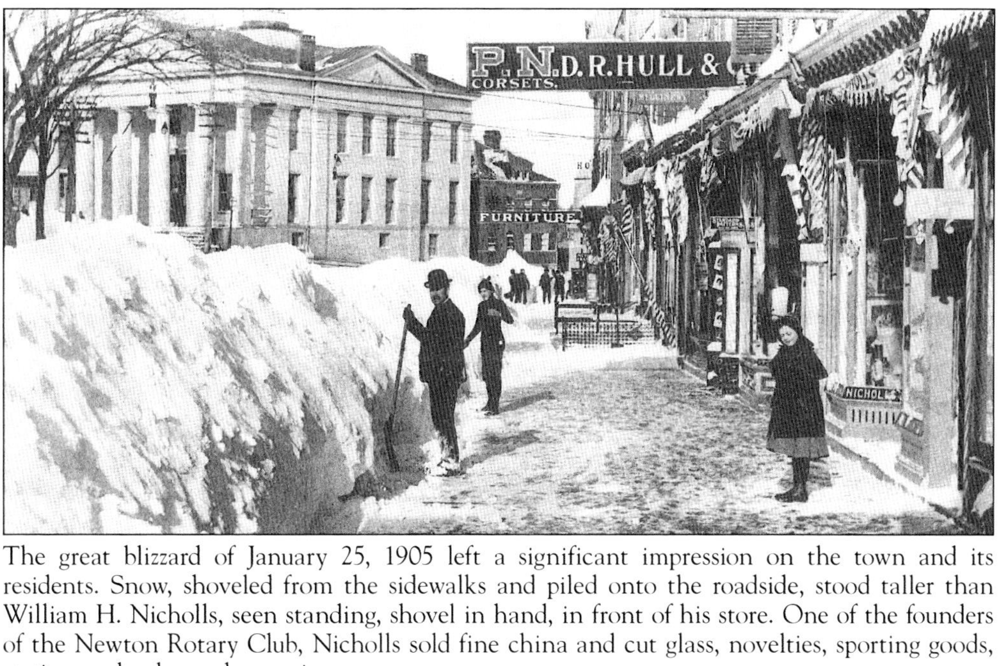

The great blizzard of January 25, 1905 left a significant impression on the town and its residents. Snow, shoveled from the sidewalks and piled onto the roadside, stood taller than William H. Nicholls, seen standing, shovel in hand, in front of his store. One of the founders of the Newton Rotary Club, Nicholls sold fine china and cut glass, novelties, sporting goods, stationery, books, and magazines.

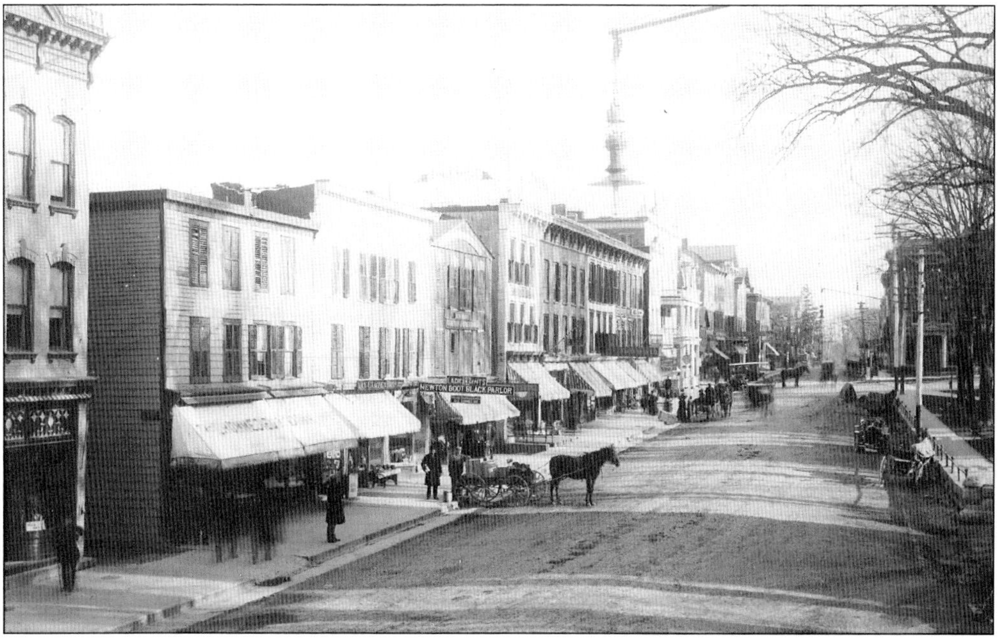

On a quiet afternoon in the spring of 1906, a horse-drawn buckboard is being loaded with goods from the VanCampen Brothers' store. An early open car can be seen parked along the square— harbinger of the horseless carriages that would soon dominate the streets of Newton.

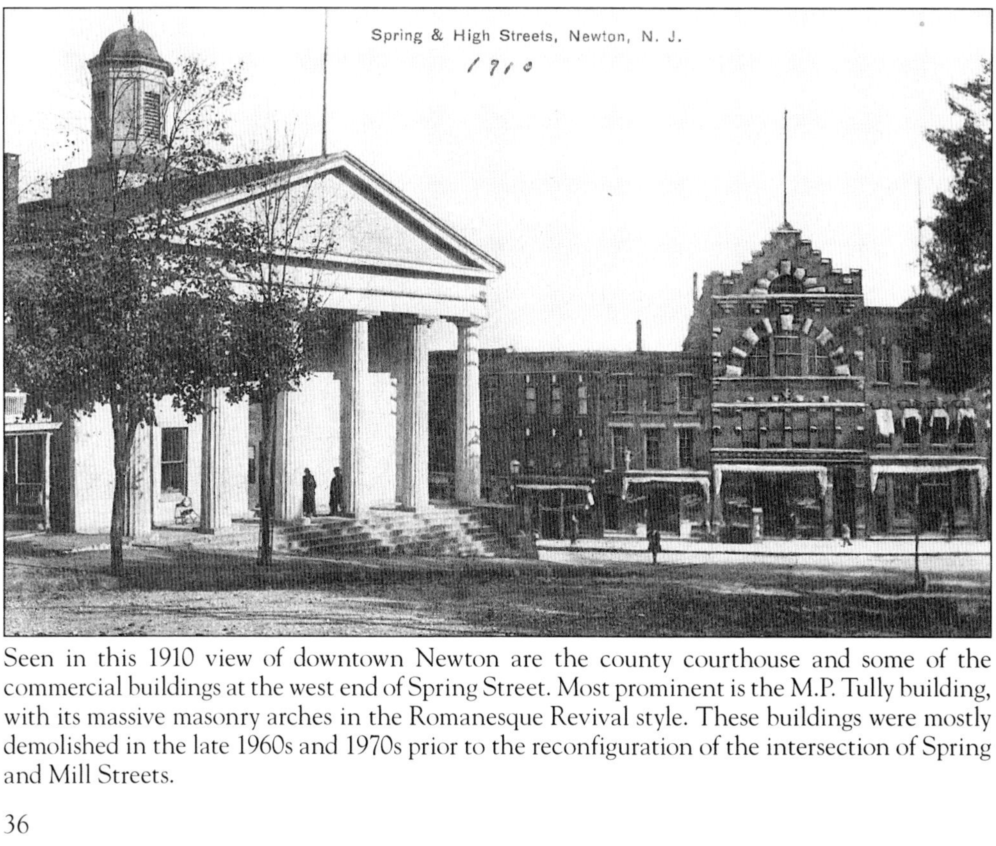

Seen in this 1910 view of downtown Newton are the county courthouse and some of the commercial buildings at the west end of Spring Street. Most prominent is the M.P. Tully building, with its massive masonry arches in the Romanesque Revival style. These buildings were mostly demolished in the late 1960s and 1970s prior to the reconfiguration of the intersection of Spring and Mill Streets.

Three

NEWTON'S COMMERCE

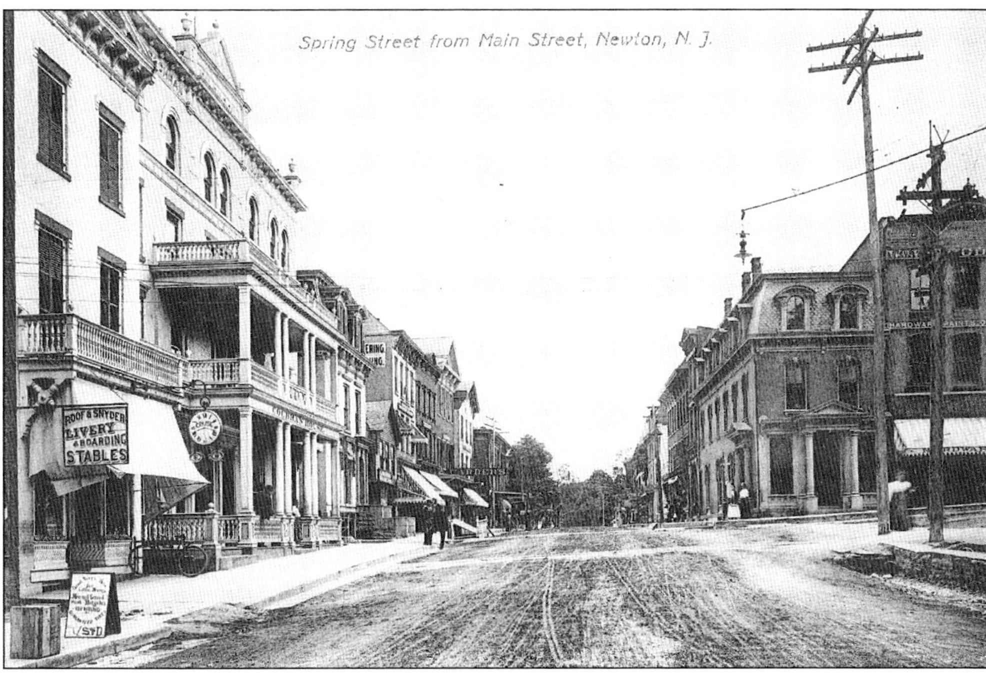

Then as now, Spring Street and the streets radiating from it formed the heart of Newton's commercial district. A bicycle shop, livery stable, watch & eyeglass store, and a hardware store can all be seen in this 1912 view of the intersection of Spring and Main Streets, not to mention two banks and the Cochran House.

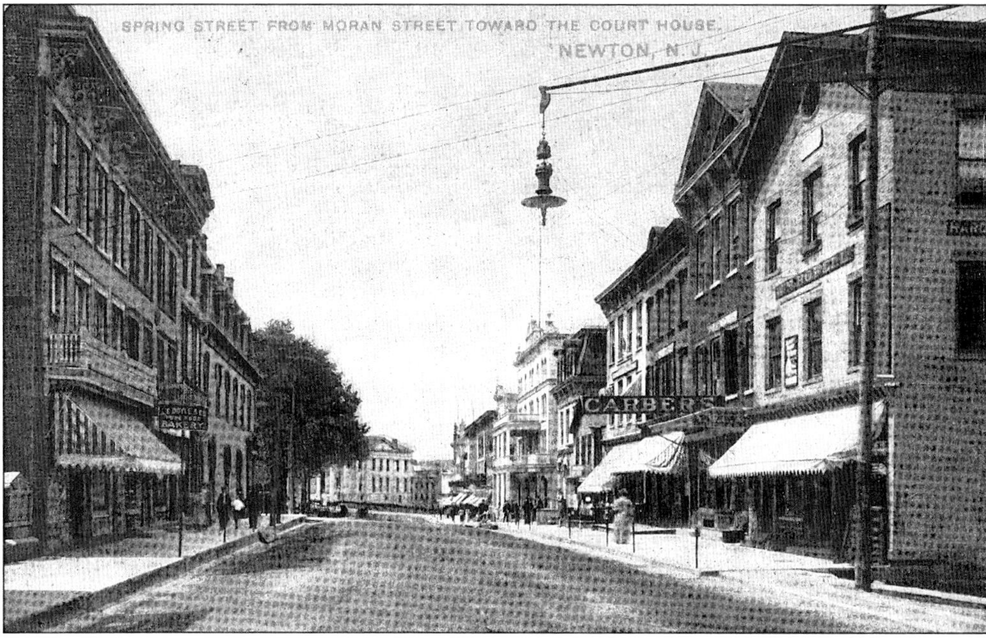

The commercial core of Newton extended on Spring Street from the courthouse, past the intersection with Moran Street, seen here, and on to the railroad station at the east end of town. Notice the new-fangled electric street light hanging over the intersection.

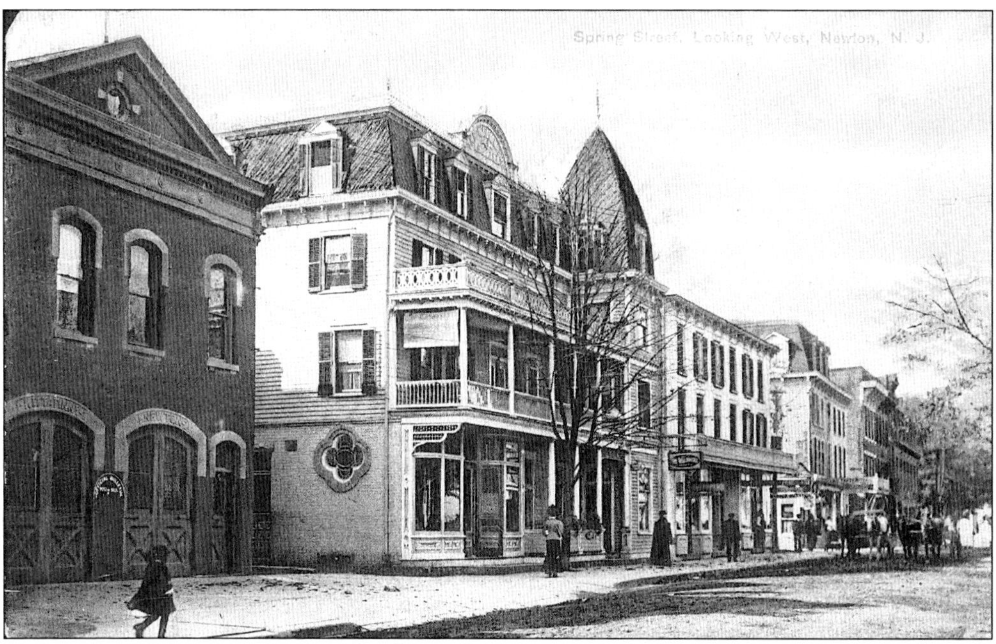

With its ornate second-story porch, the Waldmere Hotel dominated the south side of Spring Street. The firehouse, on the hotel's left, was built in 1892 as a joint facility for Newton Steamer Company No. 1 and the Kittatinny Hose Company.

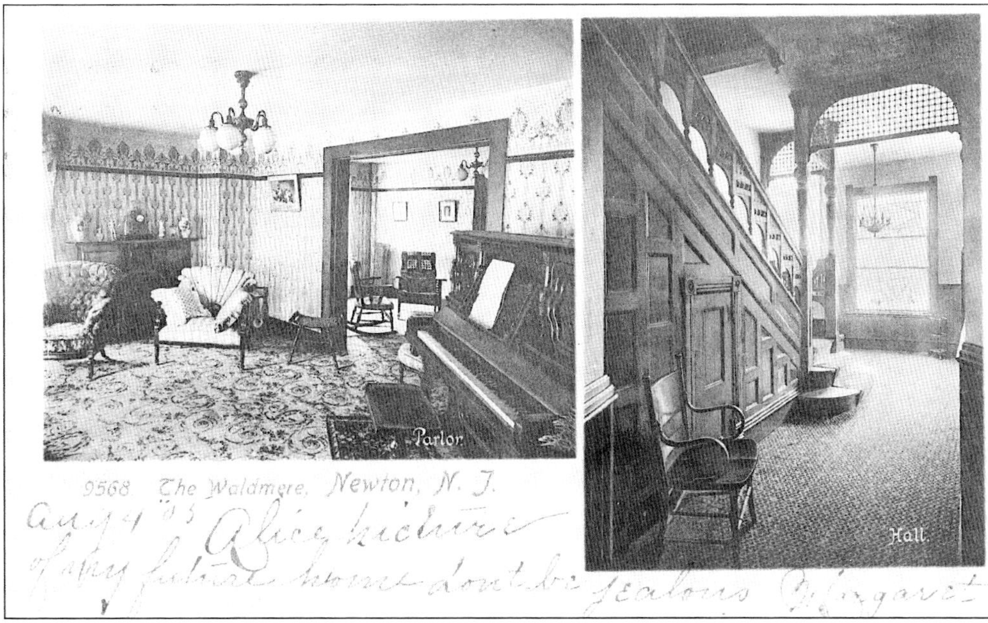

The homey atmosphere of the Waldmere was perhaps due to the fact that it was originally a private residence. The oldest portions date to about 1822, and Andrew B. Brickner remodeled the structure and opened it as a hotel in 1903. This postcard was mailed in 1905, so the pictures were taken shortly after the hotel opened. A contemporary newspaper described the staircase as "a work of art."

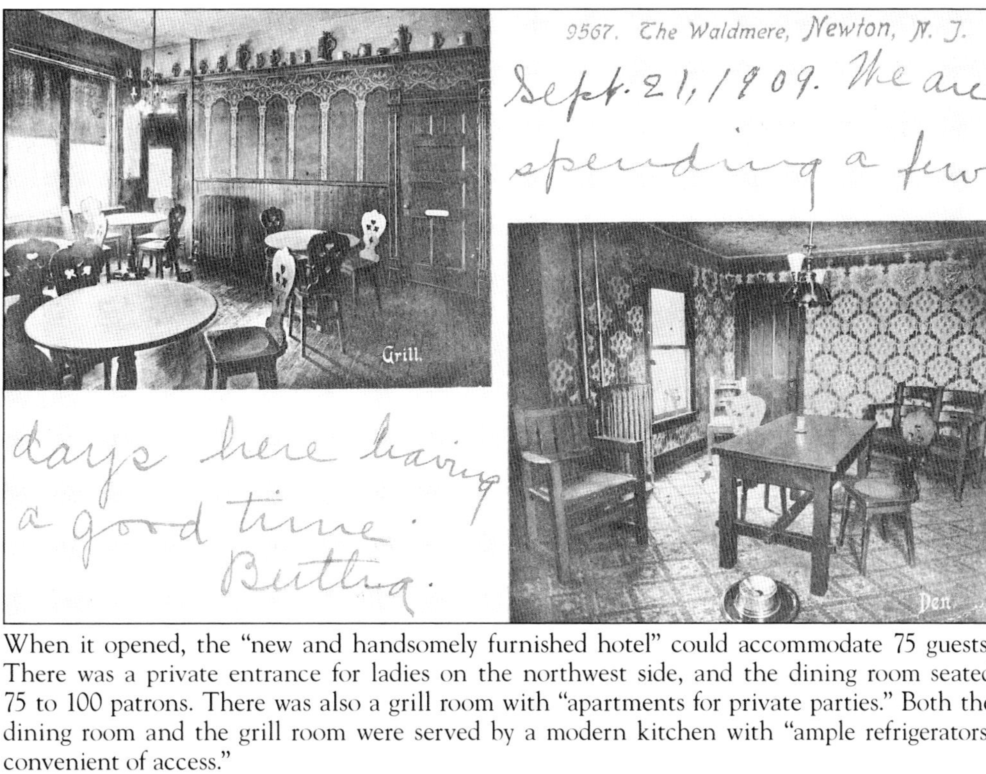

When it opened, the "new and handsomely furnished hotel" could accommodate 75 guests. There was a private entrance for ladies on the northwest side, and the dining room seated 75 to 100 patrons. There was also a grill room with "apartments for private parties." Both the dining room and the grill room were served by a modern kitchen with "ample refrigerators, convenient of access."

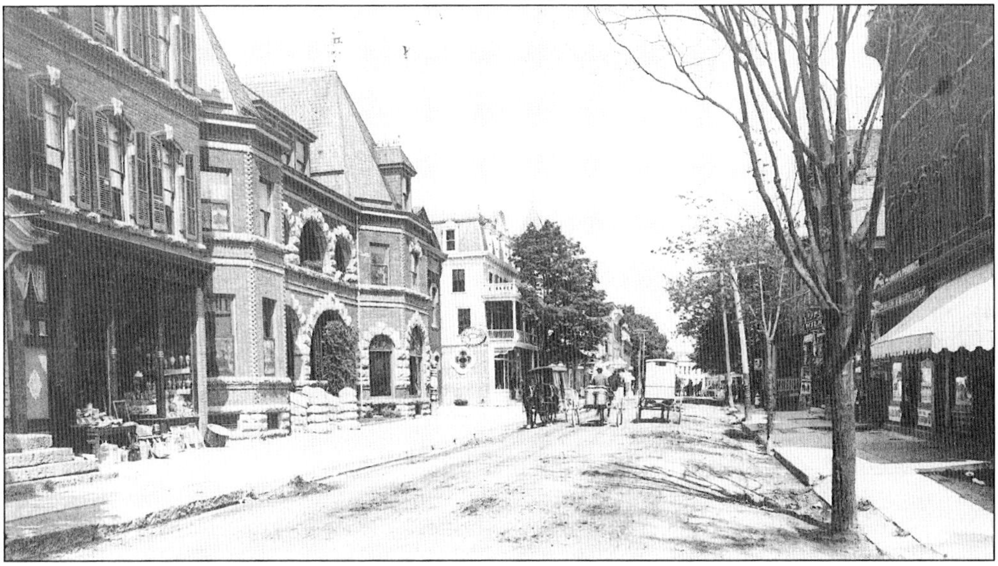

In 1895, Mrs. Cortelyou spent $20,000 on the construction of a combination residence and storehouse on the site of the old Townsend homestead. The building was designed in the Romanesque Revival style, with massive granite arches, by J.J. Merriam of Summit, New Jersey. The business portion of the building was leased to Daniel Fisher as a billiard and pool parlor.

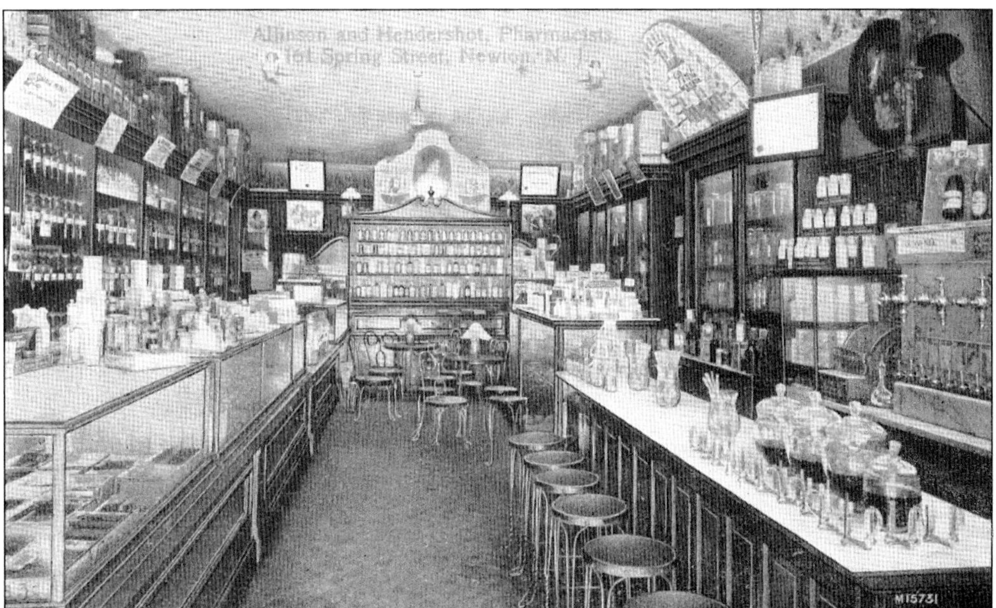

This is the interior of one of the oldest pharmacies in Newton, Allinson & Hendershot. Their store had several locations. About 1910, when this postcard was published, it was located in the English building, across the street and a bit east of the Waldmere Hotel.

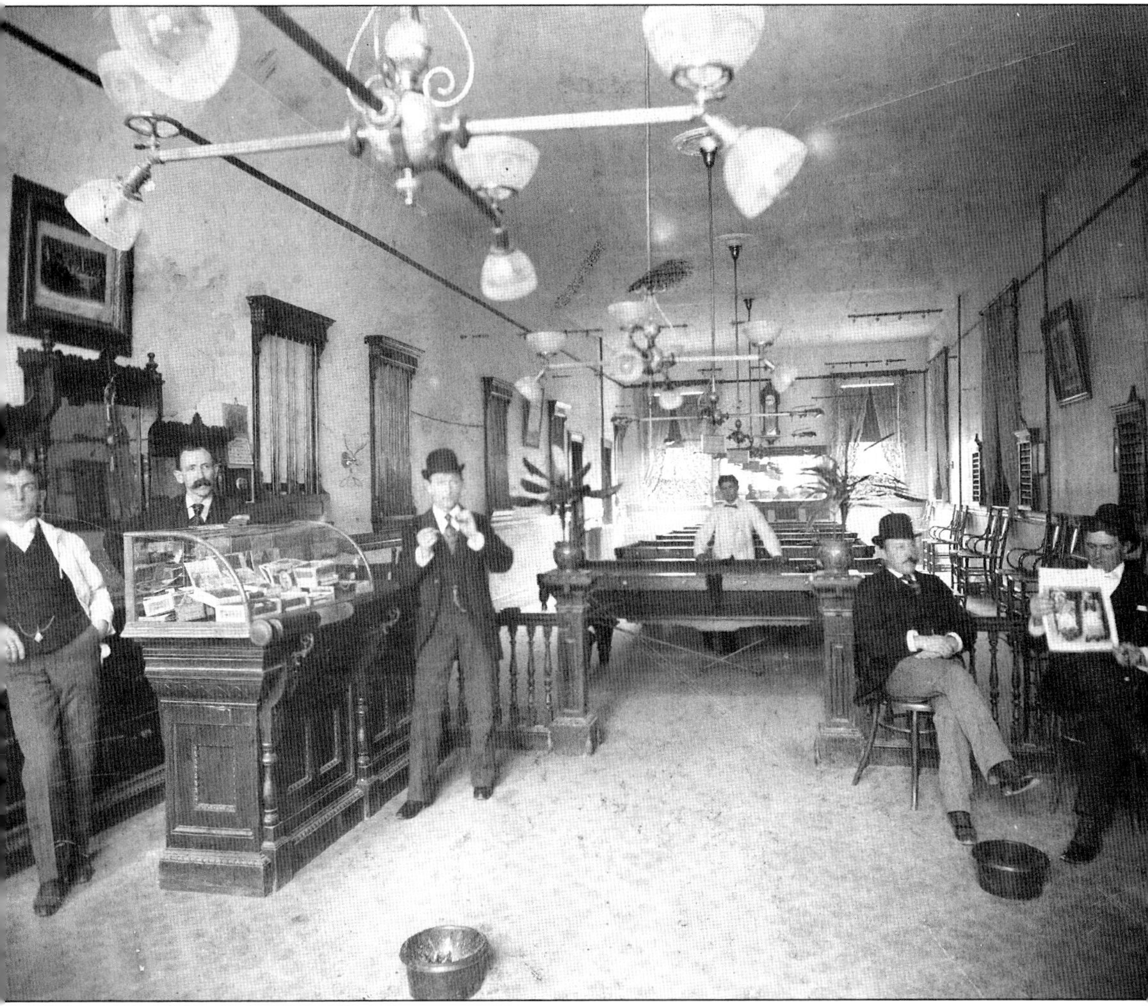

"Such is the enterprise . . . the crowd is 'all right' . . . Any slight disturbance is promptly quenched and tabooed without further comment . . . As to the stock: it is all that can be desired in the tobacco and soft drink line and is found invariably fresh . . . The tonsorial artist . . . is the genuine article . . . The billiard tables are the most attractive in town and the best conducted. The manager and proprietor, Mr. D.L. Fisher is one of the leading spirits in town and a member of several of our leading fraternal societies." This description of Fisher's billiard parlor was published by the *Sussex Register* in 1897.

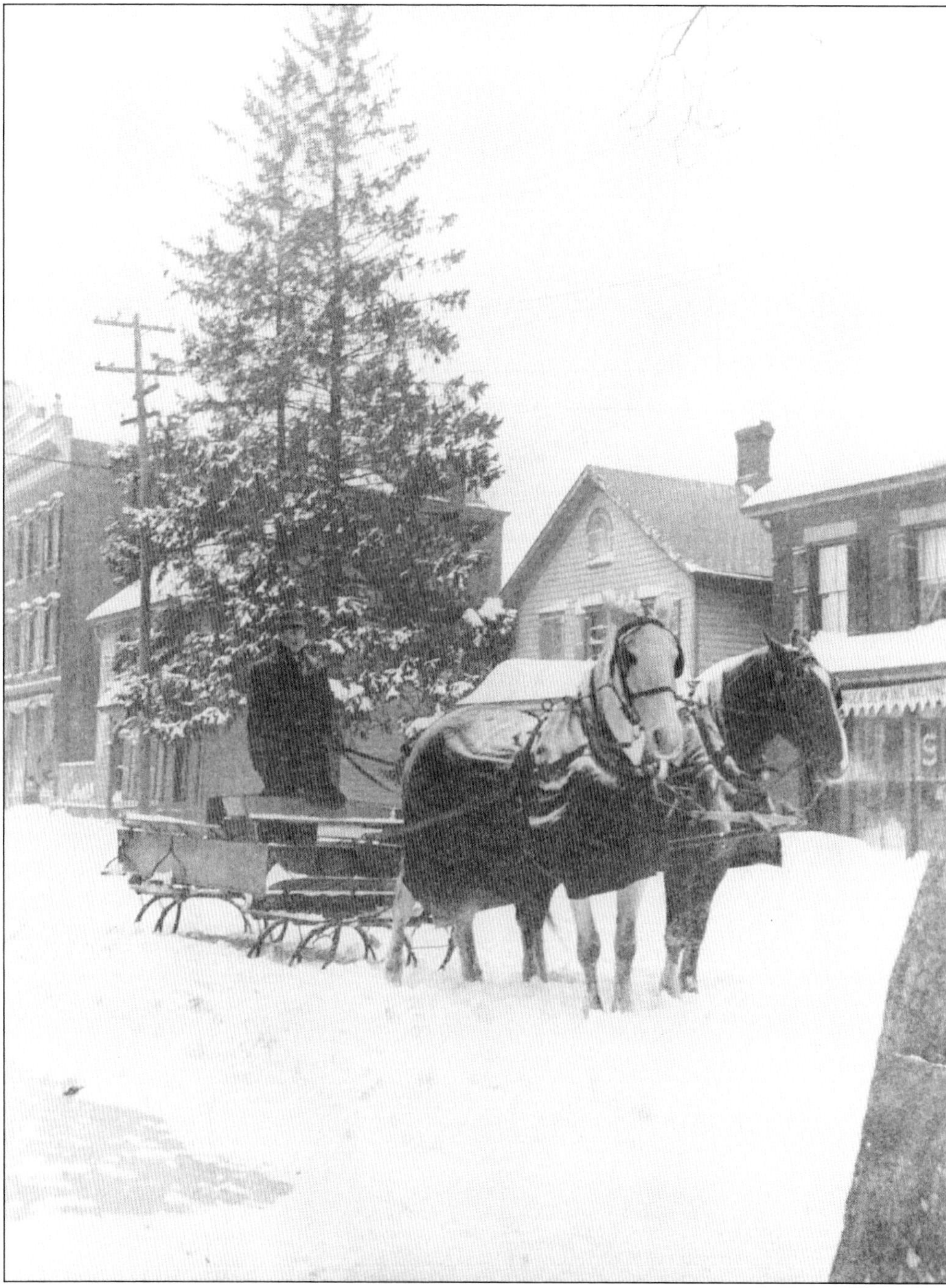

Just as today's drivers put snow tires on their cars, yesterday's farmers mounted their wagons on bobsleds. This team stands in front of the Singer Sewing Machine dealership on Spring Street, located in the former Savacool Paper Box Manufacturing facility (see page 57). The English building, with its imposing cast iron crest, can be seen on the left. Notice too, the mature trees, including the two towering evergreens, that lined the street. When this photograph was taken, about 1910, the streets were still left unplowed to facilitate travel by horse-drawn sledge and sleigh.

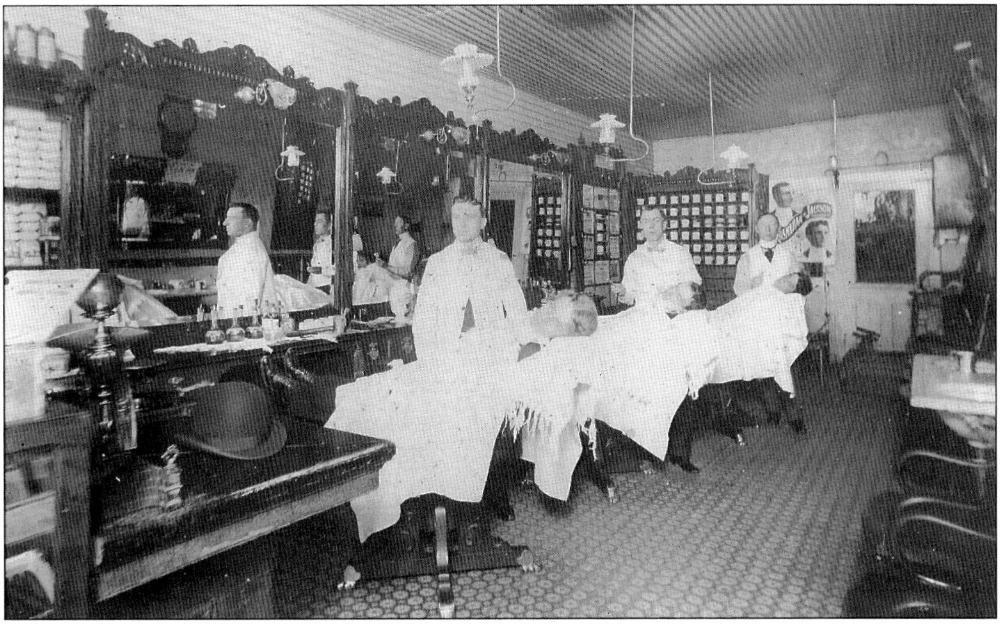

Three young men have been lathered for a shave in one of Newton's several barbershops. The cabinet at the rear contains individual shaving mugs for regular customers. The ribbed tin ceiling reflected the light from the gas lamps, allowing the barbers to ply their trade with greater speed and, we hope, accuracy.

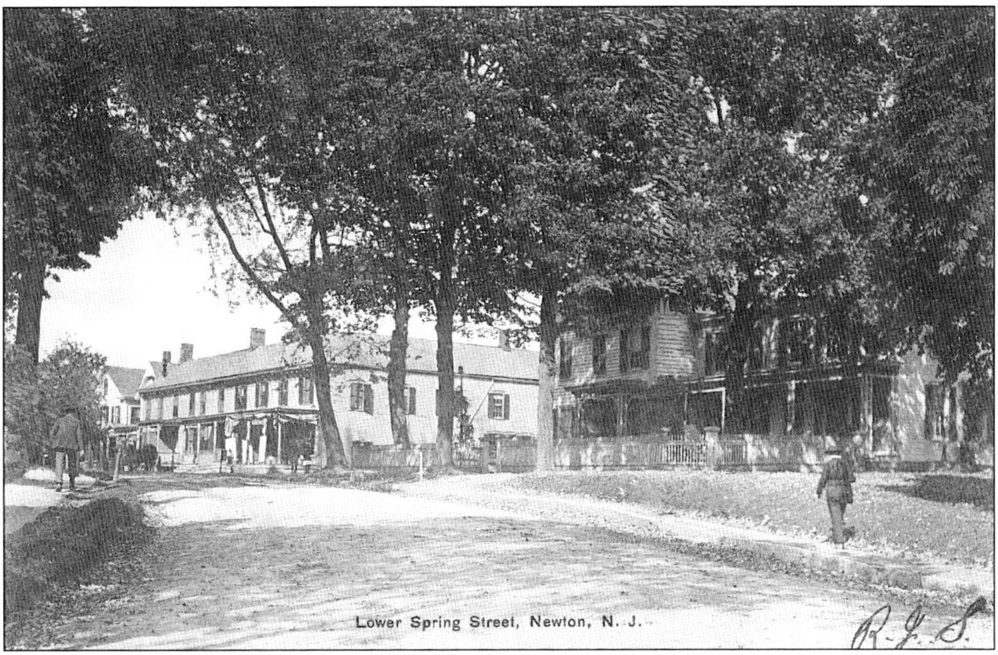

The eastern end of Spring Street contained a mixture of residential and commercial structures. The two-story frame building at the corner of Spring Street and Union Place was an apartment house, but the rooms in front on the ground floor were taken over by small businesses, as can be attested by their ramshackle porches and awnings. The house on the right was known locally as "The Homestead."

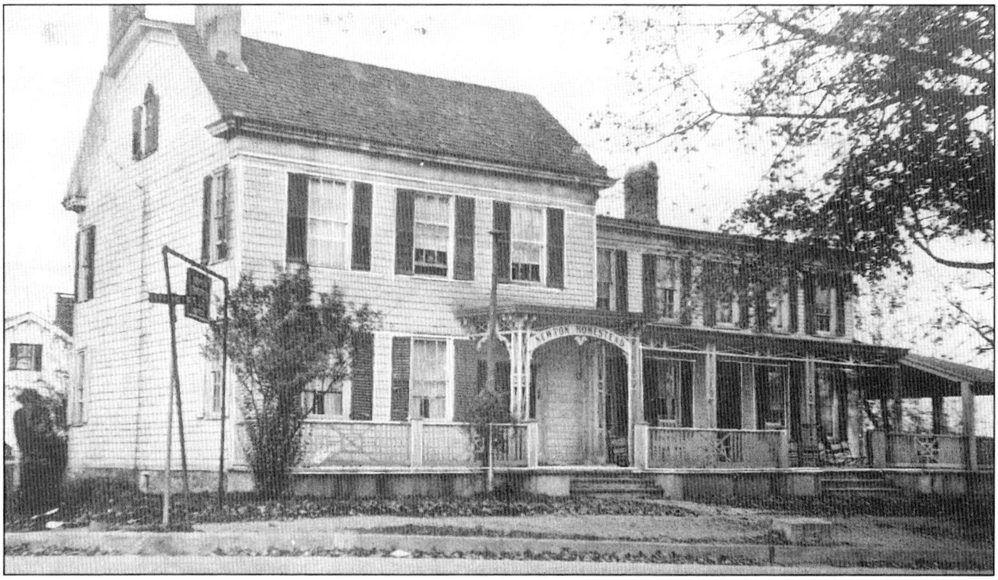

Its oldest portion built in the 18th century, "The Homestead" had a Dutch-influenced gambrel roof. In the early 19th century, the right wing was added with a Federal-style flattened roof with a deep cornice. In the late 1850s the house was purchased by Dr. John R. Stuart, an early investor in the Sussex Railway. At the turn of the century, his descendants were running it as a boarding house.

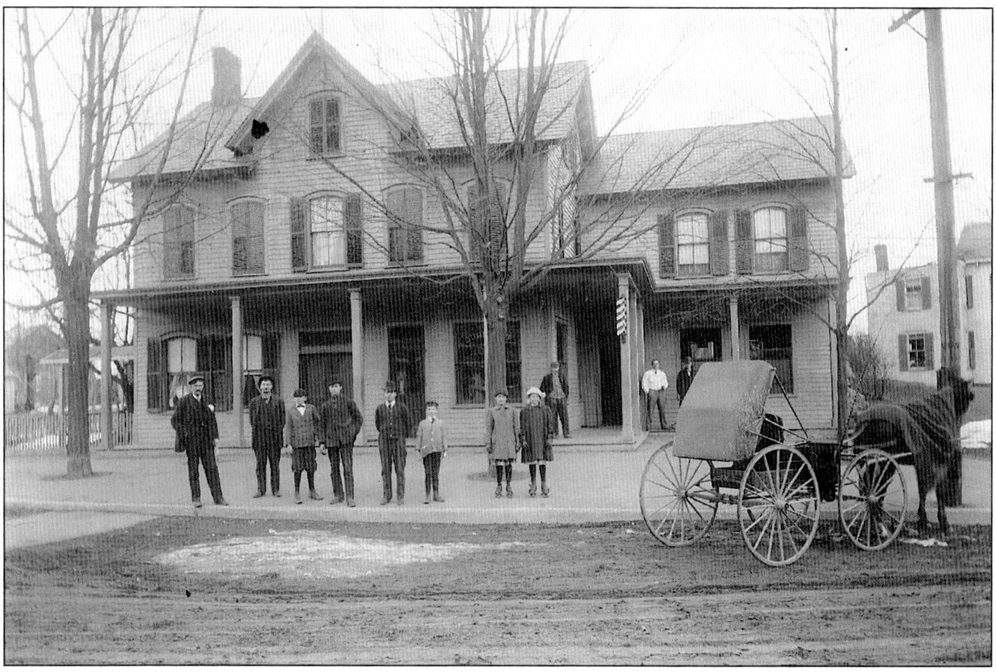

Conveniently located near the railway station at the east end of Spring Street, the Durling House was built in 1870 by Col. James Fitts as the National Hotel. Subsequent owners added to the building. In 1909, Henry Durling purchased the hotel (then known as the Lackawanna Hotel) from Charles Fredenburgh, and in 1911 extended the hotel's porch. Notice the two little girls in roller skates.

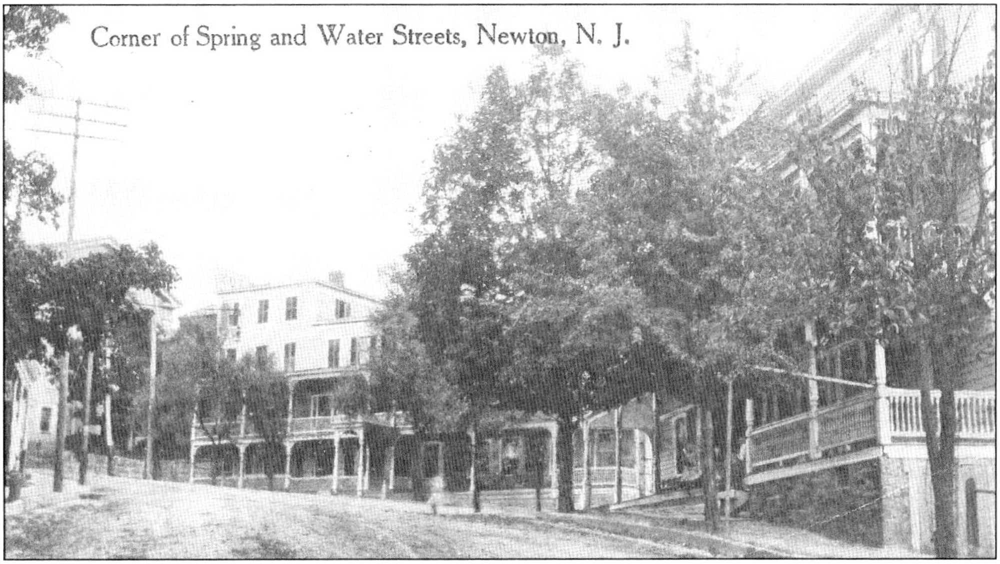

At its west end, Spring Street ended behind the courthouse in a three-way intersection with Mill and Water Streets. The Sussex Hotel, on the right with the two-story porch, stood in the confluence of Mill and Water Streets. Across from it, in the center of the view, is the Hotel Newton, one of the last buildings on the south side of Spring Street.

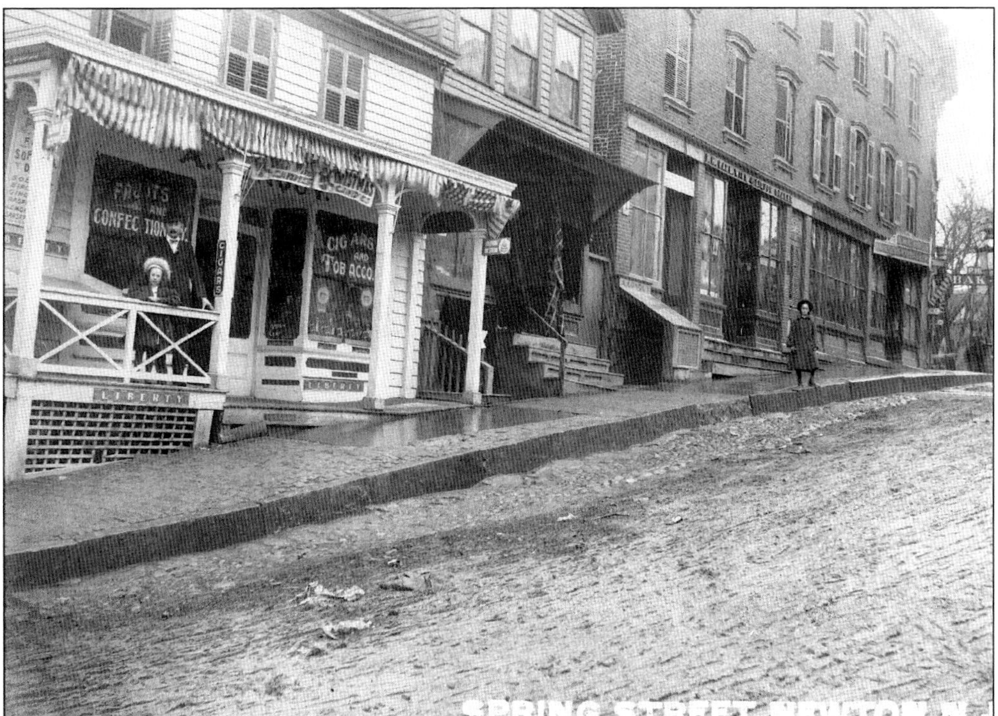

These shops stood on the north side of Spring Street, across from the Hotel Newton. Water Street began a few doors down the hill. The buildings fell victim to urban renewal in the 1970s, and Water Street was later widened and realigned, obliterating the site. We hope the little girl in this c. 1910 postcard was able to sample some goods from the candy shop.

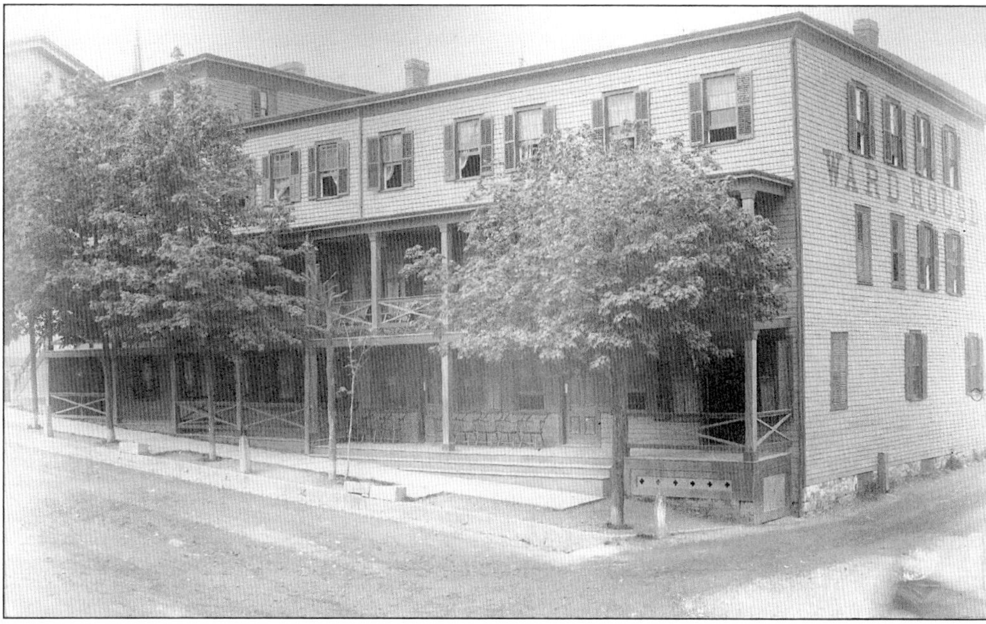

When this hotel, conveniently sited just behind the courthouse, was erected before the Civil War, it was known as the Anderson House. It changed owners and names several times, becoming the Ward House and later the Hotel Newton, finally ending as an apartment building. This photograph was taken about 1890, when the establishment was known as the Ward House.

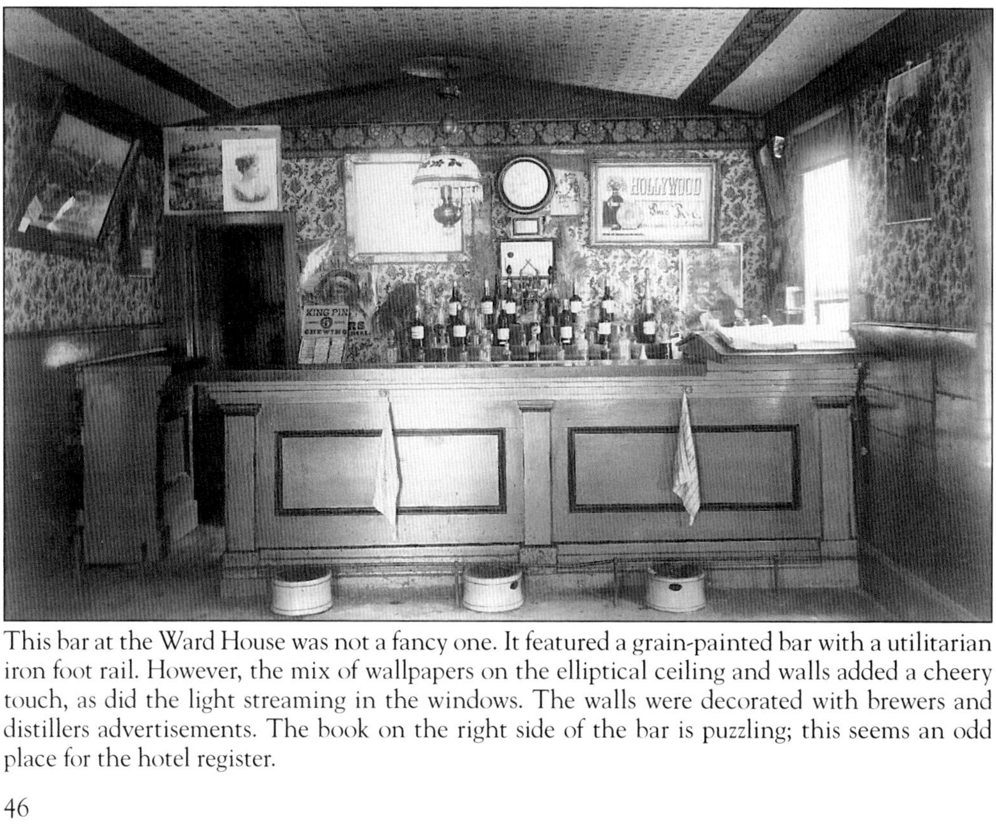

This bar at the Ward House was not a fancy one. It featured a grain-painted bar with a utilitarian iron foot rail. However, the mix of wallpapers on the elliptical ceiling and walls added a cheery touch, as did the light streaming in the windows. The walls were decorated with brewers and distillers advertisements. The book on the right side of the bar is puzzling; this seems an odd place for the hotel register.

Four

Transportation and Industry

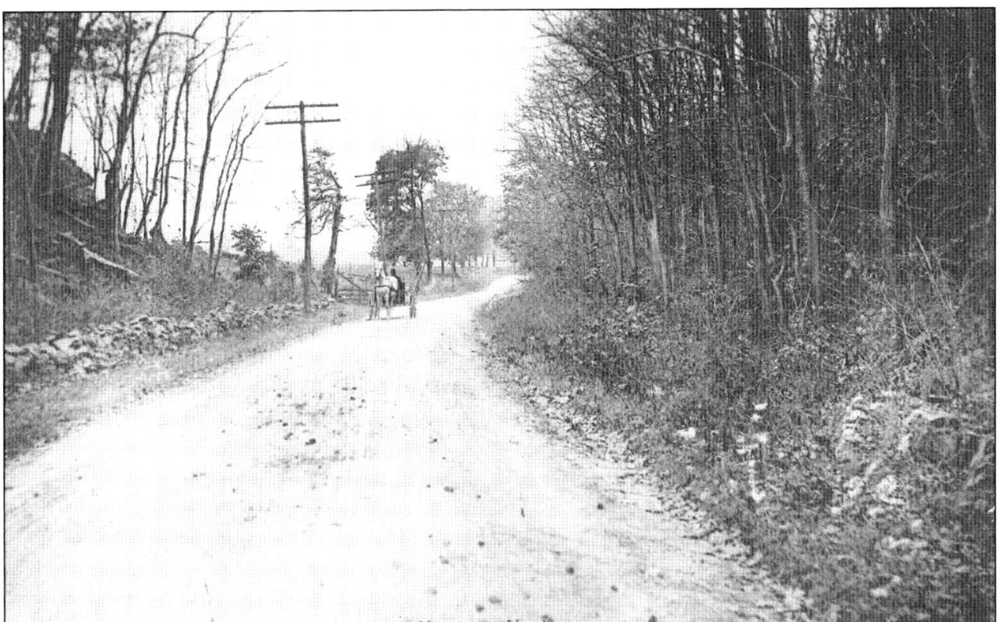

A Favorite Drive. The Narrows near Newton, N. J.

Reliable transportation is critical to the success of any community, and Newton was chosen as the county seat in part because of its location at the intersection of two ancient trails, the "New York Road" from Elizabeth to Milford, Pennsylvania, and the "Easton Road" from Easton, Pennsylvania to Kingston, New York. The New York Road entered town from the south through the Narrows, on what is now Route 206. From the days of the earliest settlers until the early decades of this century, it was a quiet dirt road and all the vehicles were horse-drawn, like the one seen in this 1910 image.

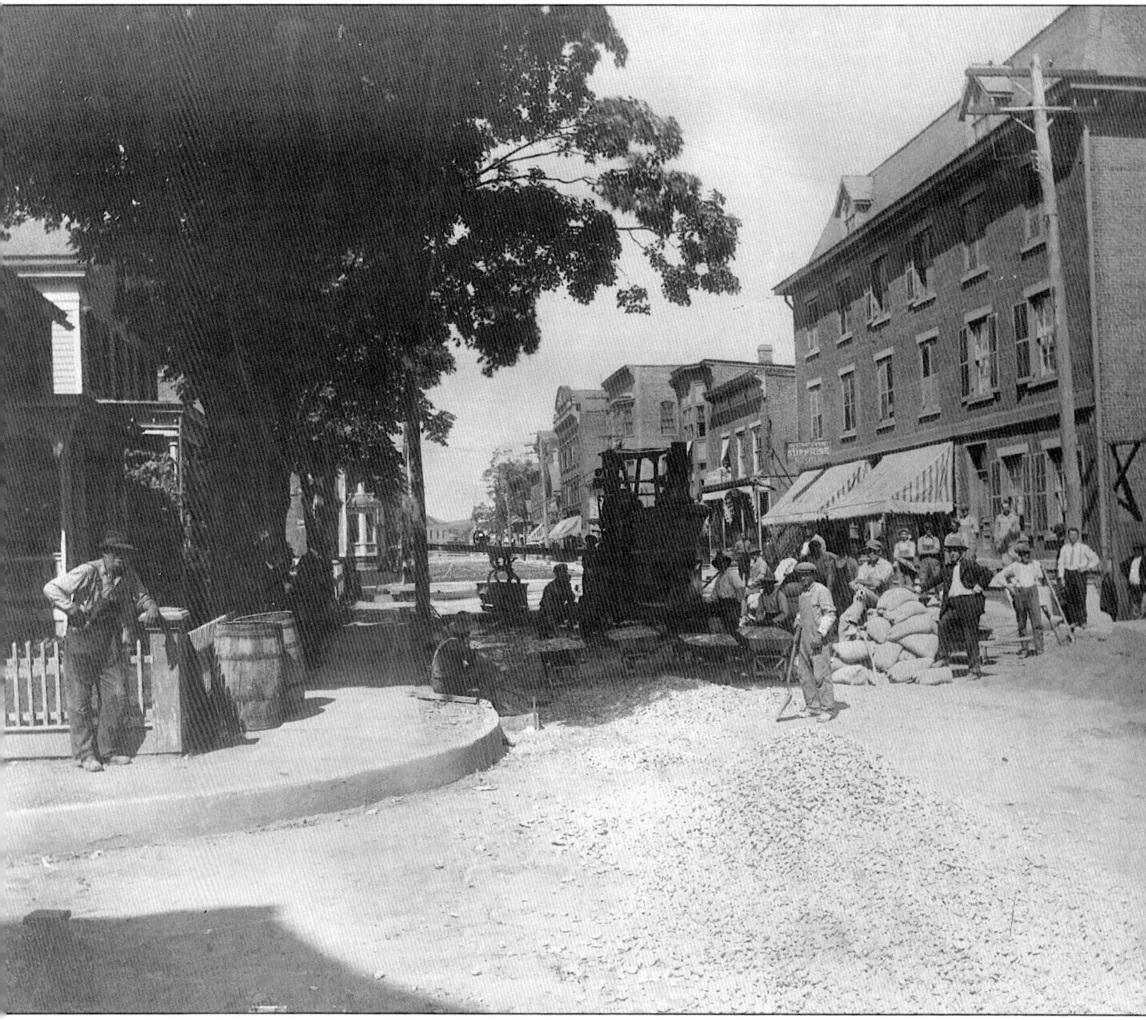

From April until July 1915, the citizens of Newton engaged in a heated debate over the paving of Spring Street. Some businessmen argued that brick was more durable than concrete and the surface gave better traction for horses pulling heavy wagons. Despite this argument, the town committee moved forward in mid-July. A contract to pave the road in concrete from Union Place to High Street was awarded to the Sothman Company of New York. The L.S. Iliff Company, and Hart & Iliff, both of Newton, split the contract to provide the concrete.

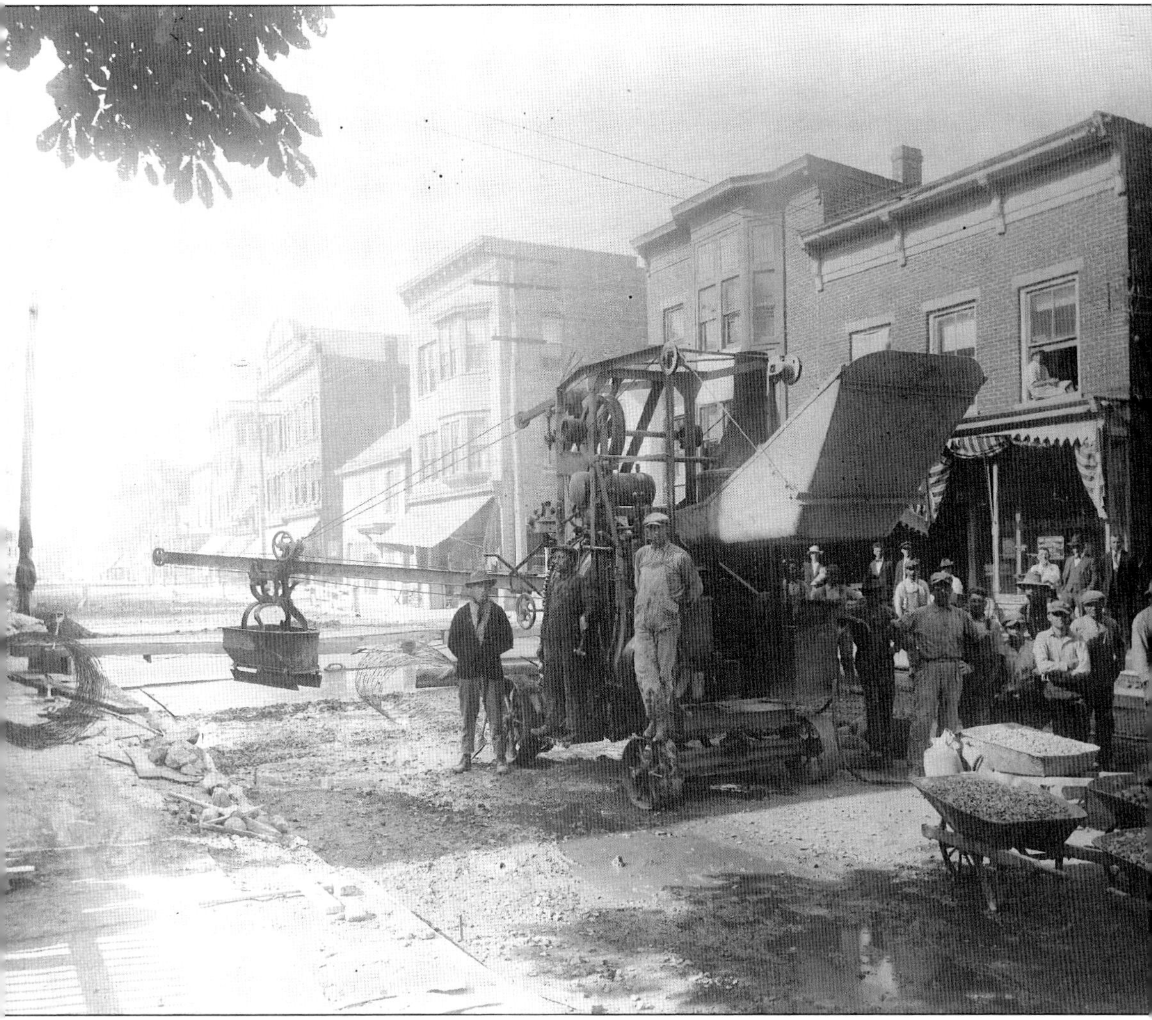

Work began a few weeks after the contract was awarded, and was well underway by September, when these photographs were taken. Here the workman pose next to their combination cement mixer and spreader. When the machine was in operation, they dumped barrow loads of aggregate into the big moveable hopper, and then raised it to add the stones to the cement in the mixer drum. The finished concrete was then poured into the bucket on the extended boom and dumped in the proper place.

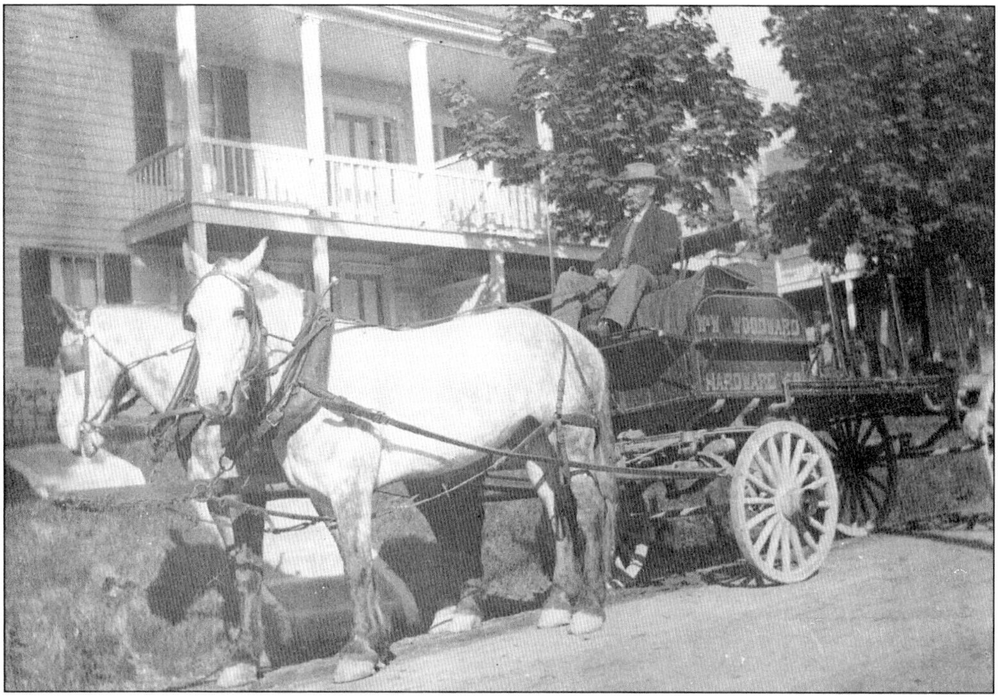

Like many local merchants, William Woodward relied on horsepower to deliver goods to his customers. His store, at 3 Main Street, carried all types of hardware and tools, plus farm implements, seeds, paint, firearms, sporting goods, and housewares. In 1897, the stock was valued in excess of $50,000. (Courtesy of Jan Gminder.)

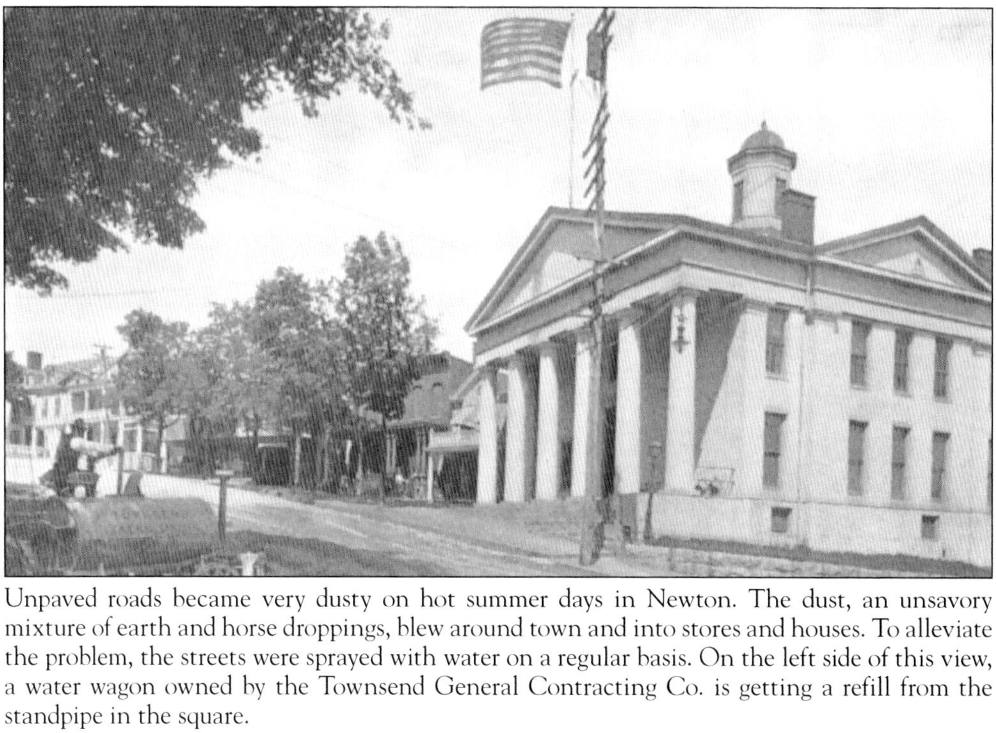

Unpaved roads became very dusty on hot summer days in Newton. The dust, an unsavory mixture of earth and horse droppings, blew around town and into stores and houses. To alleviate the problem, the streets were sprayed with water on a regular basis. On the left side of this view, a water wagon owned by the Townsend General Contracting Co. is getting a refill from the standpipe in the square.

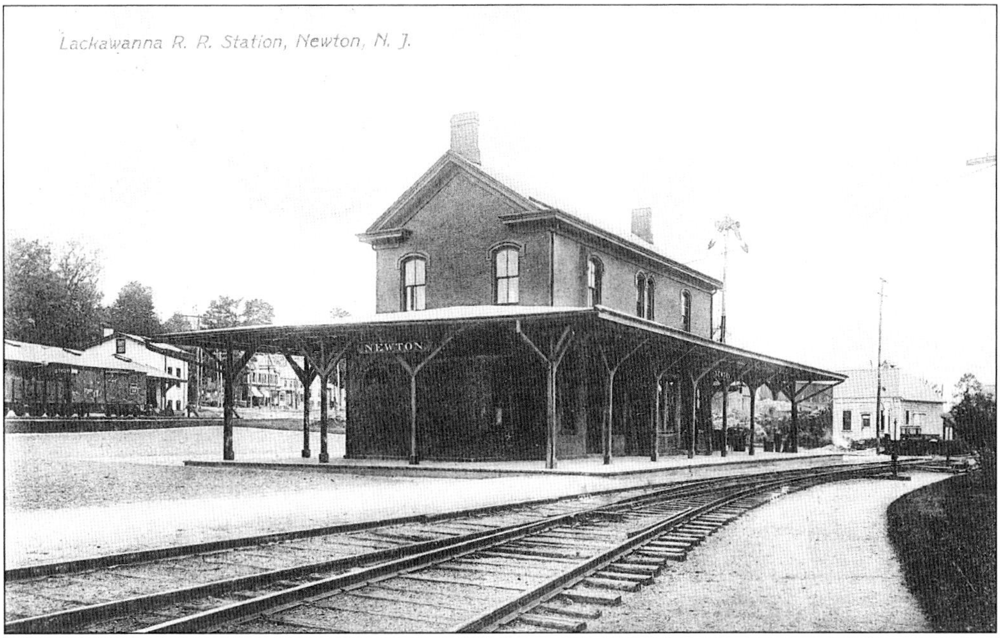

When the railroad first came to Newton in 1854, passengers and freight shared the same terminal building. However, by 1873 rail traffic was booming, and the Delaware, Lackawanna and Western Railroad built this handsome new passenger station at the end of Spring Street. The freight depot can be seen behind it on the left, built in 1907 on the site of the original terminal.

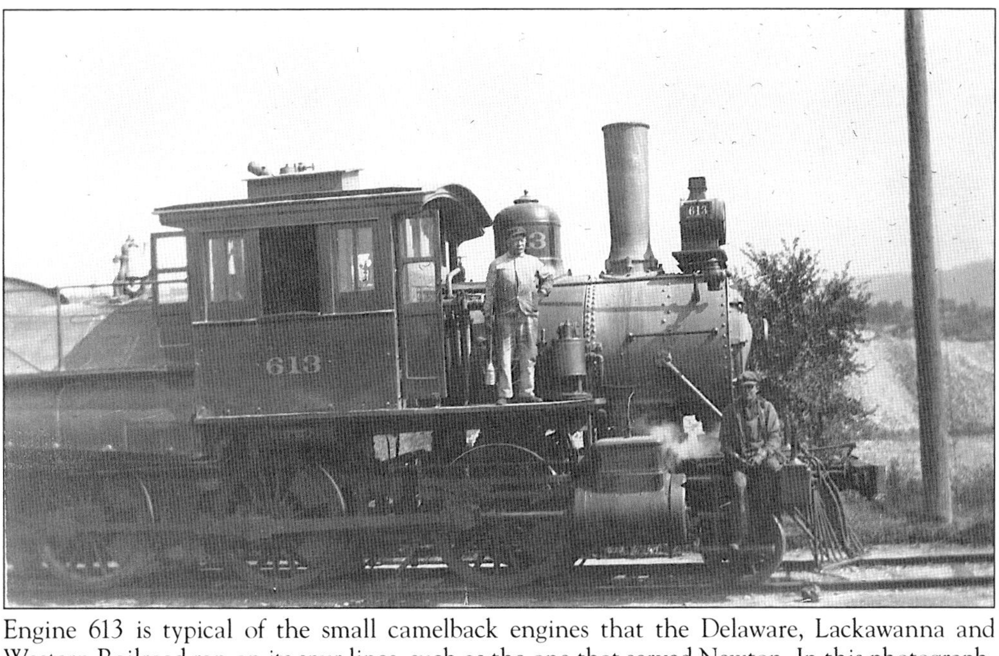

Engine 613 is typical of the small camelback engines that the Delaware, Lackawanna and Western Railroad ran on its spur lines, such as the one that served Newton. In this photograph, taken about 1910, the engineer, George Jones, is standing in front of the open cab door, while his fireman, John Decker, sits over one of the lead wheels.

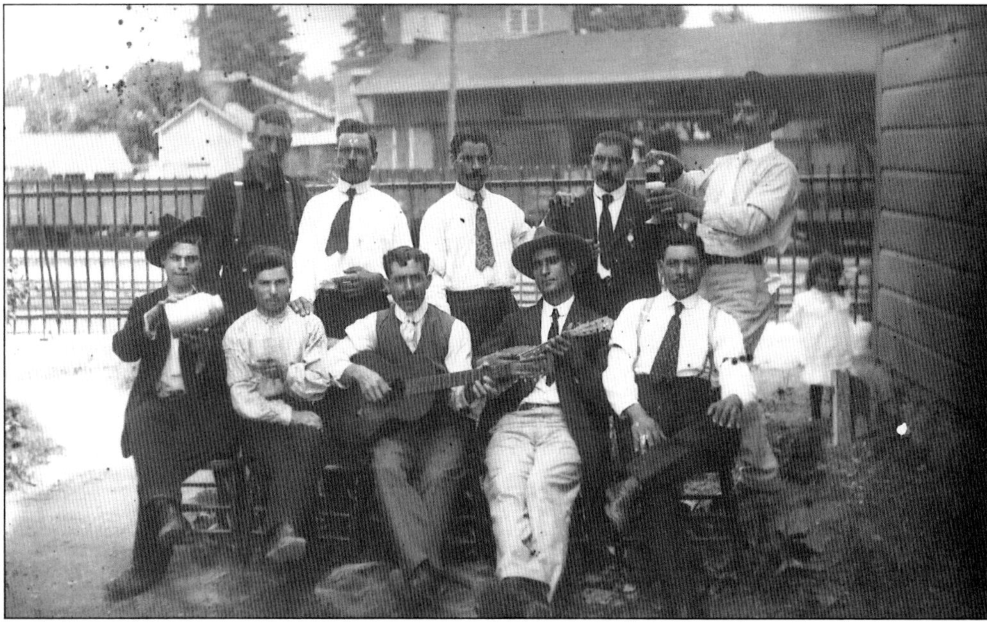

These men, possibly recent immigrants, most likely worked in the rail yard, or in the creamery and shoe factories nearby. Here they sit in their Sunday best between their houses on Railroad Avenue. Railroad Avenue, which ran between the rail line and Sparta Avenue, was eliminated by urban renewal in the 1970s .

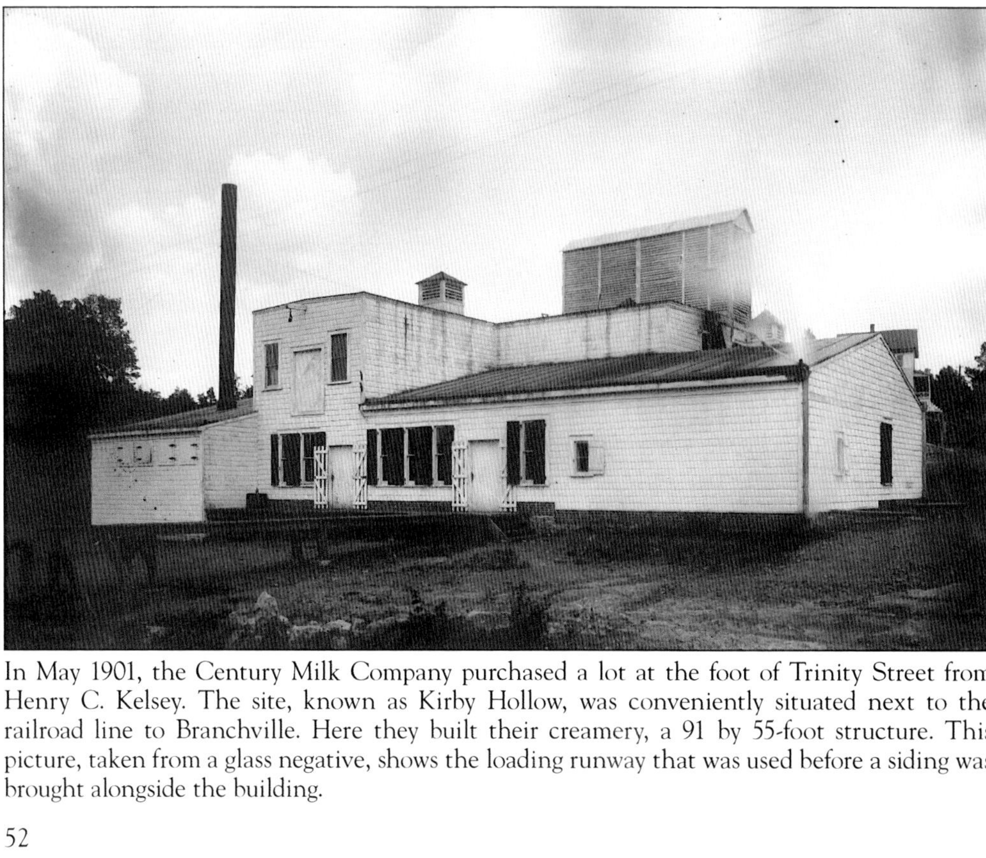

In May 1901, the Century Milk Company purchased a lot at the foot of Trinity Street from Henry C. Kelsey. The site, known as Kirby Hollow, was conveniently situated next to the railroad line to Branchville. Here they built their creamery, a 91 by 55-foot structure. This picture, taken from a glass negative, shows the loading runway that was used before a siding was brought alongside the building.

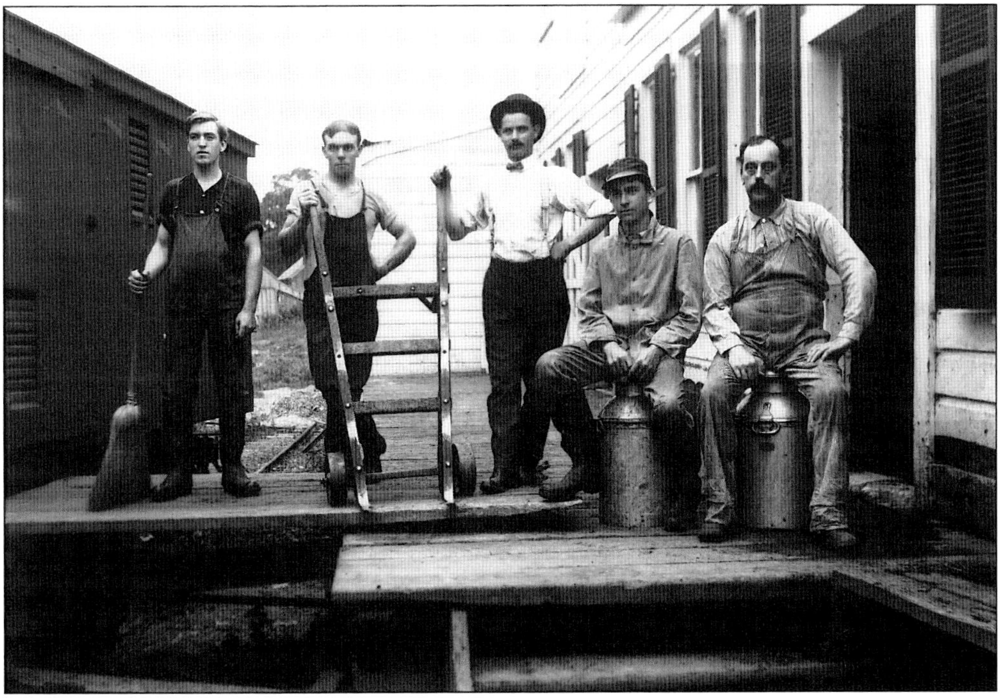

By 1910, a siding had been built alongside the creamery. Here five workers pose on the loading dock next to one of the Lackawanna Railroad's wooden refrigerated cars used to transport creamery products to Newark, New York, and other cities in the eastern part of the state. When this photo was taken, the creamery was producing one full carload of milk and cream per day.

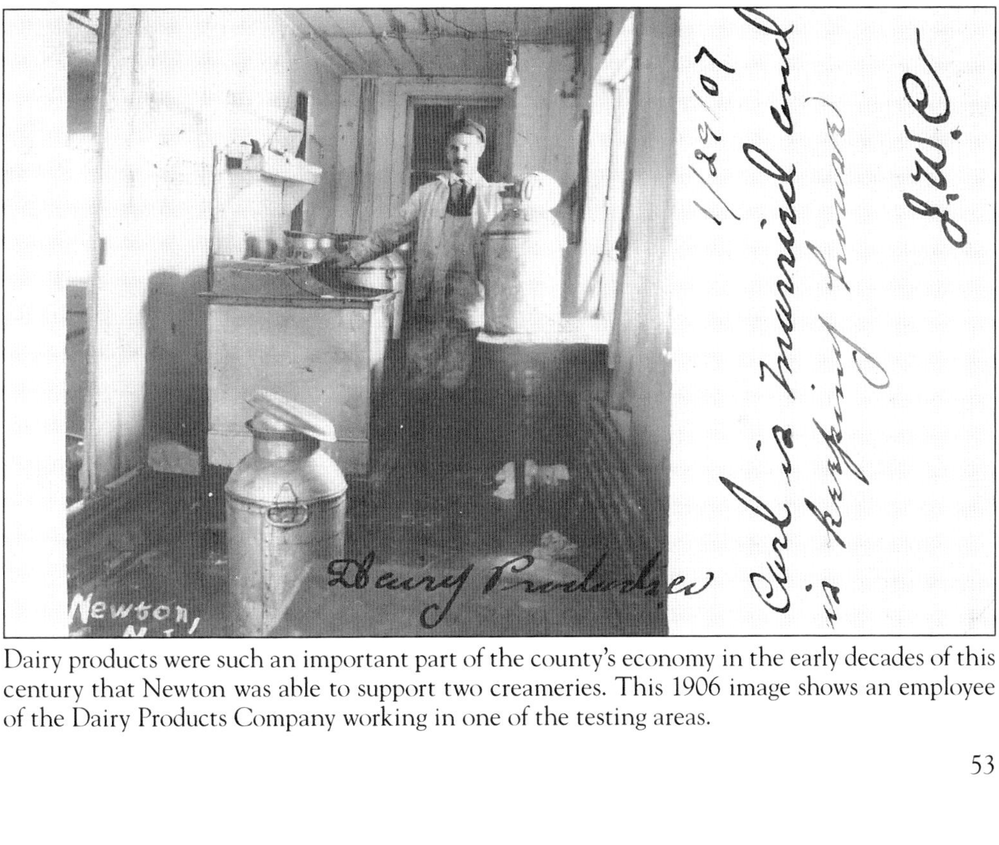

Dairy products were such an important part of the county's economy in the early decades of this century that Newton was able to support two creameries. This 1906 image shows an employee of the Dairy Products Company working in one of the testing areas.

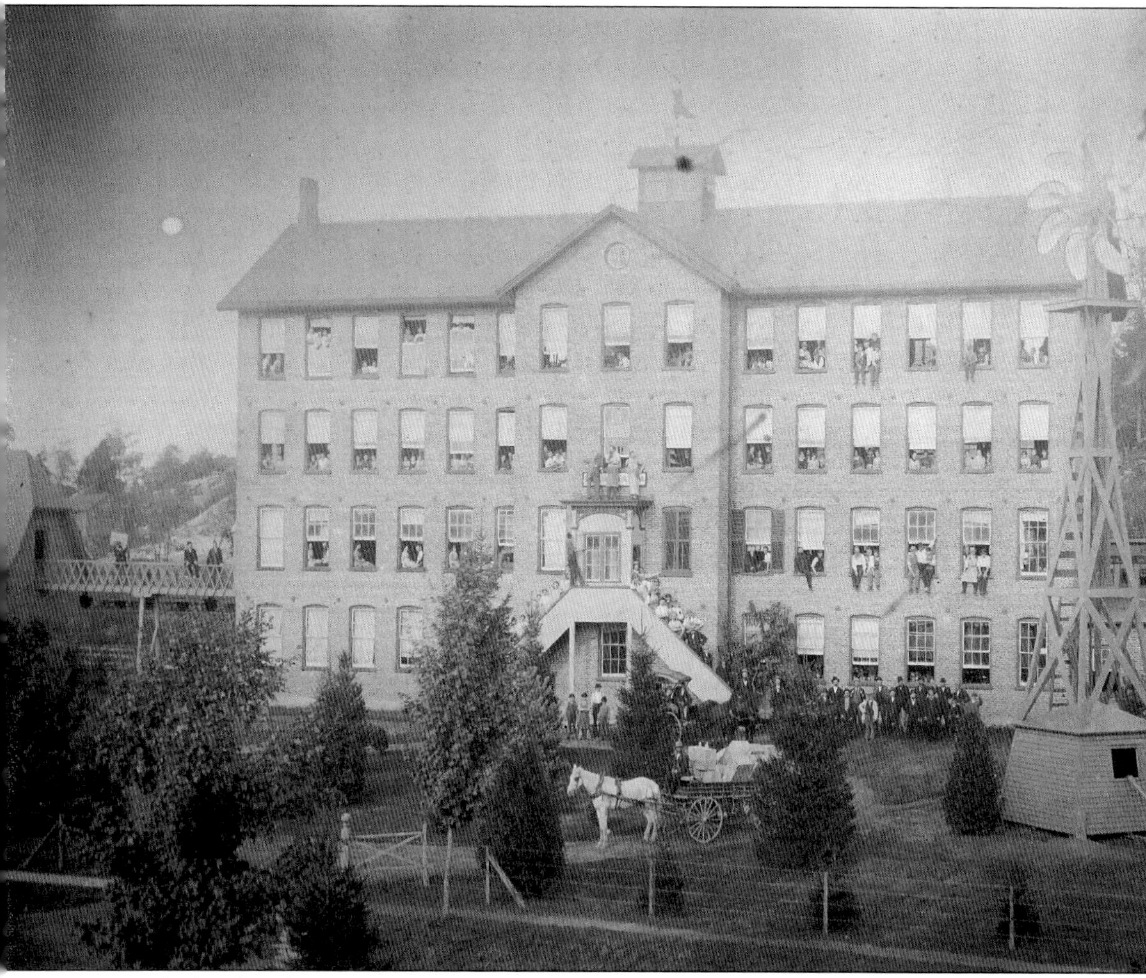

At the height of its success, the Henry W. Merriam Shoe Company was the largest employer in Newton, with over 550 workers by 1913. Merriam got his start in New York City during the Civil War, making boots and shoes for the Union Army. In 1873, Newton's Land Improvement Company persuaded him to move his operations to Newton, where he built this handsome brick factory building for his operations. Merriam shifted his focus from men's to ladies' and children's shoes, and began his Newton operation by producing 500 pairs of ladies' shoes per week. By 1883, he was producing over 1,000 pairs of ladies' and children's shoes per day, and had purchased the factory building from the Land Improvement Company. This photograph of the factory was taken about 1882. The small building on the left is the box factory completed in 1881, the same year as the windmill, which powered a water pump. (Courtesy of the Merriam House.)

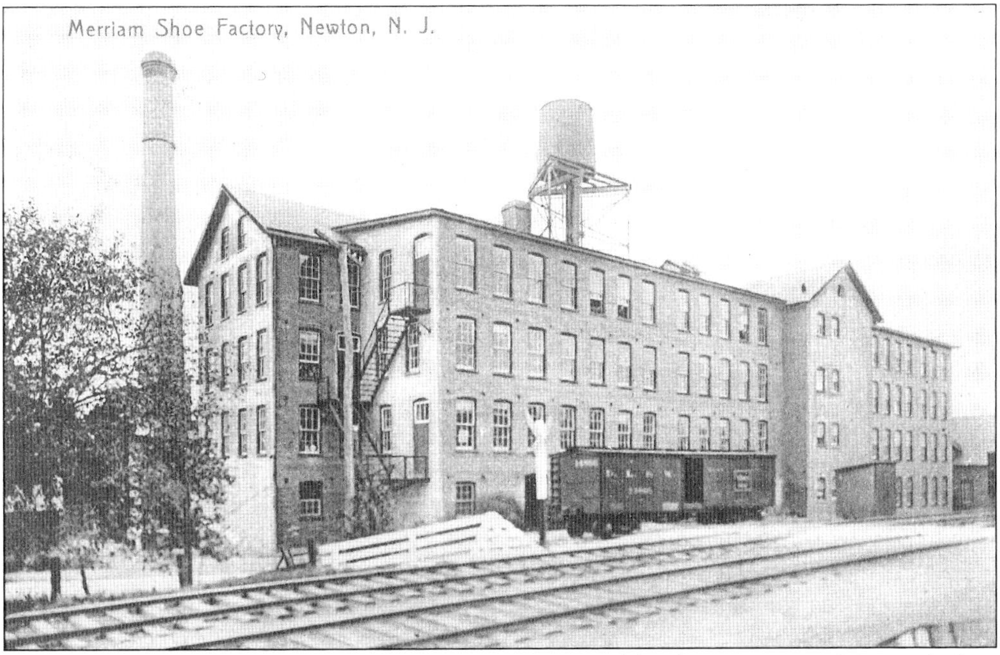

Rail transport was crucial to industrial development; so, like the creameries, Merriam's shoe factory was built next to the railroad tracks with a private siding for bringing in raw materials and shipping out finished goods. By the time this postcard was published in 1907, the factory had grown considerably and a steam plant had been added to power the sewing machines and other equipment.

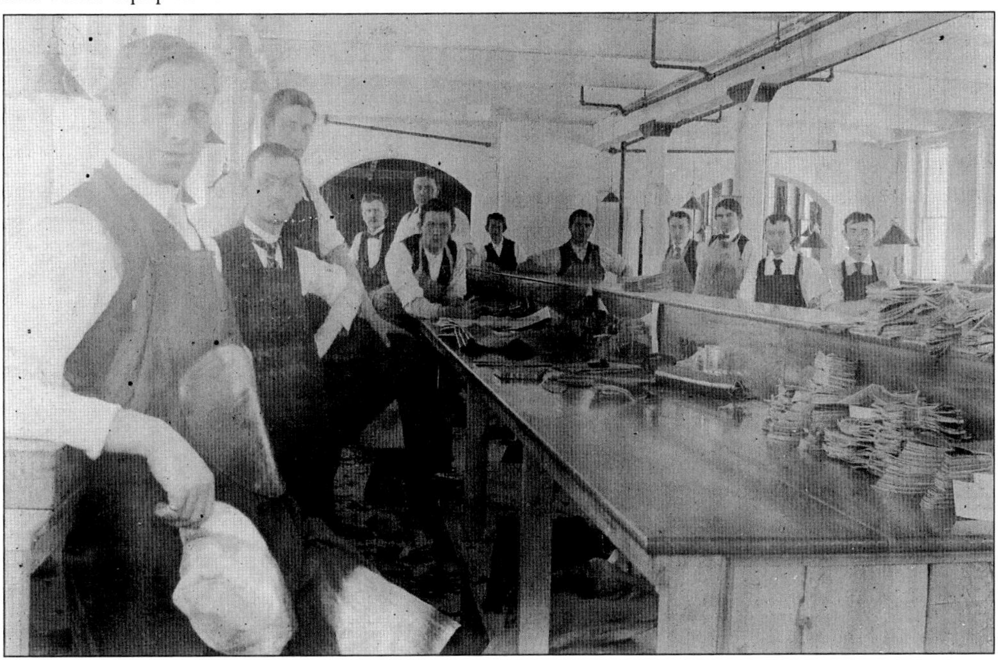

In 1906, some of Merriam's employees posed for this photograph, gathered around the workbenches where leather was cut into shoe soles. Even though they are working in a factory, notice how many of the men are wearing vests and ties.

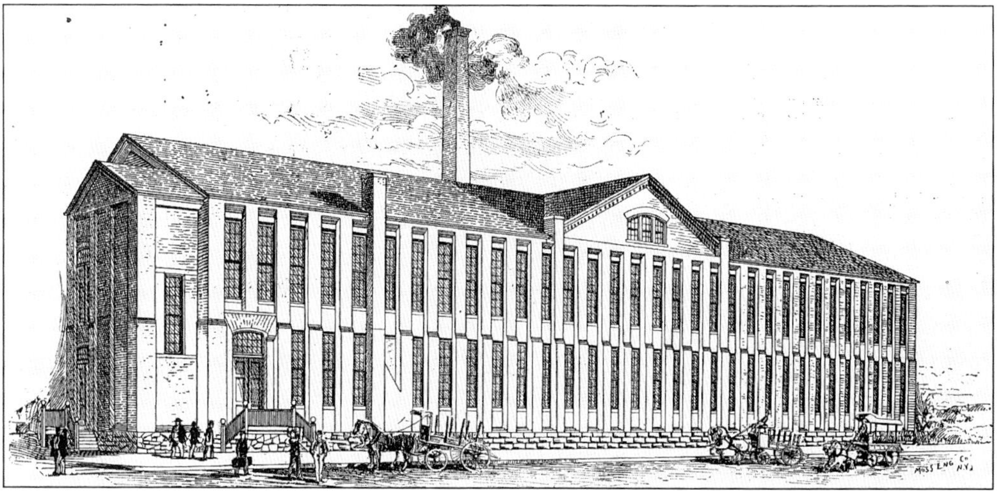

On October 25, 1895, a groundbreaking ceremony was held for the Sterling Silk Mill's imposing new brick building, and the company was in production by May the following year. According to the *New Jersey Herald*, the Paterson company was persuaded to build a mill in Newton due to "the untiring efforts of the Retail Merchants' Mutual Protective Association, of which W.W. Woodward is President."

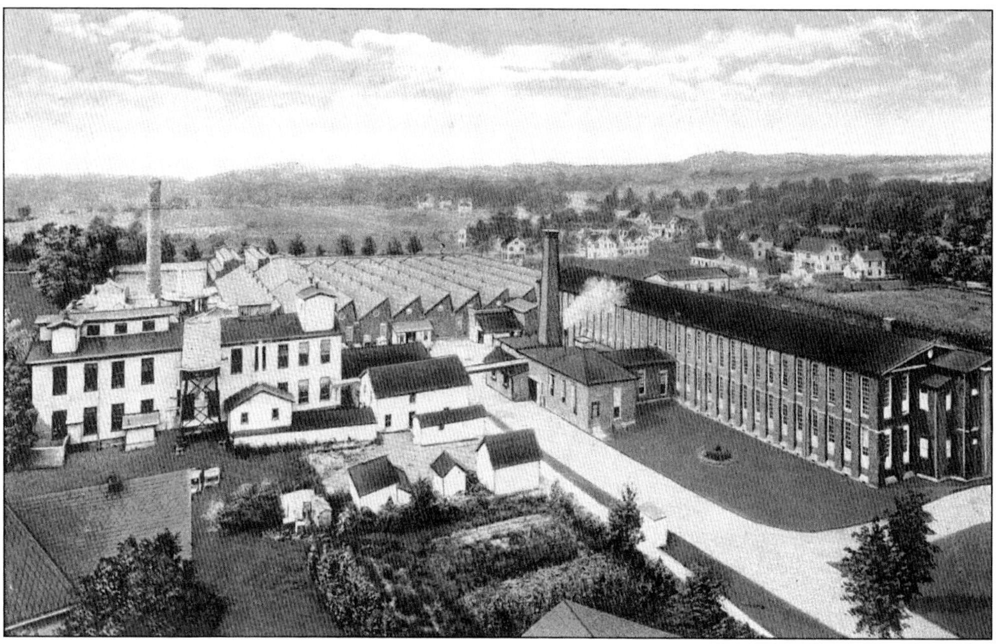

This view of the silk mill was taken about 1912 from the roof of the Merriam Shoe factory. The saw-toothed annex, with 400 looms, was added in 1899, and the large white dye house the following year. The company went through several name changes, finally becoming the Sussex Print Works in 1911.

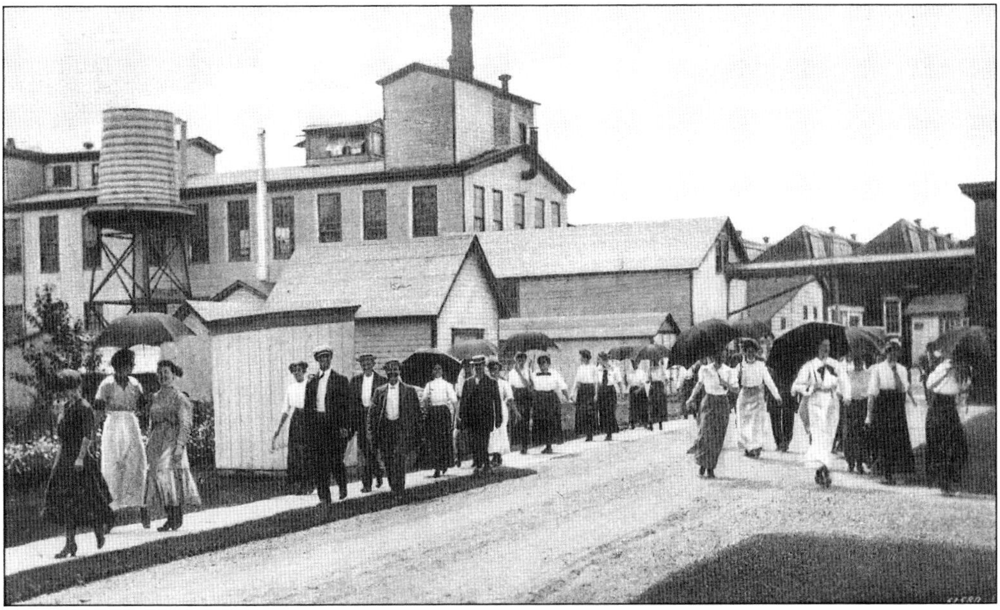

Employees of the Sussex Print Works leave the factory for lunch in this photograph taken during the summer of 1912. Many of the women carry umbrellas to provide dual protection from the hot sun and sudden downpours. Nevertheless, the workers' clothing makes few concessions to the season. The men are still wearing jackets, and the women's dresses cover layers of petticoats and corsets.

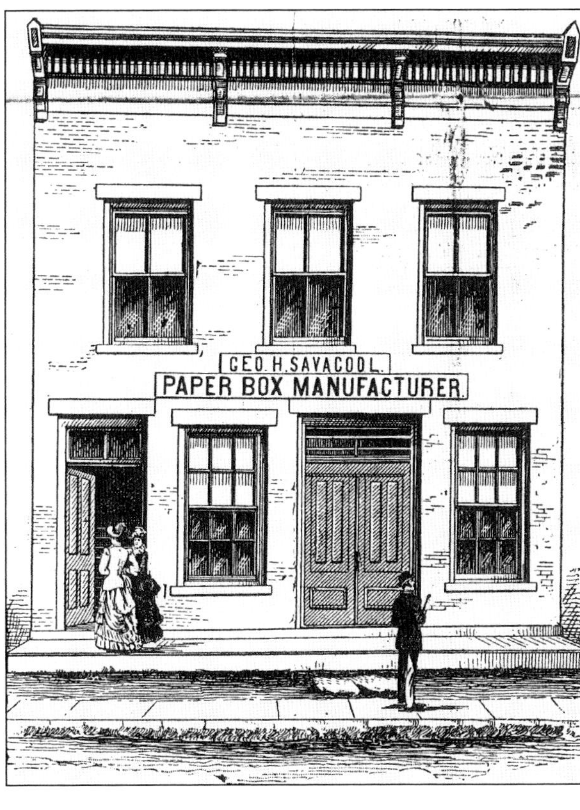

George Savacool purchased this paper box factory at 185 Spring Street in 1888 from the McEwen brothers of Whippany. At that time, the factory employed six girls and two boys to make between 1,000 and 1,500 boxes per day. The boxes were sold to the town's two shoe factories for packing the finished shoes. By 1895, Savacool employed 12 girls and four men to produce 4,000 boxes per day.

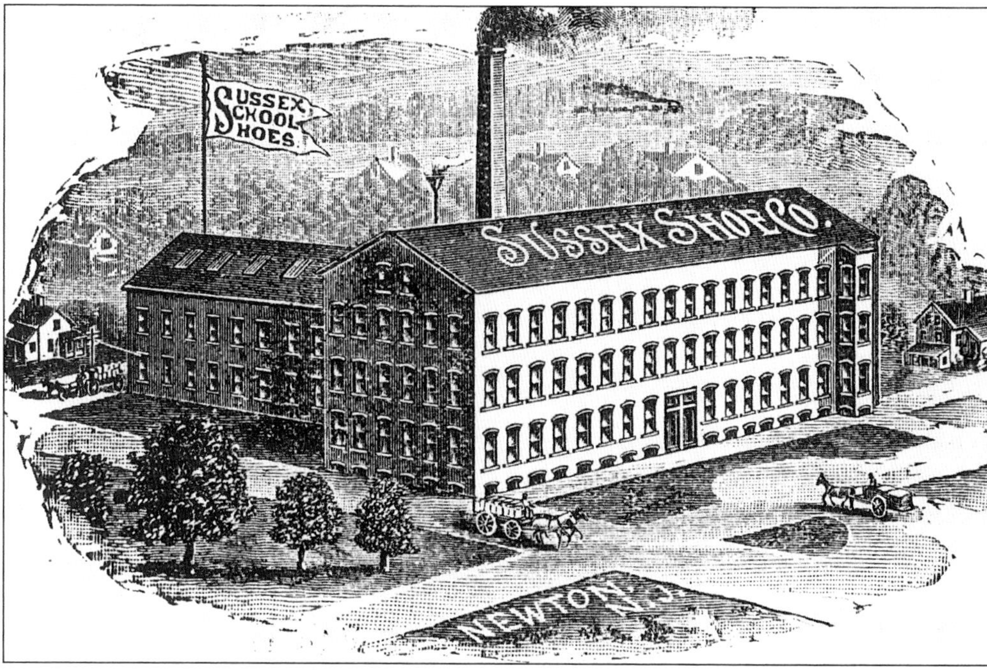

Henry Merriam's success in the shoe business lead to competitors. In 1890, the Sussex Shoe Company set up operations in this building on Mill Street. According to the *New Jersey Herald* in 1895, the company employed 200 people and produced 6,000 pairs of shoes per week, specializing in boys' and girls' school shoes, and ladies' and children's "spring heels."

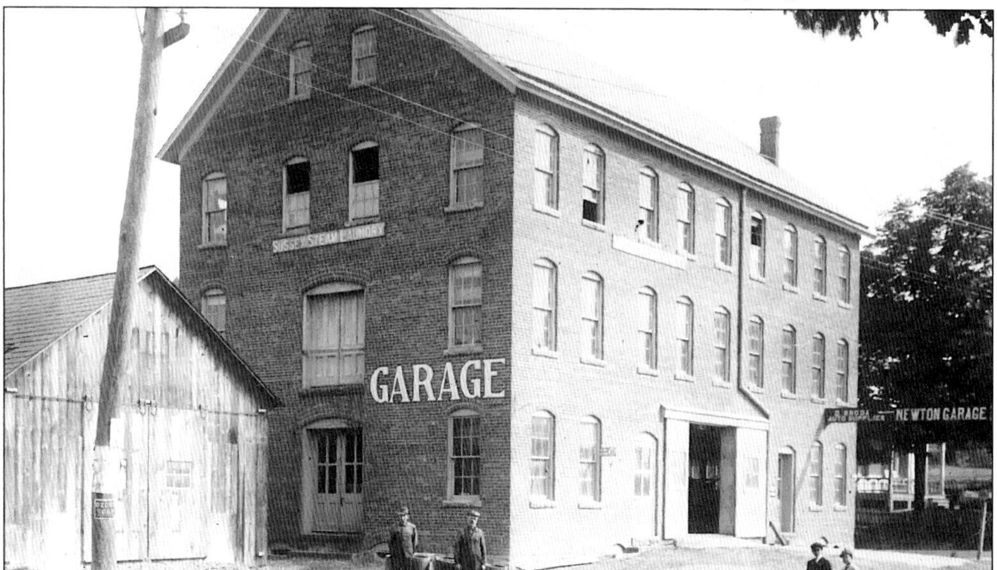

Even though 62 Water Street, at the corner of Clinton and Water Streets, now contains apartments and a restaurant, it was originally built as an industrial building. In 1907, William H. Mellor opened a towel factory in the building, producing cotton towels for major New York department stores. The building also housed a steam laundry and the county's first automotive repair facility, operated by Damian Broda.

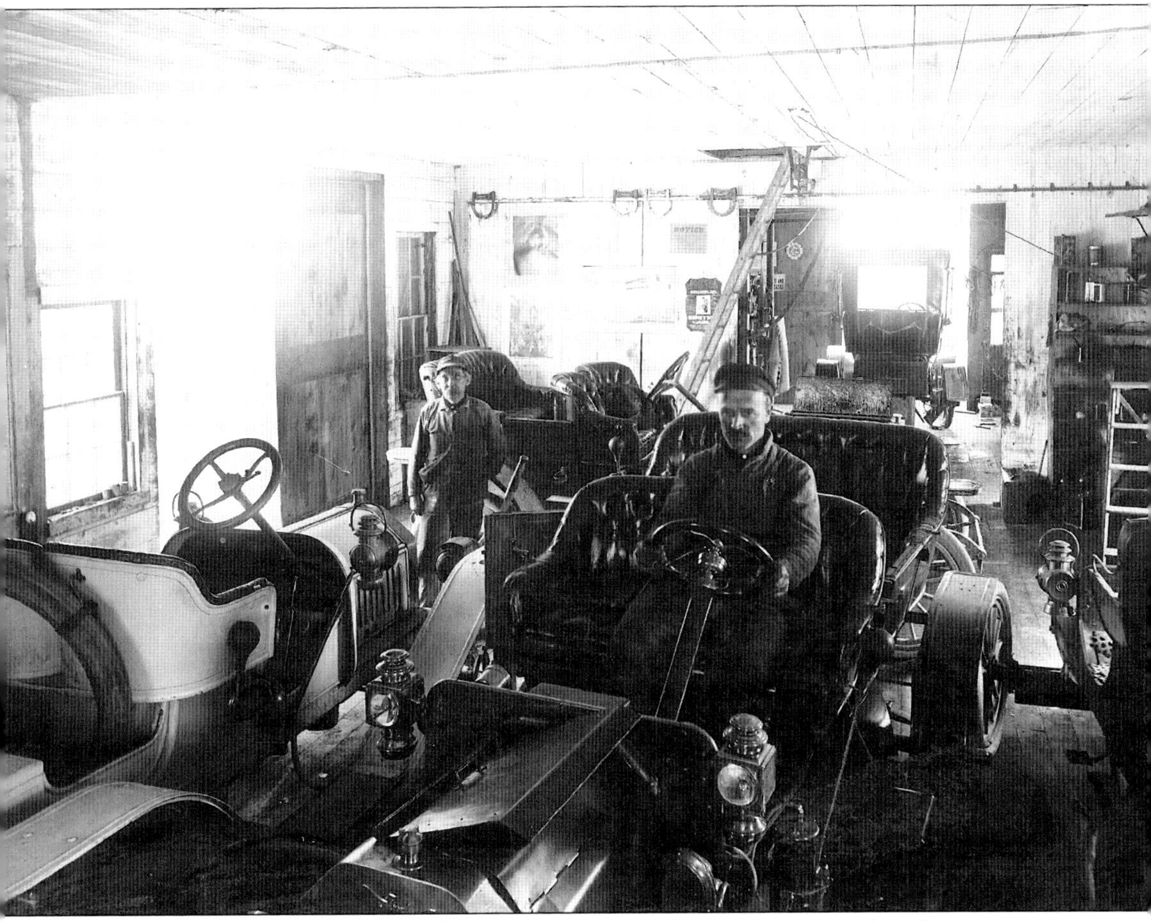

Damian Broda sits proudly behind the wheel of an open Ford touring car while his assistant looks on in this photograph taken about 1907. As the owner of the first automotive repair shop in Sussex county, Broda had the opportunity to work on a wide variety of horseless carriages. If you look on the back wall of the garage, you can see that the tradition of decorating workshops with pin-up girls has been around for many years. The car in the background is standing where the central bar of the County Seat Restaurant stands today.

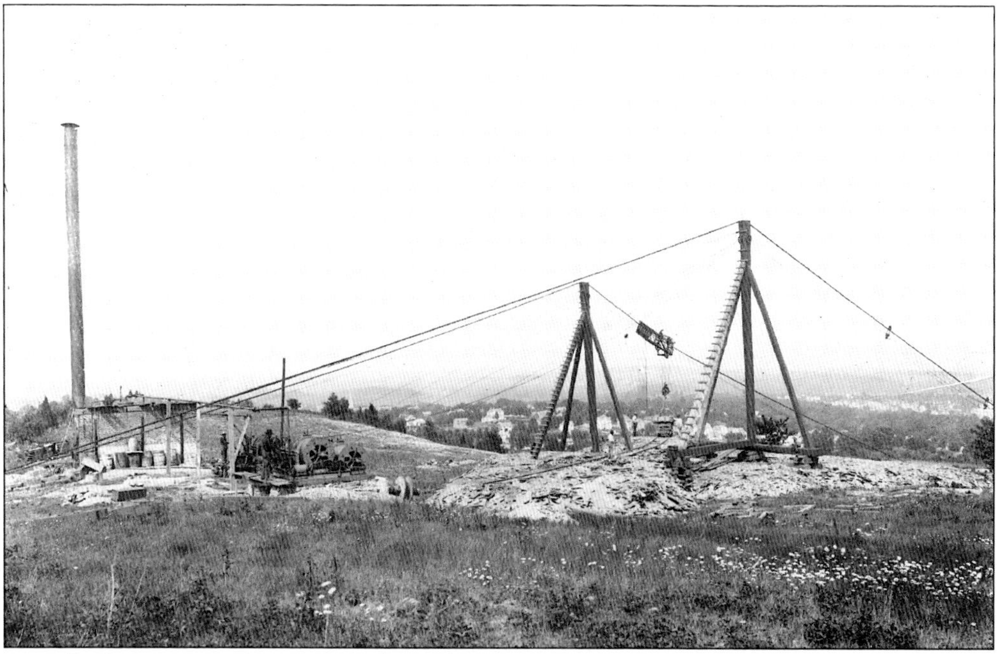

Not all of Newton's industries were located in mill buildings. This slate quarry was located on West End Avenue about a mile south of the center of town. From the late 19th century until 1923 it provided roofing tiles for all of the buildings in the town and surrounding countryside. This view shows the hoists used to bring the slate out of the quarry pit.

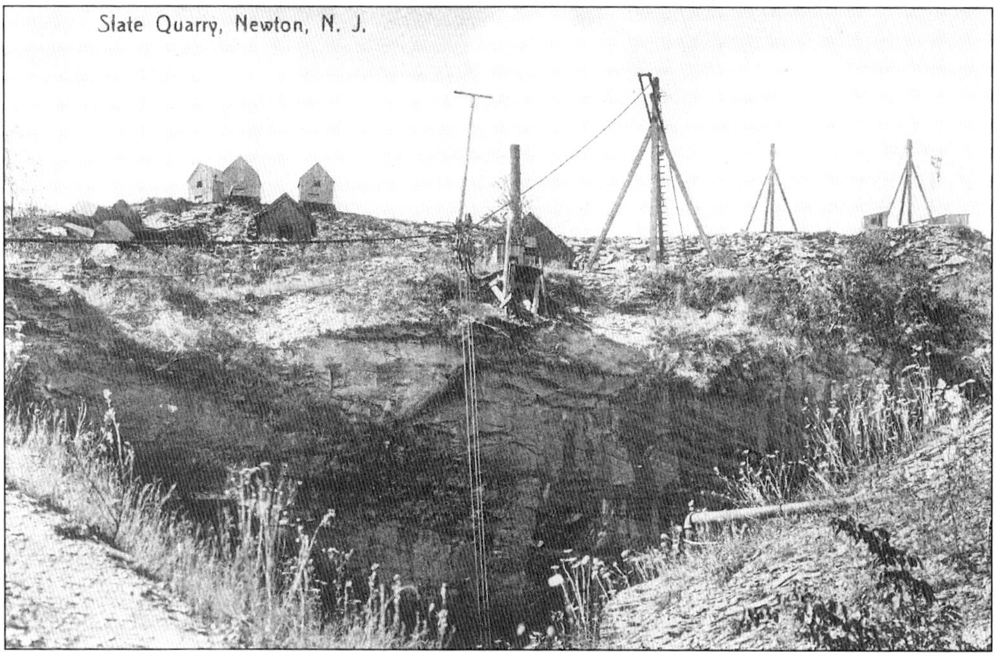

This early 20th-century postcard shows the quarry with the hoist lines descending into the pit. In the foreground is a pipe, part of the pumping system that kept the pit dry. When the quarry was abandoned in 1923, it rapidly filled with water. In fact, water now fills the pit completely, and the overflow is piped into a nearby brook.

Five

NEIGHBORHOODS

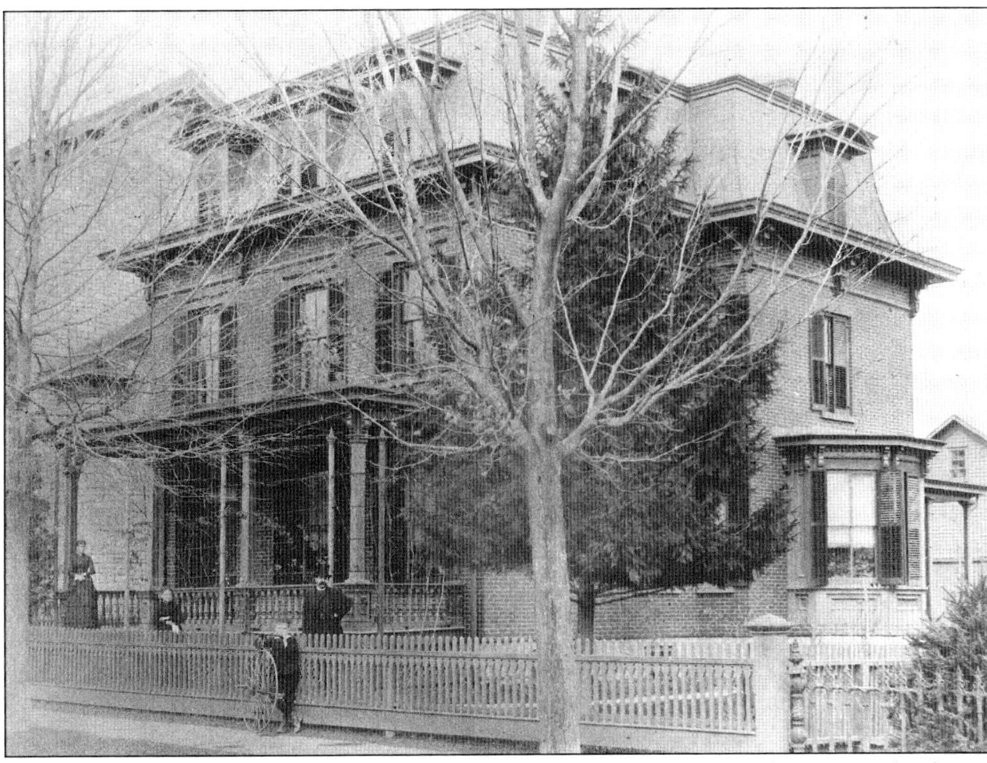

Newton's neighborhoods boast many splendid examples of Victorian architecture. This home, on Church Street, was built in 1869 by General Lyman Edwards. The house was designed in the Second Empire style with a mansard roof and pedimented dormer windows. The brick for the walls was fired locally, and the roofing slates came from the quarry on West End Avenue. As was typical of the period, the house had louvered shutters on all of the windows to keep the furniture and carpets from fading in the sunlight, while still providing ventilation. Edwards was a local tinsmith and stove dealer. He was also in charge of the municipal militia for several years in the early part of the century.

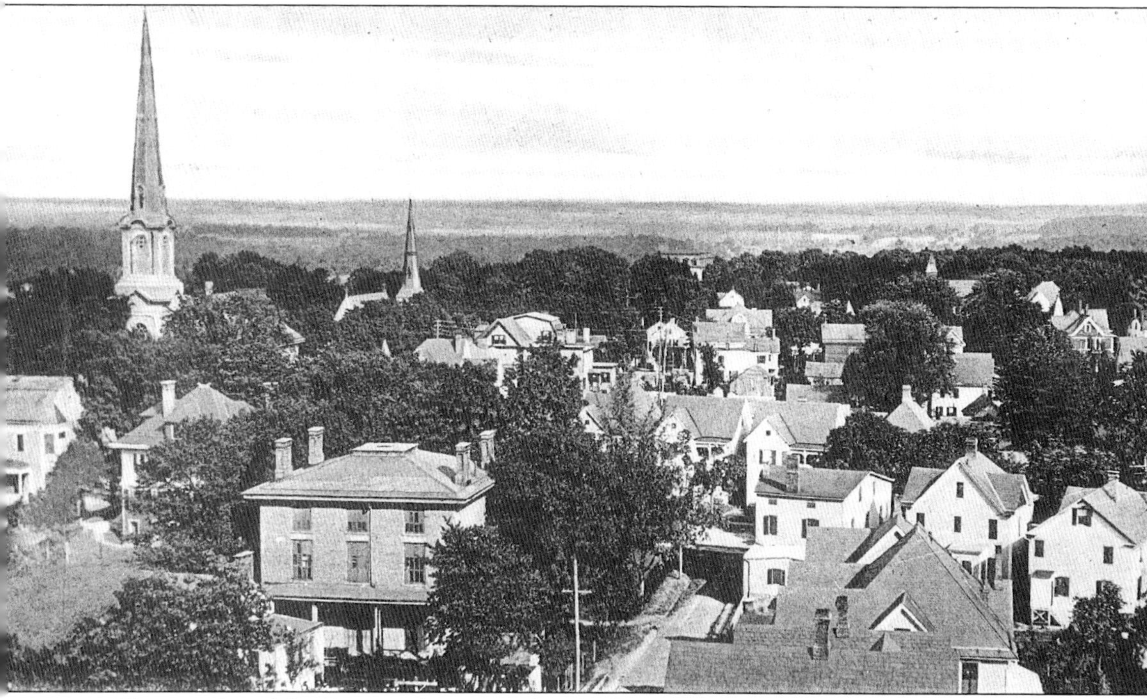

The steeples of the First Presbyterian Church (left foreground) and the Episcopal church (left background) tower over the residences and businesses in this panoramic bird's-eye view of Newton, taken from the Academy Street hill. When this photograph was taken, in the early years of the 20th century, Newton was experiencing a period of rapid growth. The Waldmere Hotel was first opened in 1903, while the old Hoppaugh House on High Street was reopened

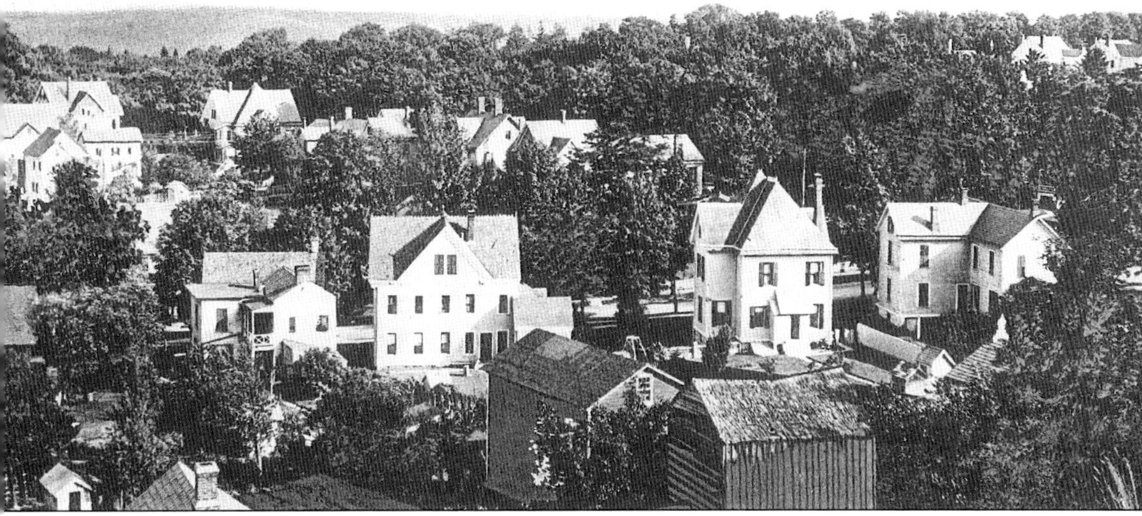

as the Park Hotel the same year. Also during that year, ground was broken for the new electric plant on Water Street. The following year saw the enlargement of the Cochran House with the addition of the fourth floor and refurbishment of the barroom. New stores were being built on Spring Street and new homes were being constructed throughout the town. By 1905, Newton had 4,422 year-round residents.

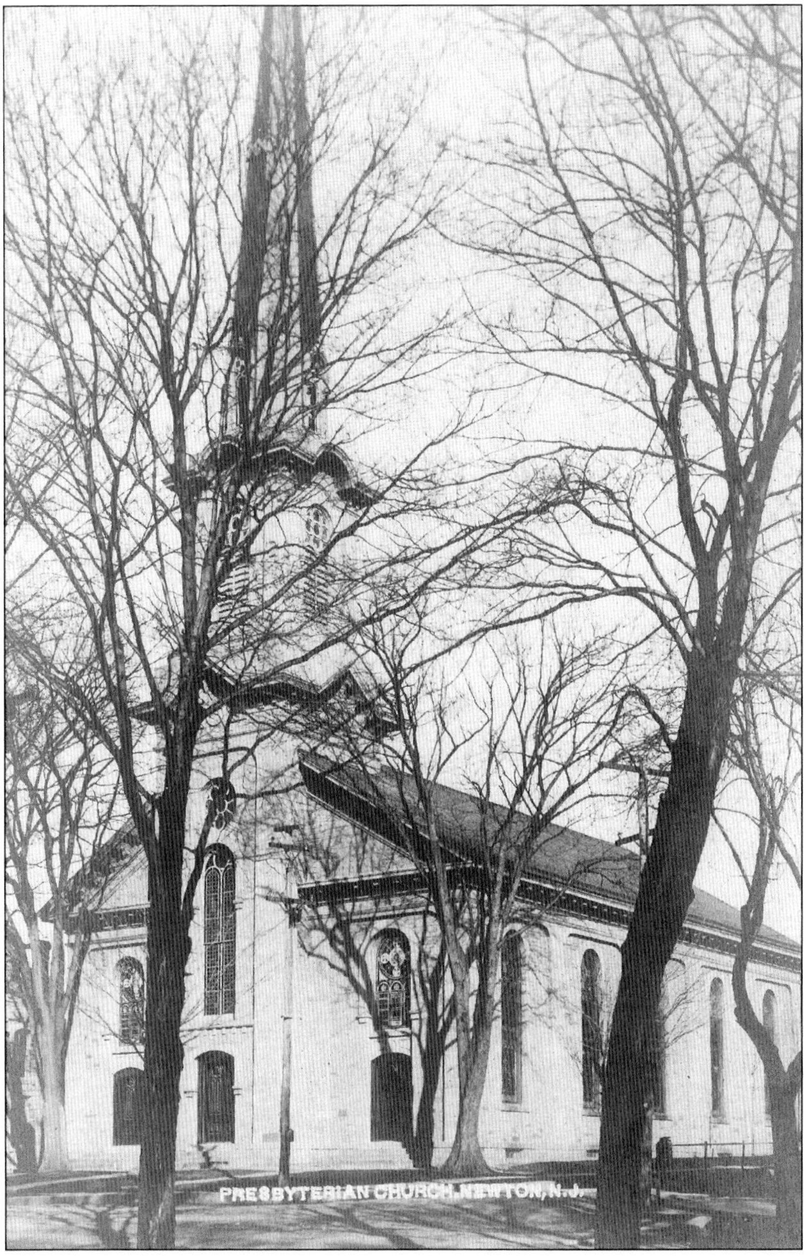

By the time the Civil War came to an end, Newton's Presbyterian congregation had outgrown their 1828 building on High Street. Consequently, they tore it down, and in 1869 broke ground for their third and present sanctuary. The new building was designed by architect Chauncy Graham, a specialist in church architecture. He designed the church in the fashionable Italianate style with deep bracketed eaves and flattened arches over the windows and doors. However, the overall form and proportions of the church pay homage to the classical Georgian and Greek Revival churches of New England. The sweeping steeple climbs to a total height of 178 feet and the walls were made of native blue limestone. The church was officially dedicated in May 1871. The steeple and belfry had to be removed in 1978 due to structural deficiencies, and were replaced in 1988.

This photograph of the choir and organist of the First Presbyterian Church was taken in the 1828 church, just before it was demolished in 1869, to make room for the new church, seen on the previous page. From left to right are: David Foster, John Simmons, Gabriel Dunning, Mr. Shafer, Charles Rorbach, organist, Miss Shafer, Hortense Couse Dutcher, Margaret Neldon Havens, and Margaret Rorbach Dunning.

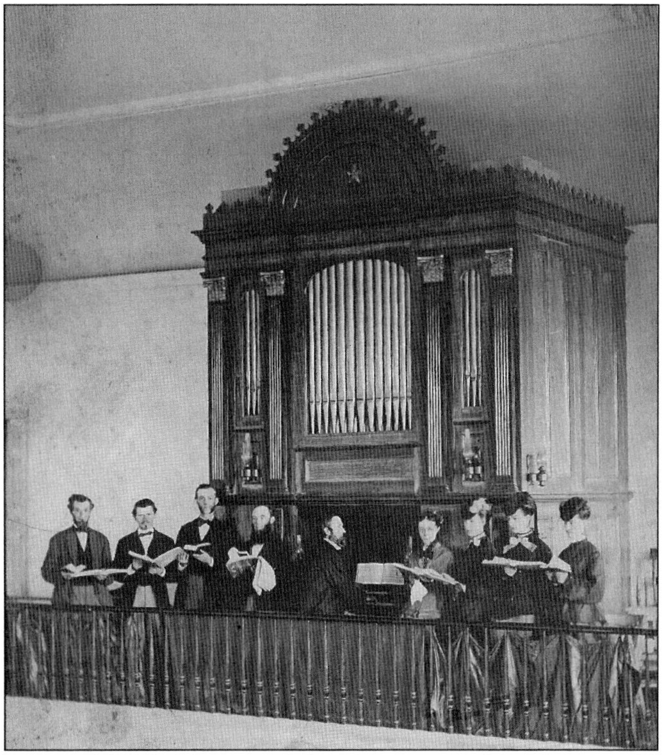

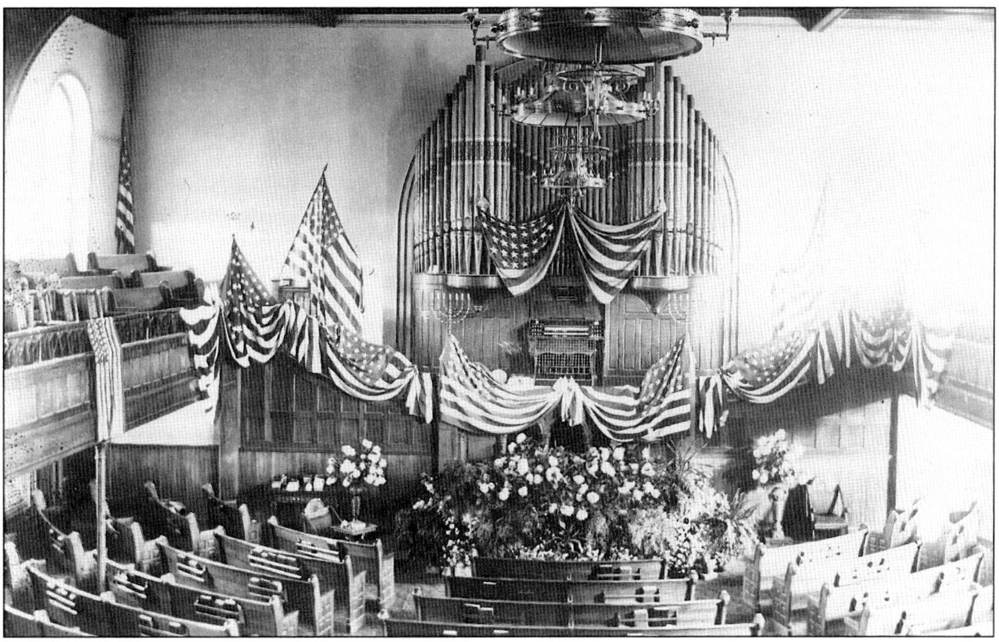

Both the Methodists and Presbyterians celebrated Children's Day each spring. Here the First Presbyterian Church is decorated for Children's Day on June 12, 1898. The front of the sanctuary is elaborately decorated with American flags and flowers. Note the very ornate gas chandeliers, with gas jets in the form of candles. In 1893, Henry W. Merriam donated $10,000 to the church for interior renovation, including new pews.

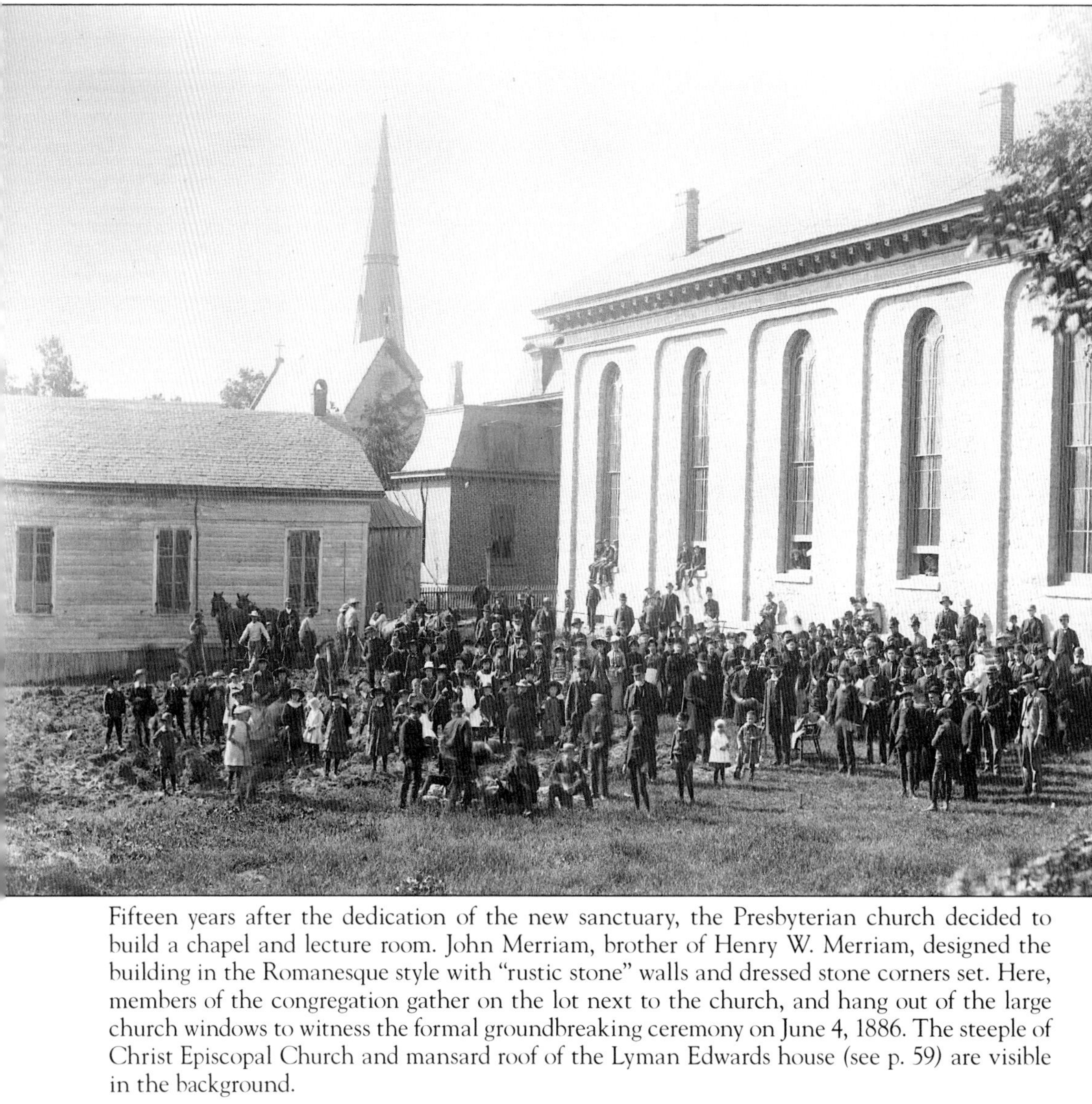

Fifteen years after the dedication of the new sanctuary, the Presbyterian church decided to build a chapel and lecture room. John Merriam, brother of Henry W. Merriam, designed the building in the Romanesque style with "rustic stone" walls and dressed stone corners set. Here, members of the congregation gather on the lot next to the church, and hang out of the large church windows to witness the formal groundbreaking ceremony on June 4, 1886. The steeple of Christ Episcopal Church and mansard roof of the Lyman Edwards house (see p. 59) are visible in the background.

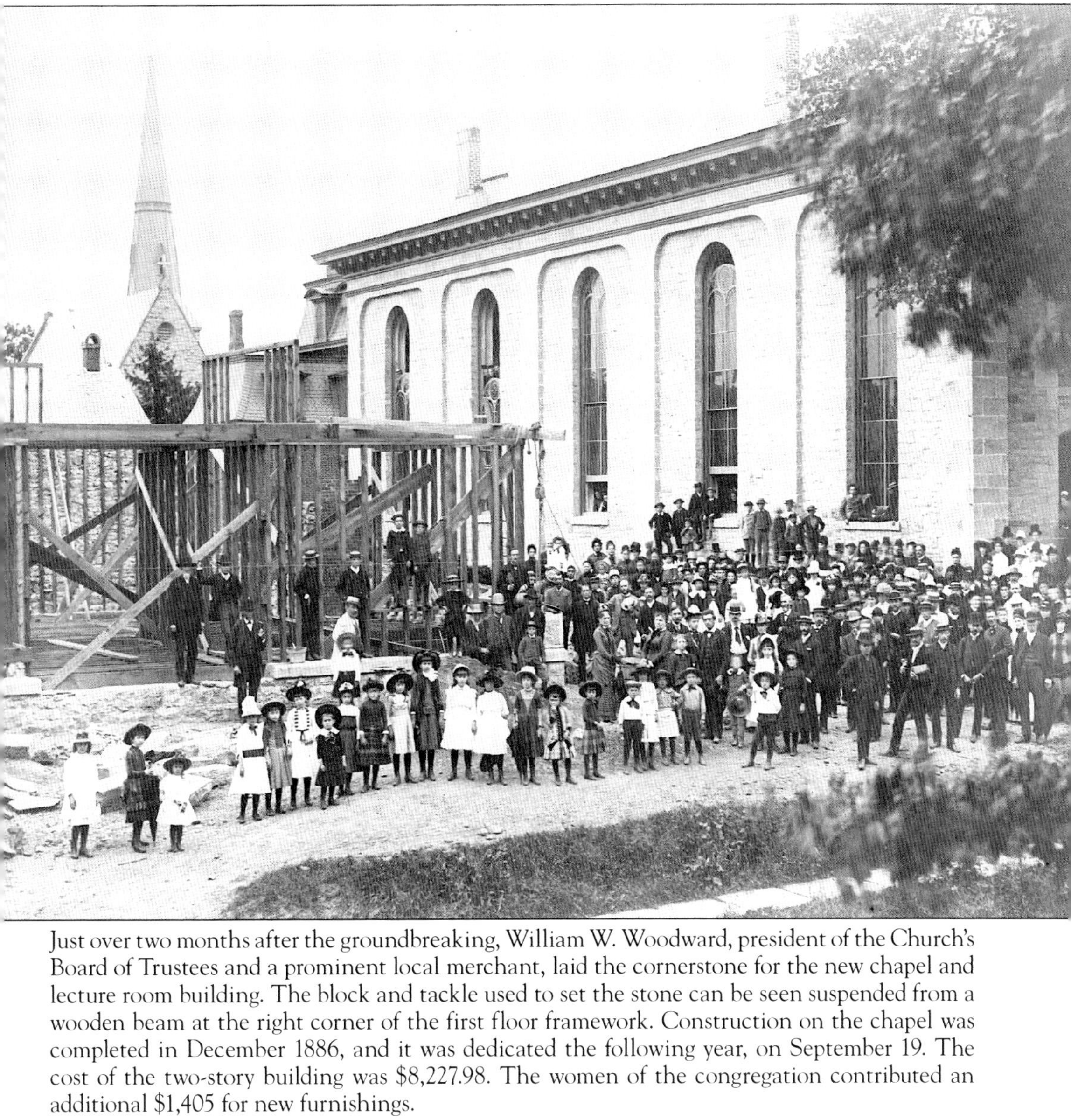

Just over two months after the groundbreaking, William W. Woodward, president of the Church's Board of Trustees and a prominent local merchant, laid the cornerstone for the new chapel and lecture room building. The block and tackle used to set the stone can be seen suspended from a wooden beam at the right corner of the first floor framework. Construction on the chapel was completed in December 1886, and it was dedicated the following year, on September 19. The cost of the two-story building was $8,227.98. The women of the congregation contributed an additional $1,405 for new furnishings.

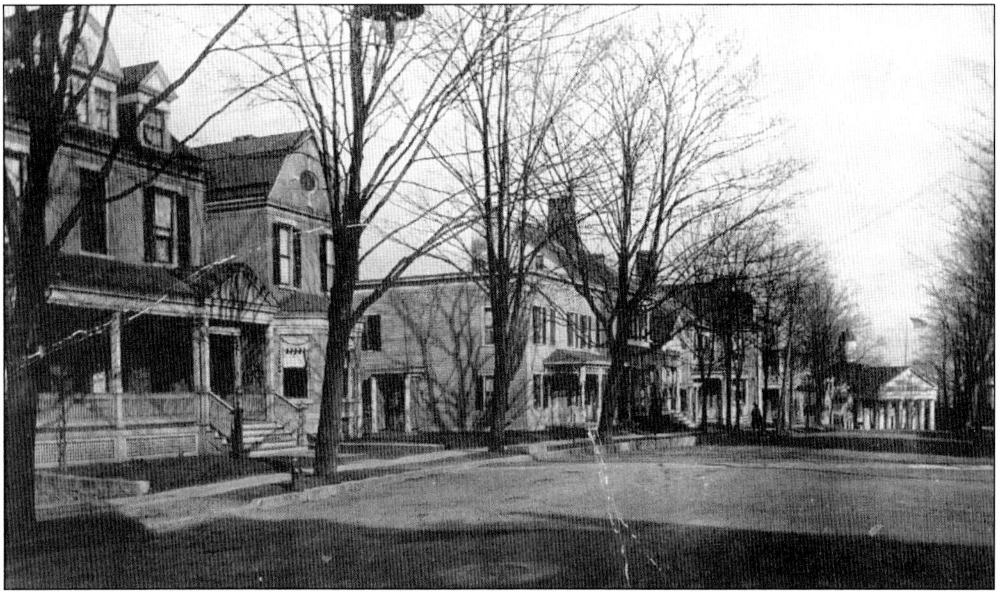

Across High Street from the Presbyterian church stands the large brick McCarter-Morrison House and the smaller wood frame Hallock House, along with the other buildings extending down to the county courthouse. The McCarter House was originally constructed in 1819, and a major addition was added in 1891. The earliest section of the Hallock House was built around 1795 and it was probably first enlarged about 1823.

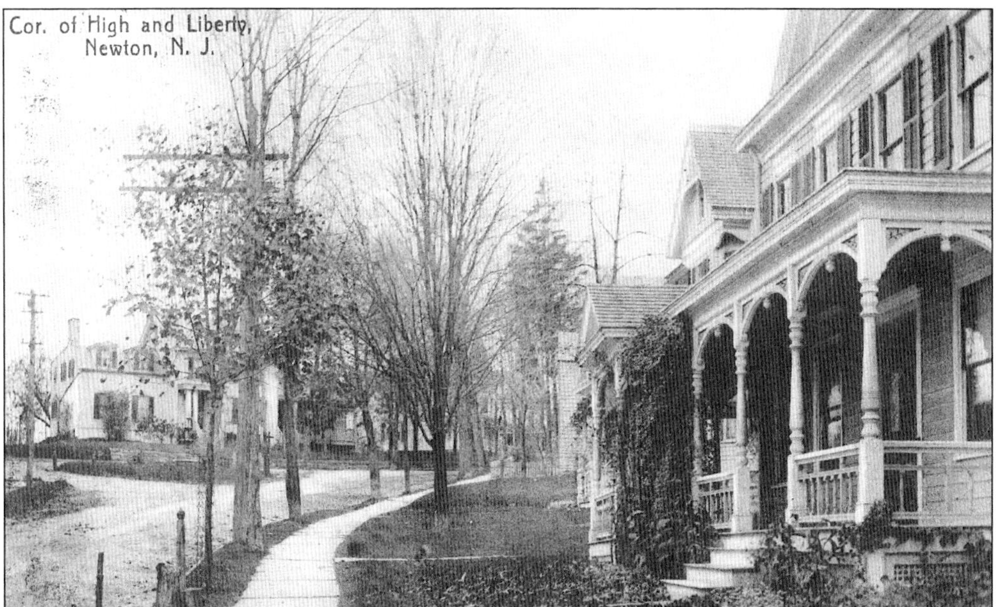

This c. 1911 postcard view looks south along High Street to the intersection with Liberty Street, with Victorian houses facing the slate sidewalk. This scene also shows the grassed triangle in the road intersection with its cast iron fountain, which has long since been removed.

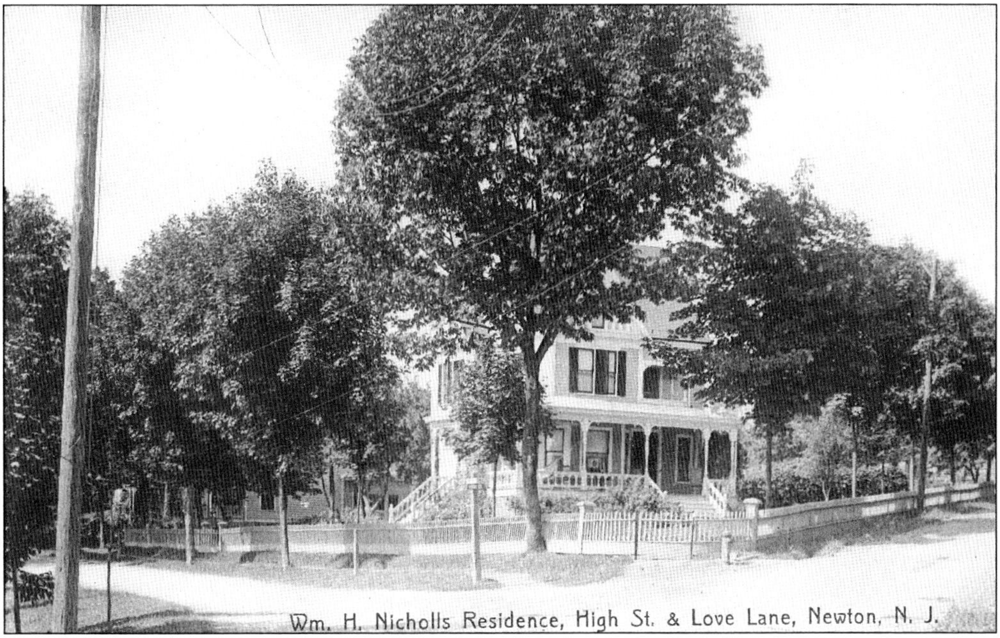

William H. Nicholls was a printer for the *New Jersey Herald* for 21 years. Then he opened a store on Spring Street and sold china, glassware, toys, sporting goods, stationery, books, and did job printing. He also served on the town committee, was town treasurer, and keeper of school funds. This photograph of his house at the intersection of High Street and Love Lane (West End Avenue) was taken about 1907.

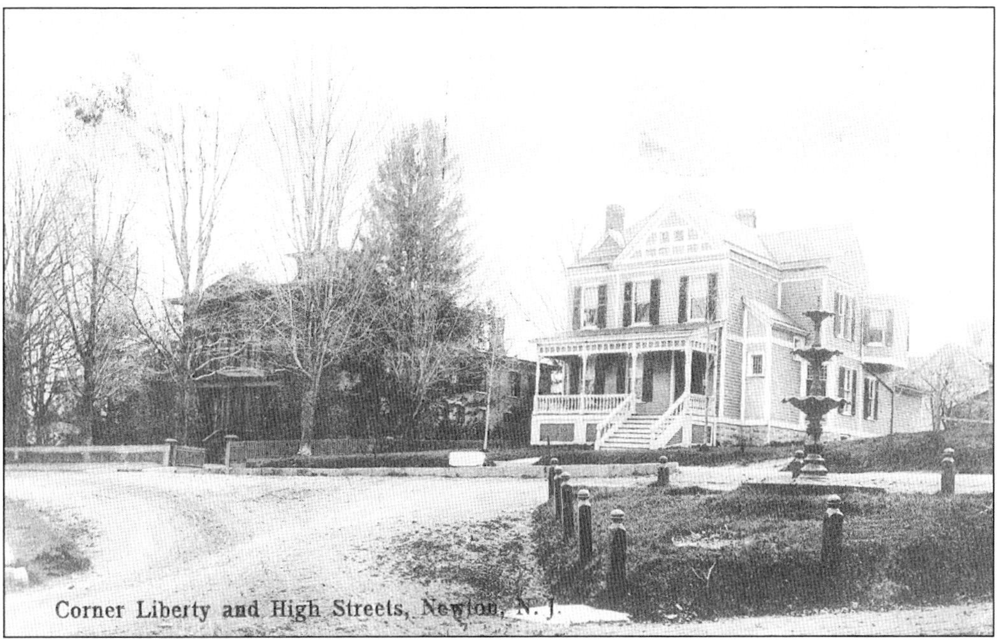

This c. 1909 postcard provides an excellent view of the cast-iron fountain that once graced the intersection of High and Liberty Streets. Behind it is the house belonging to William F. Howell. The house on the left, partially hidden by trees, was built in the 1850s for the Linns. After the death of the last owner, Miss Mary Kanouse, in 1965, it housed the county YWCA.

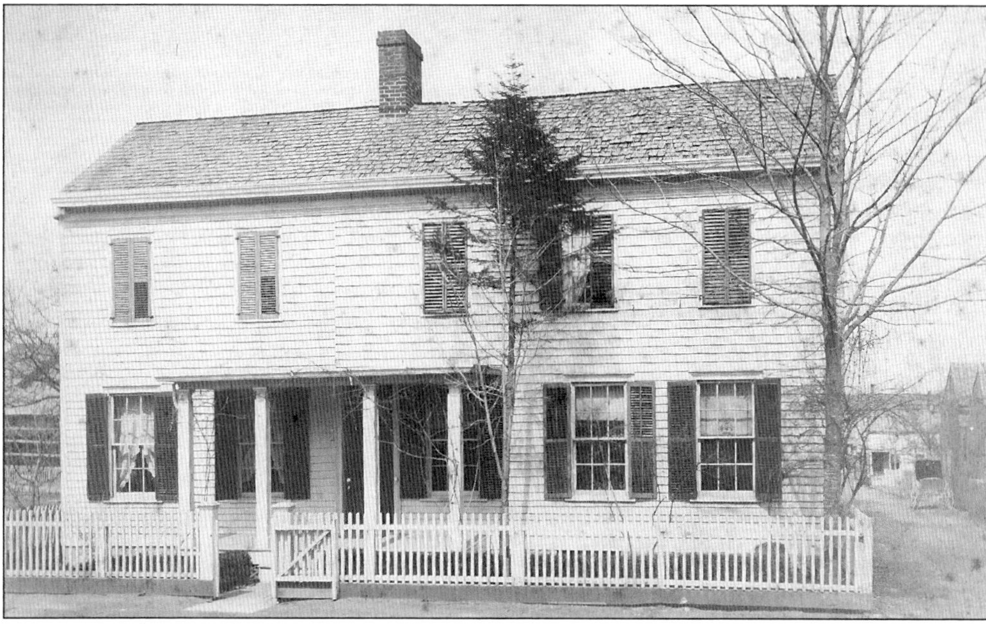

This 1875 photograph shows the boyhood home of Samuel Johnson, a prominent local businessman. Johnson operated a dry goods store at the corner of Main and Spring Streets (see page 14). The house fronts on Liberty Street, with Linwood Annex extending down the right side of the building.

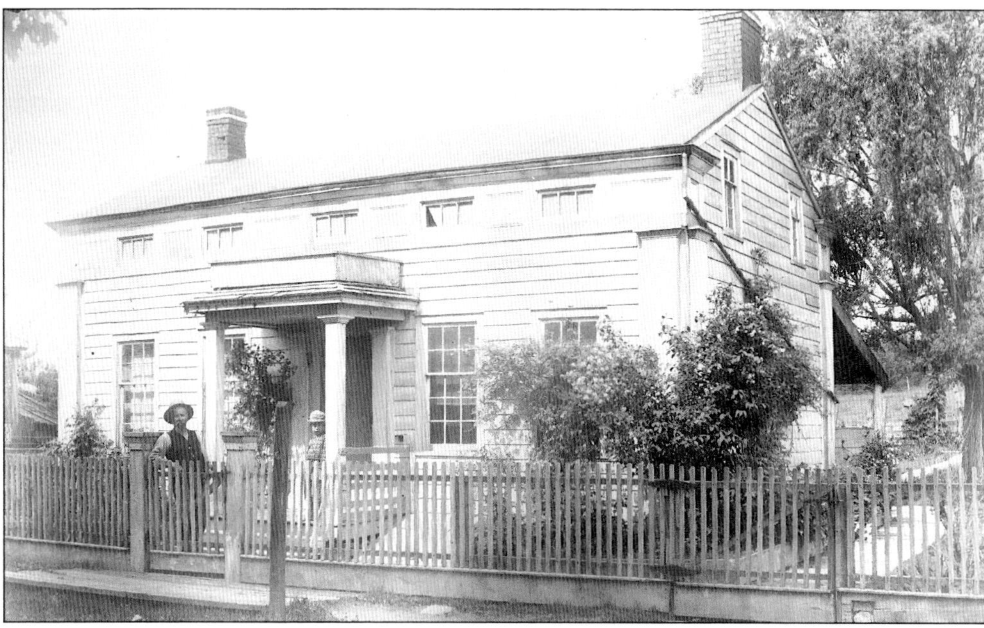

A classic example of the small one-story houses found in many rural parts of Sussex County is this little house on Liberty Street. Built in the mid-19th century, it has been treated to fashionable Greek revival trimmings, including pilasters at the corners, and a decorative frieze punctuated by the small "eyebrow" windows on the second floor.

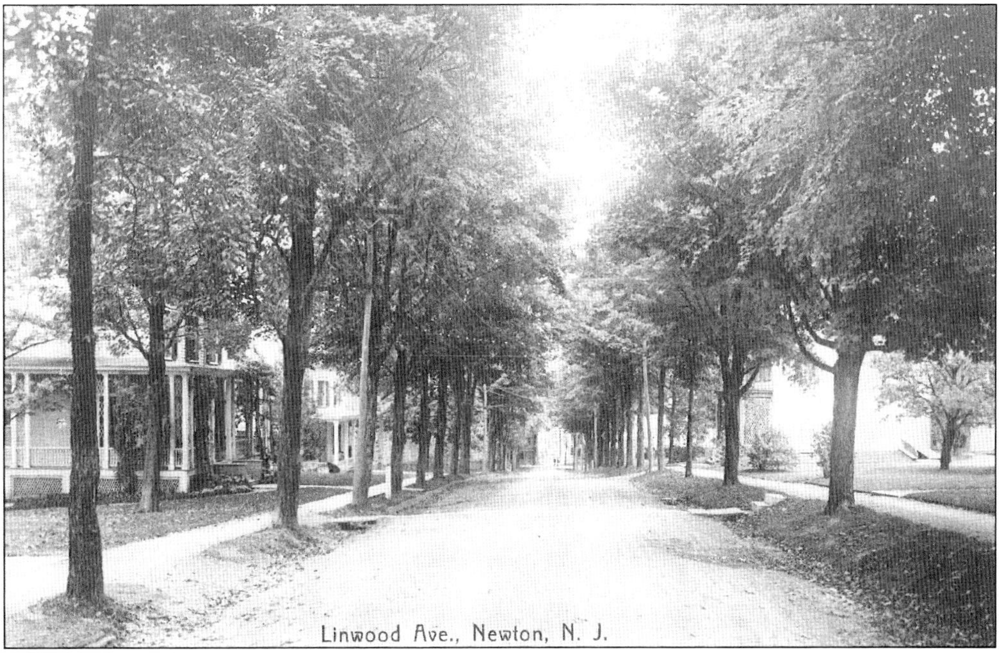

By 1883, the section of Linwood Avenue between Liberty and Thompson Streets was developed with beautifully ornate homes. This 1907 image by Nicholls shows the hard-packed dirt roadway, flanked by mature trees, and the 19th-century houses. This scene could be found in numerous places throughout Newton in the late 19th century.

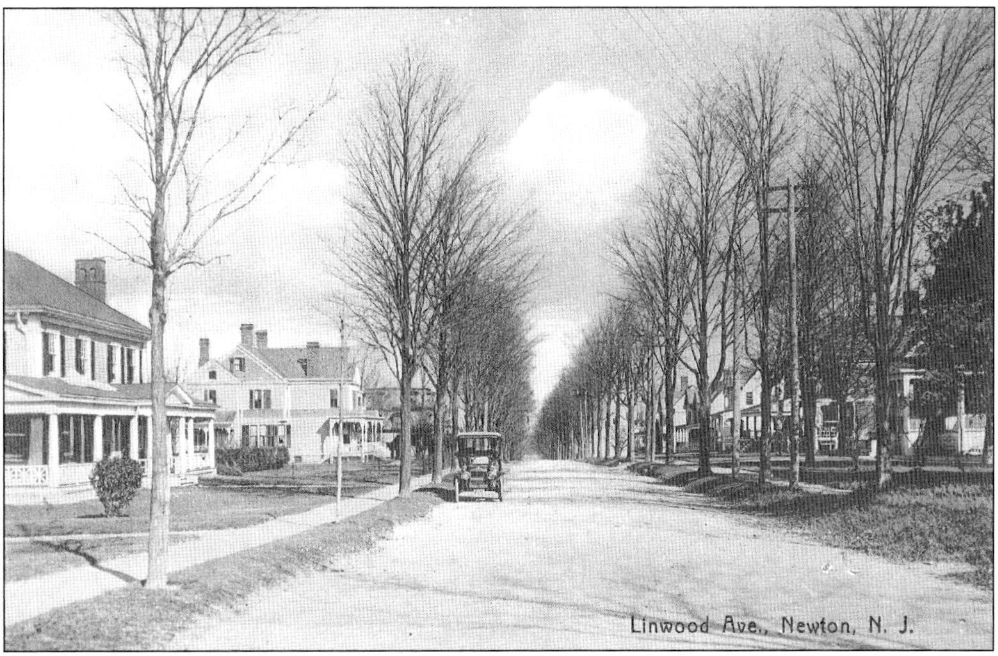

Four years later, in 1911, Nicholls published this image of the southern portion of Linwood Avenue, extending from Thompson Street to Foster Street. Newer and larger homes are seen here, along with an early model automobile.

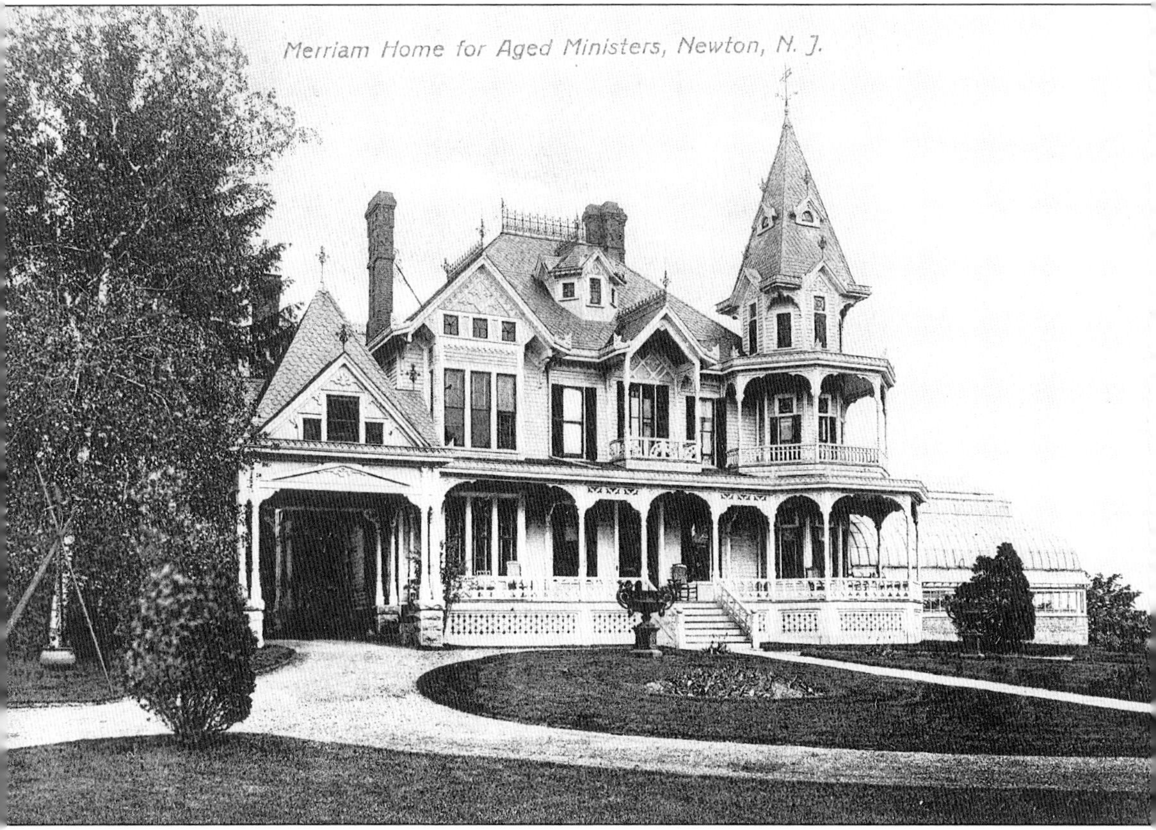

Henry W. Merriam, the Newton shoe manufacturer, acquired the triangular tract of land at the intersection of Main Street and Maple Avenue in June 1883. The following month workmen began blasting away the slate ridge to level the lot in preparation for Merriam's new showcase home. When it was completed the following year, the Merriam's house had the distinction of being the largest private dwelling in Sussex County. In 1889, he enlarged the house, adding a 60-foot-long hothouse and conservatory for his wife, who was an invalid. The house, seen in this 1908 postcard, is a perfect example of a Victorian gentleman's country villa, with its exuberant Queen Anne-style turrets and porches. Merriam and his wife had no children, so he bequeathed the house to the Presbyterian Synod as a home for retired ministers.

The First Baptist Church of Newton was organized in June 1830. However, the congregation did not have a building until they acquired the lot at the corner of Main and Liberty Streets in 1841. It took several years to raise funds to build the sanctuary, which was dedicated February 25, 1847. This picture shows the building before the devastating fire in March 1910. It was rebuilt and rededicated the following year.

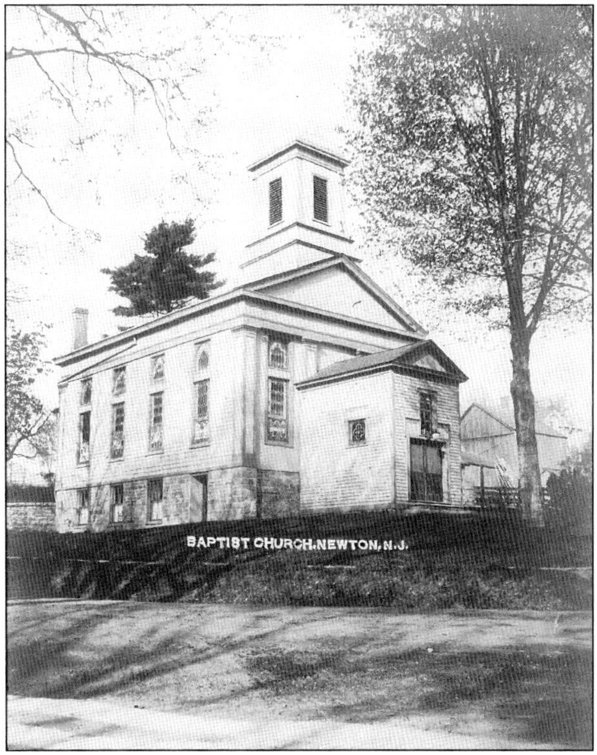

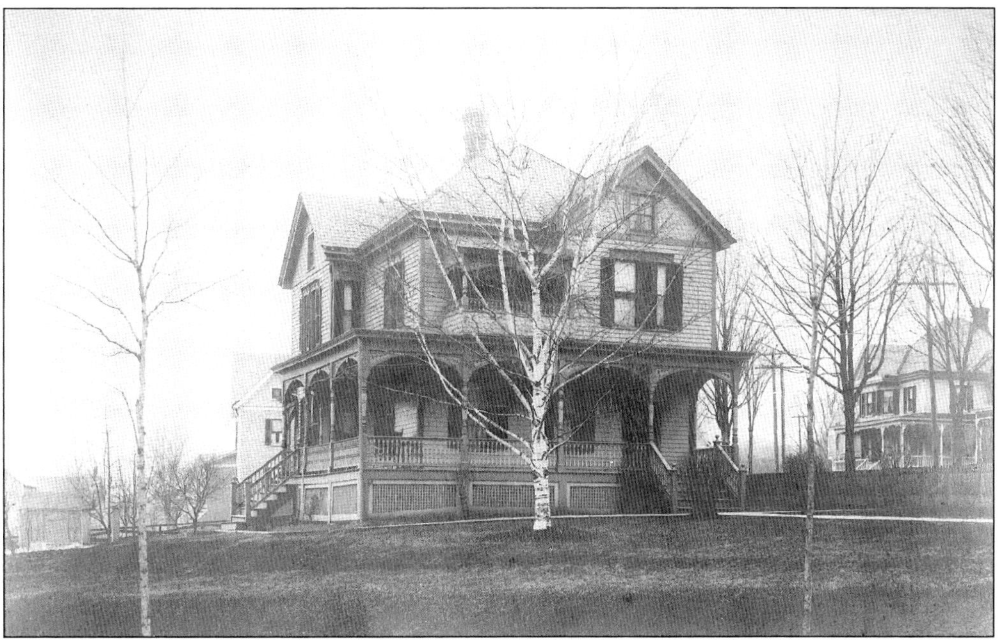

This 1903 photograph taken by George Kintner shows the Queen Anne-style house at the intersection of Main Street (in the foreground) and Ryerson Avenue. The deep porch, ornate second-floor balcony, fish-scale shingled gable ends, and corbeled brick chimney are all typical of this style of architecture. The building has undergone extensive remodeling and several additions, and is now the Iliff-Ruggiero Funeral Home.

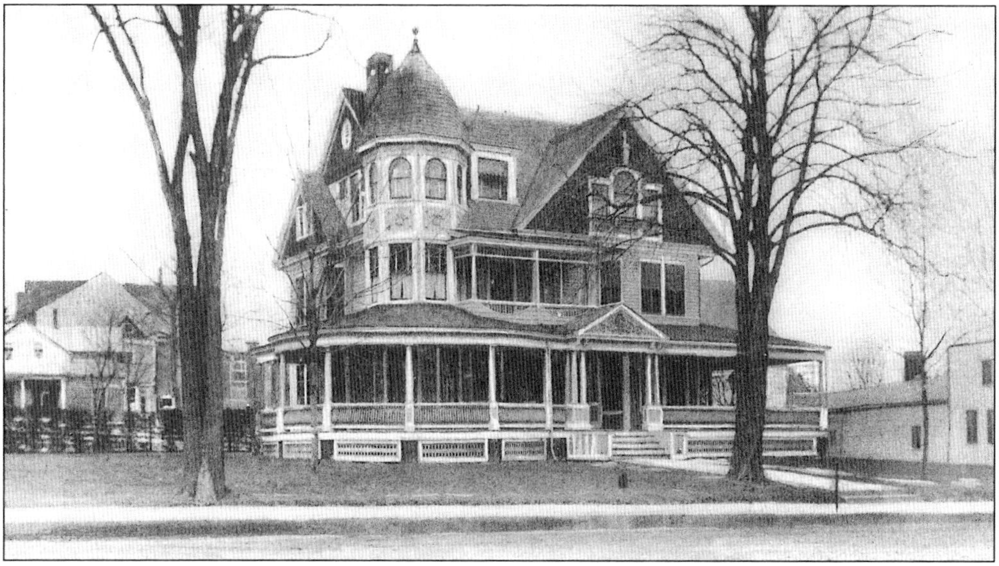

Wickham M. Clark was an undertaker who began his career in Newton in 1873. In 1892, he engaged the Walker Brothers' contracting firm to erect this massive Queen Anne-Colonial Revival hybrid house at the corner of Main and Liberty Streets. Clark retired in 1896, turning his business over to his son, Harry F. Clark, who went into partnership with William H. Hawk, and combined it with a furniture business.

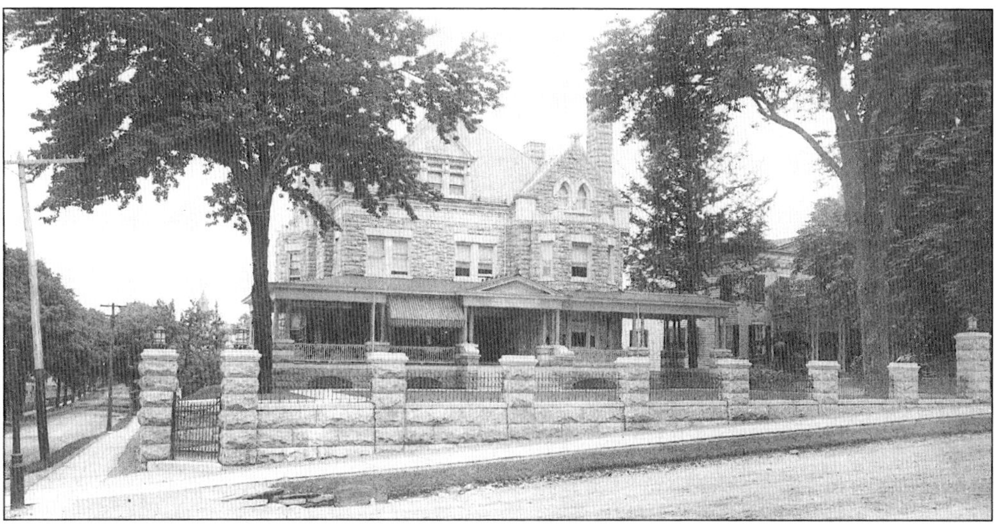

Thomas W. Bentley's mansion, at the corner of Main and Halsted Streets, was designed by the architect M. Houman. His design combined elements of the Romanesque Revival and Chateau styles, with massive stone walls and peaked roofs. Ground was broken for the house in April 1901, and Bentley, co-owner of the Sterling silk mill, moved in the following year.

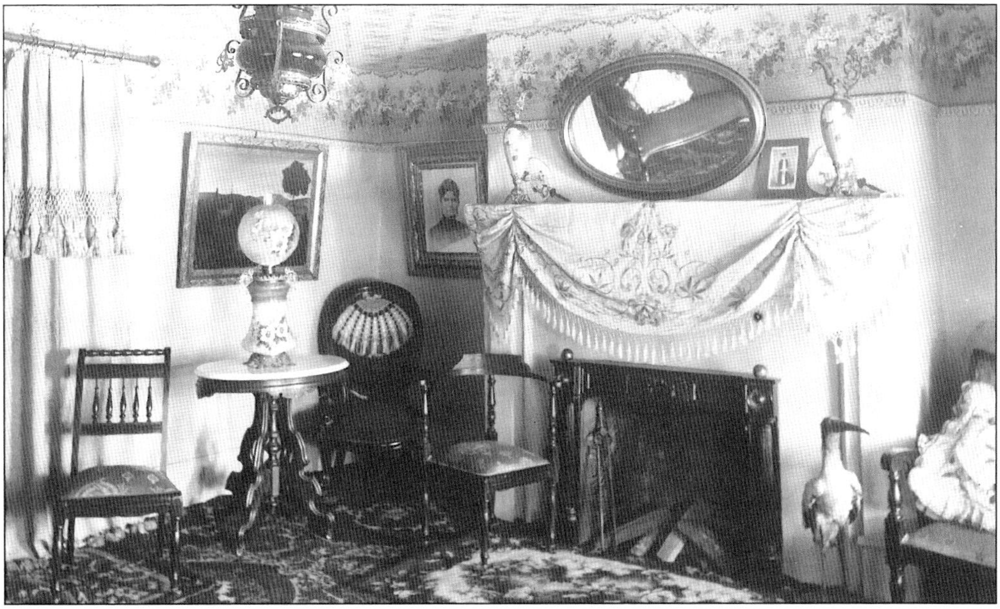

Although the low ceilings indicate that this parlor was not in one of Newton's elegant mansions, it still has many decorative touches fashionable at the turn of the century, including a draped mantle, a portiere curtain over the door to the next room, a wall-to-wall flowered rug, patterned ceiling paper, and pictures on the walls. An exotic stuffed ibis stands to the right of the fireplace.

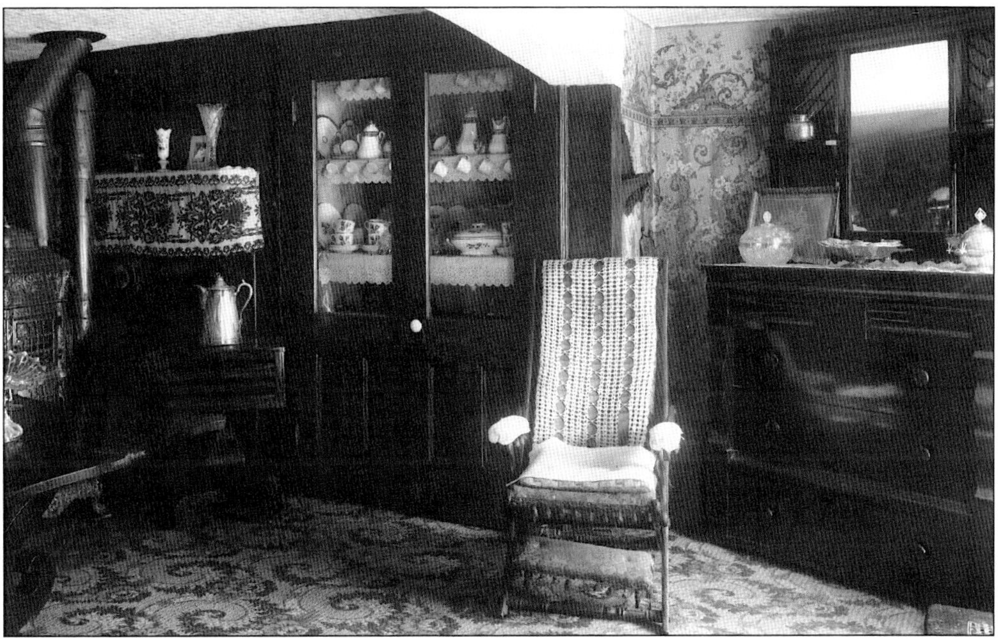

This room is typical of the Victorian period with its contrasting patterns and colors in the wall, ceiling papers, and carpet. The china cabinet, sideboard, and center table indicate that this room could have served as a combined sitting and dining room for daily use. The family probably also had a formal parlor like the one above for special occasions. Both of these interior views were taken by Newton's Townley studio.

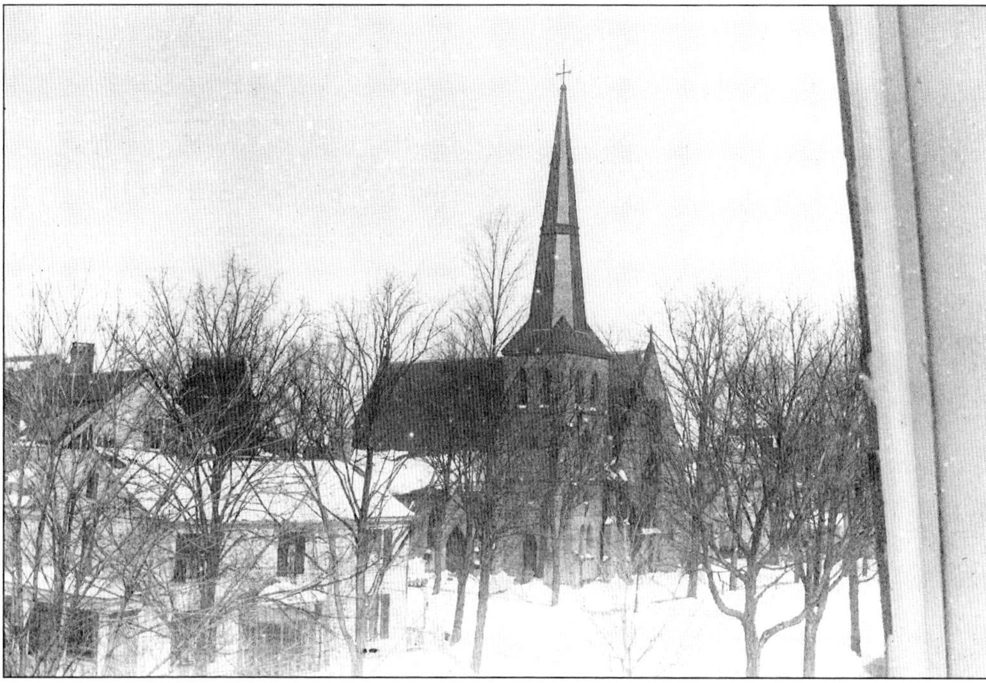

This photograph of Christ Episcopal Church, with its steeple still intact, was taken from the second floor balcony of the Franklin E. Losee house at 85–87 Main Street during the winter of 1910. Like most streets in town, Main Street was lined with trees. The house on the lower right was demolished in 1916 to make way for the Hill Memorial Building, home of the Sussex County Historical Society.

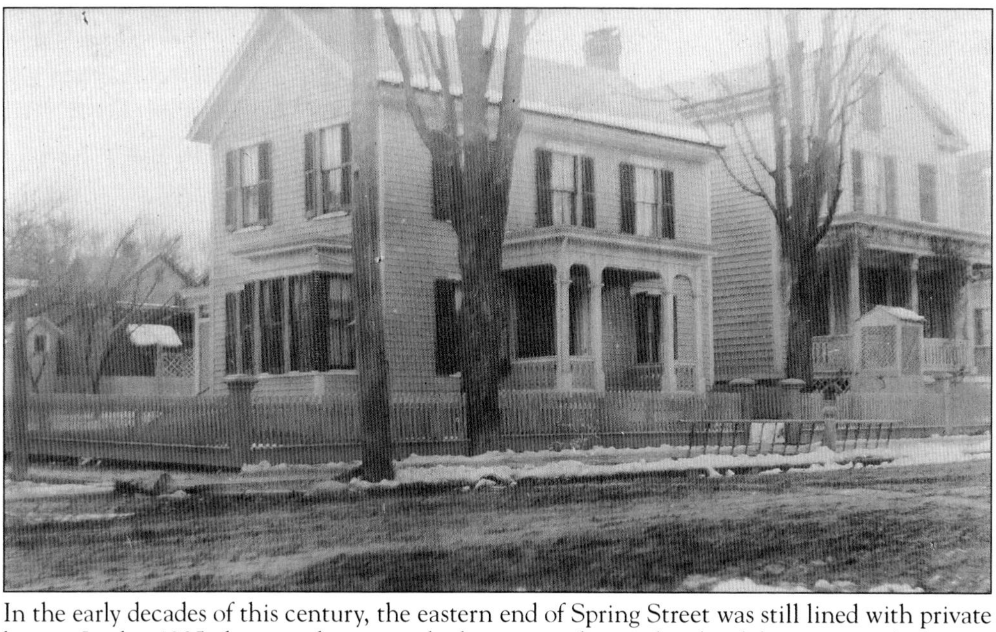

In the early decades of this century, the eastern end of Spring Street was still lined with private homes. In this 1905 photograph, we see the houses on the south side of the street at the corner of Jefferson Street. Notice the picket fences surrounding the houses, and the small well-house in front of the corner building. Who knows why a ladder is leaning against the hitching post?

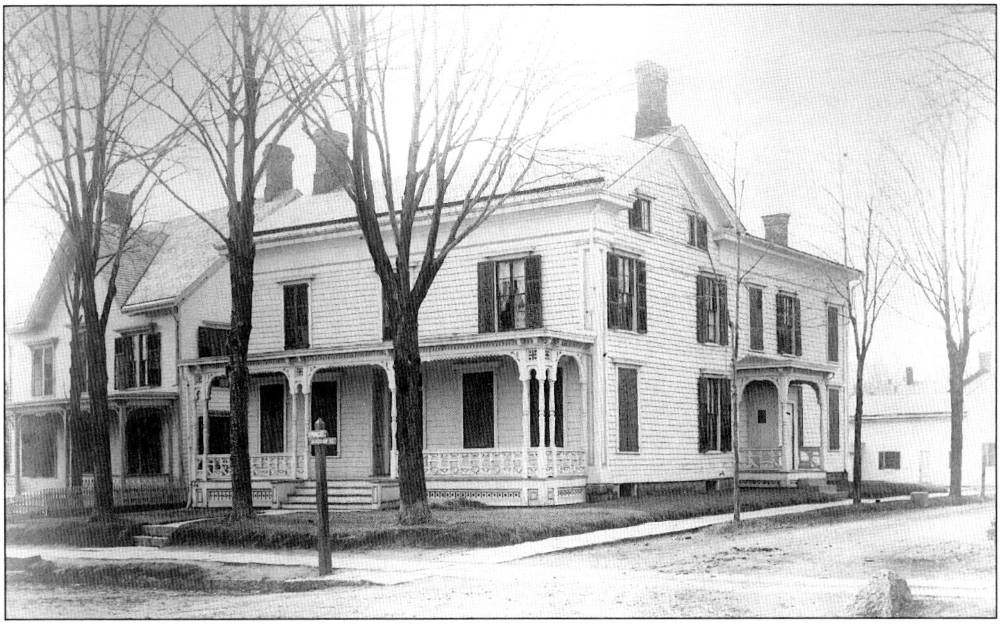

Despite the Victorian porches, the Jackson Cole house at the intersection of Spring and Madison Streets is a very good example of the Greek Revival style, built in the mid-19th century. The front and side porches with their Eastlake-influenced ornaments were added later, probably just before the turn of the century. To the left is the Pinkney house, now replaced by a strip of small stores.

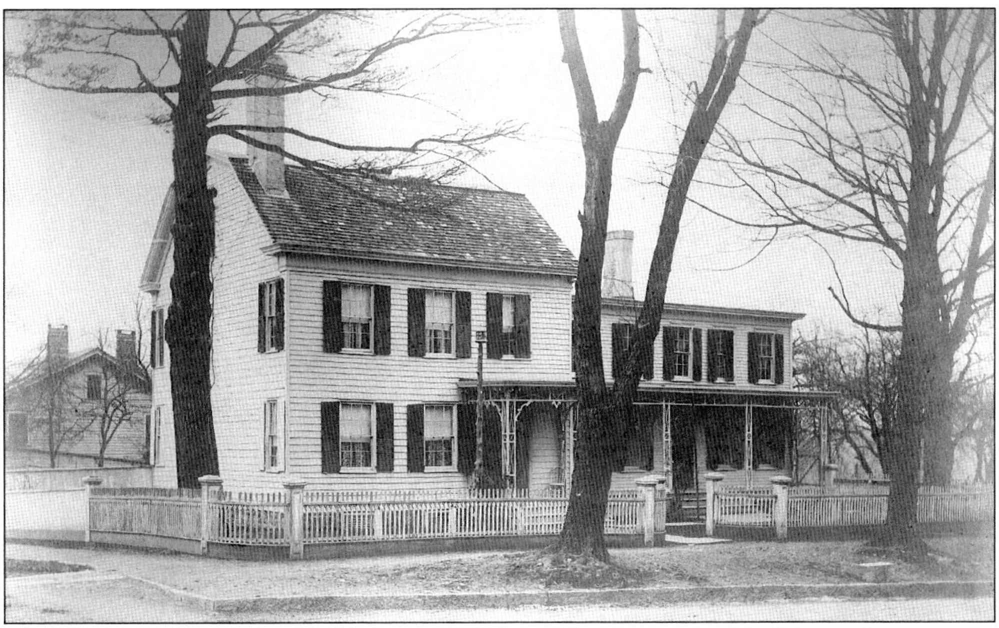

This house on Spring Street at the corner of Union Place was owned by Maggie Stuart at the turn of the century. Since the earliest portion dated to the 18th century, it was known as "Miss Stuart's Colonial Residence" or "The Homestead." This photograph, taken in 1903, shows the house surrounded by a wooden picket fence. The house was eventually replaced by a Pontiac dealership, now a drugstore.

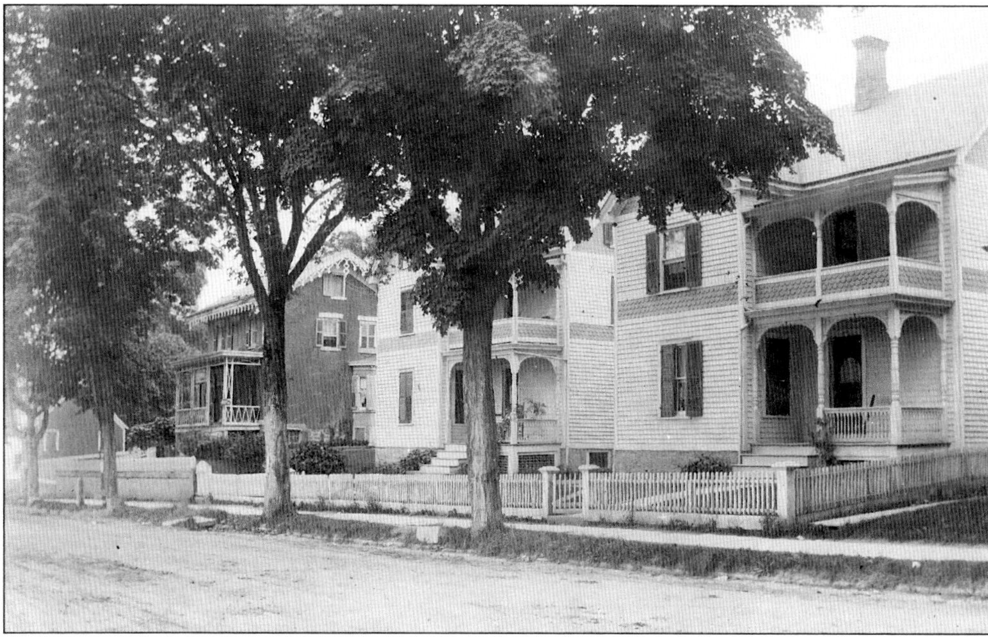

These houses are some of the last surviving residential buildings on Spring Street. Located at the east end of Spring Street, between Madison and Cedar Streets, they are excellent examples of the houses provided for workers in Newton's shops and factories at the end of the 19th century. Although modest, the houses feature fashionable Queen Anne-style touches such as porches and fish-scale shingles.

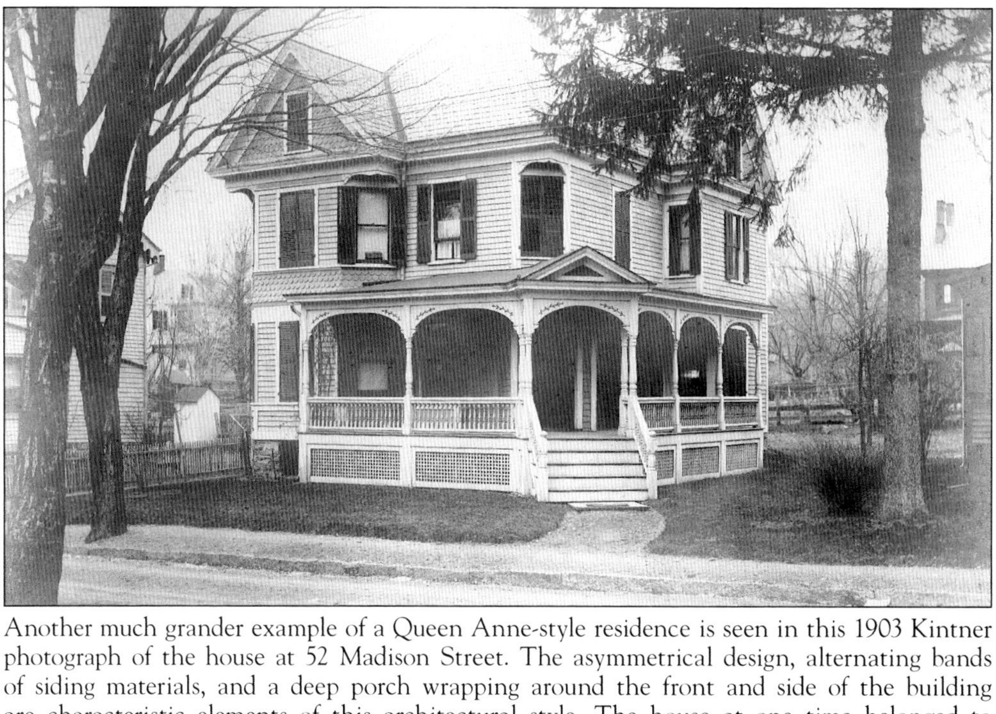

Another much grander example of a Queen Anne-style residence is seen in this 1903 Kintner photograph of the house at 52 Madison Street. The asymmetrical design, alternating bands of siding materials, and a deep porch wrapping around the front and side of the building are characteristic elements of this architectural style. The house at one time belonged to Dr. Edward K. Hawk, who also had his office there.

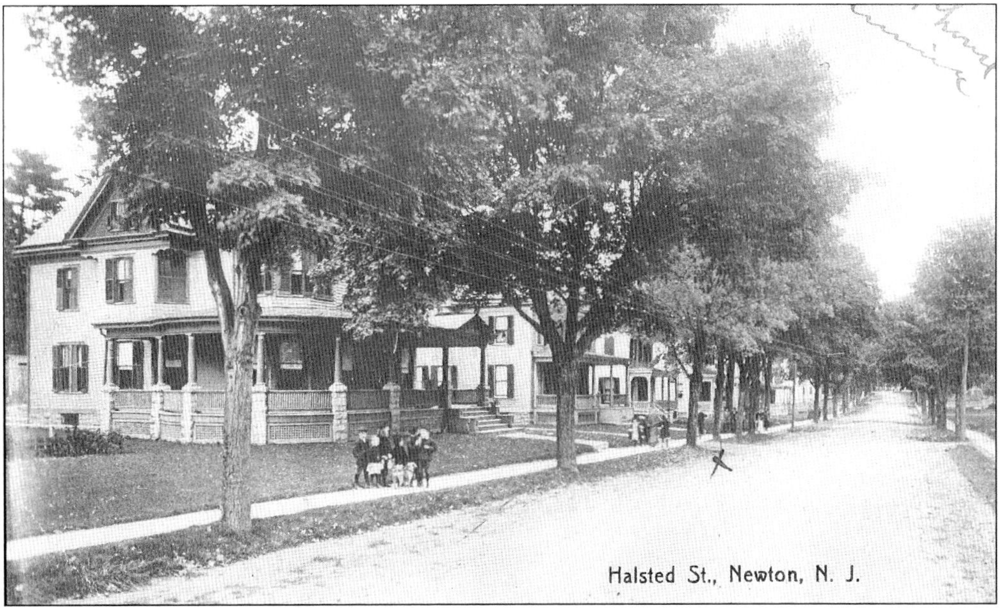

Looking down Halsted Street from Main Street, two groups of children are seen walking home from the public school, a block and a half away. Jacob L. Bunnell, publisher of the *New Jersey Herald*, proudly proclaimed "the third house is mine" when he sent this postcard to a friend in 1907.

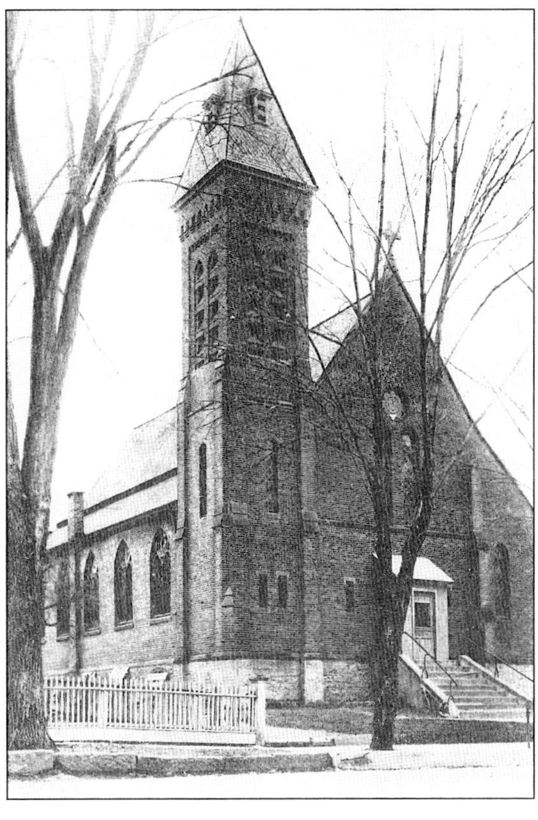

In 1871, the parishioners of St. Joseph's Catholic Church engaged Michael Quinn and Thomas Malloy to build a new church on Halsted Street, replacing one in the Old Catholic Burial ground. The church was dedicated the following September. The architect, Lawrence O'Connor, was apparently unconcerned by the rigors of Sussex County winters, since the congregation subsequently found it necessary to enclose the front door with a small vestibule.

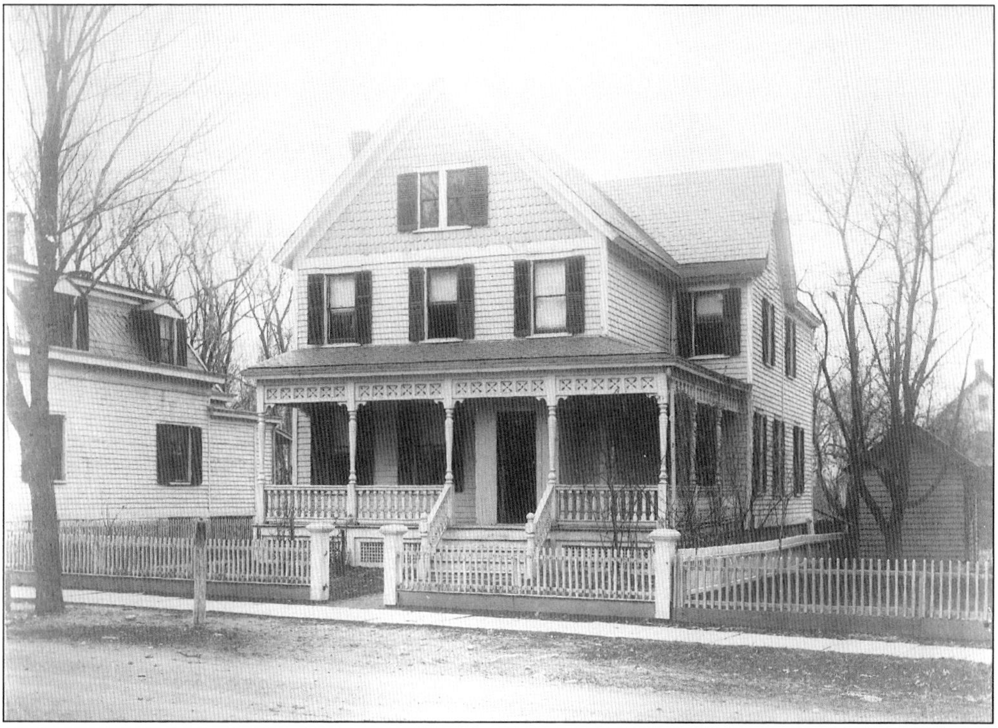

William H. Dunn built this house in 1889 at the east end of Halsted Street, across the street from the public school. Dunn was the superintendent of the H.W. Merriam Shoe Company factory, located about three blocks from his house. This house, and its neighbor—the only two-story mansard-roofed house in Newton—still stand.

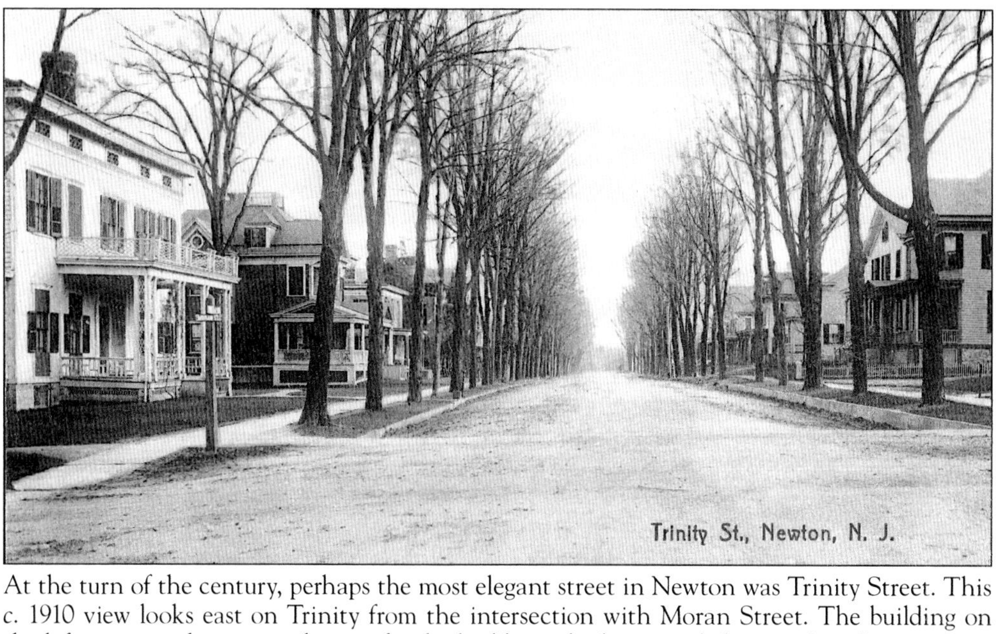

At the turn of the century, perhaps the most elegant street in Newton was Trinity Street. This c. 1910 view looks east on Trinity from the intersection with Moran Street. The building on the left was torn down to make way for the building which presently houses the administrative offices of the Newton Trust Company.

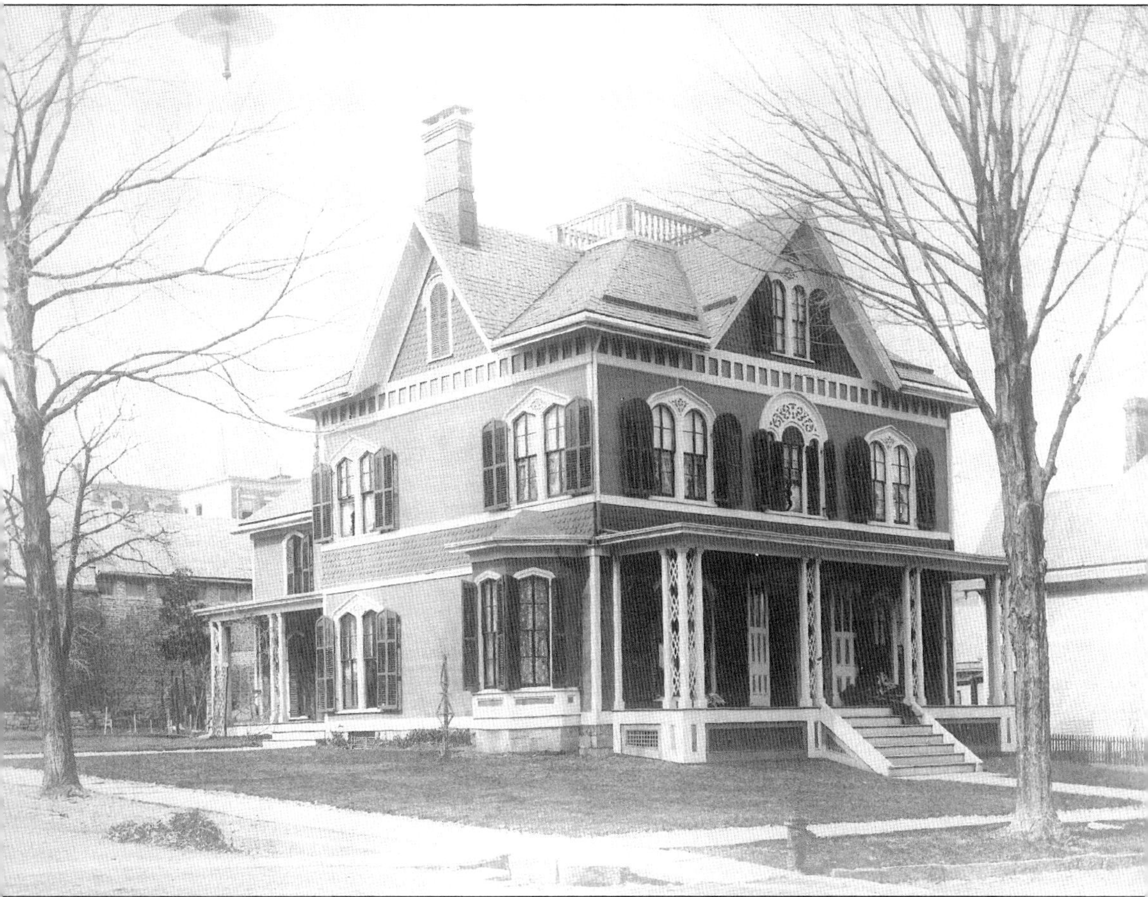

This 1903 photograph shows the elaborate two-story brick house that belonged to Charles Hendershot, proprietor of the Cochran House. Facing Trinity Street, at the southwest corner of the intersection with Moran Street, this stately Italianate mansion reflected the growing wealth of the local business community. The Town of Newton eventually purchased this and other houses along this section of Trinity Street and demolished them to make way for a parking lot.

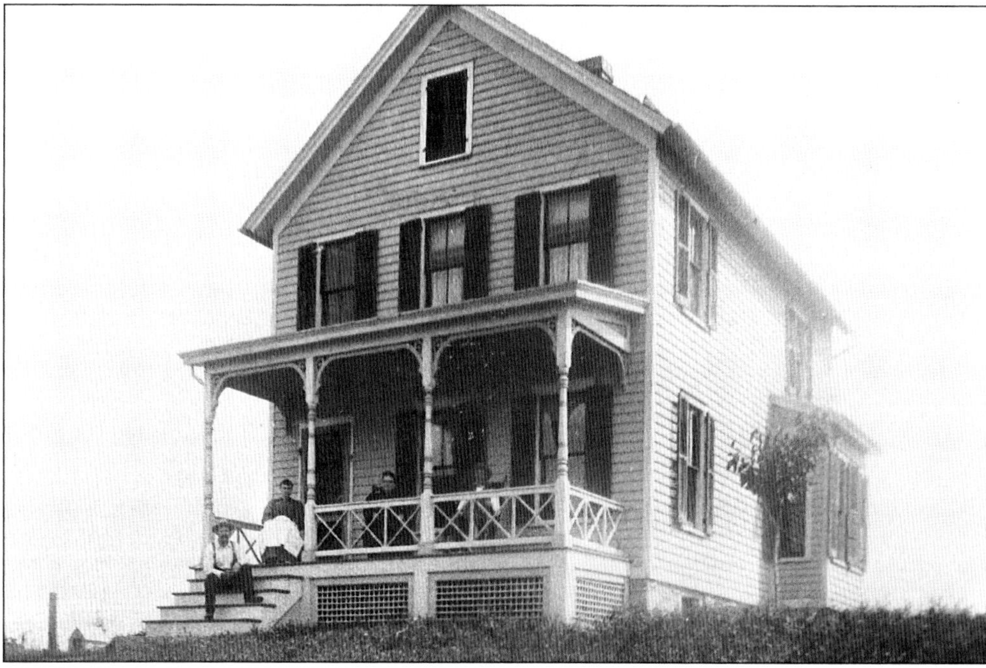

This house at 15 Sussex Street was one of a number of single-family residences built in Newton in the 1890s. Although it stands alone in this *c.* 1897 view, it was soon surrounded by other houses erected to house the employees of Newton's growing industries. The house still stands and retains the vast majority of its original features.

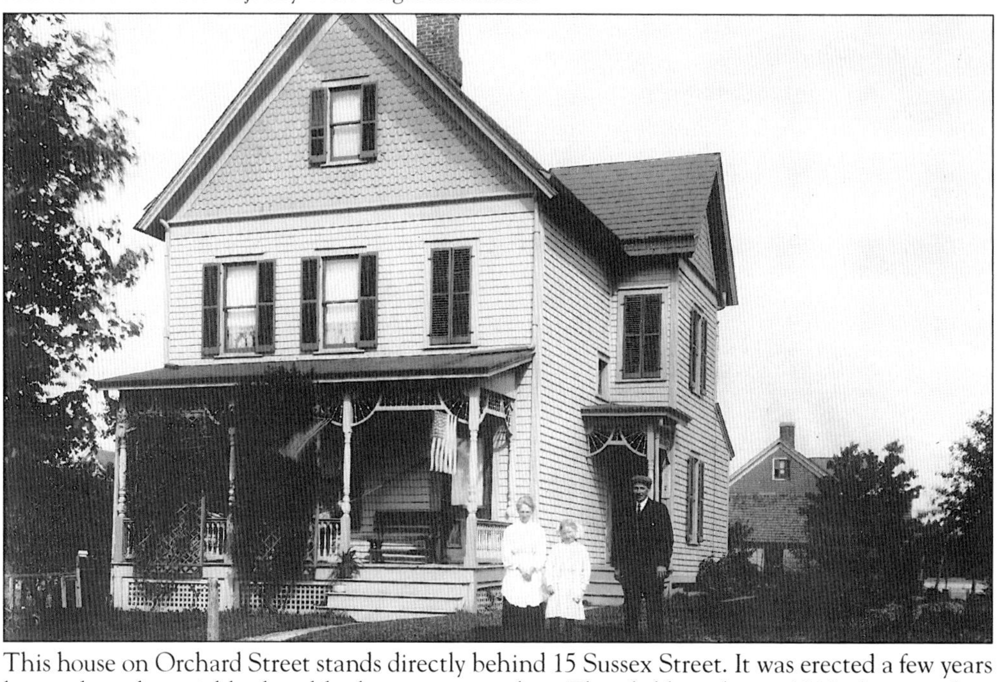

This house on Orchard Street stands directly behind 15 Sussex Street. It was erected a few years later, when the neighborhood had grown somewhat. The child in this *c.* 1905 photograph is Mildred Smith, flanked by her mother and father. She inherited the house from her parents and lived there all her life.

Six

SCHOOLS

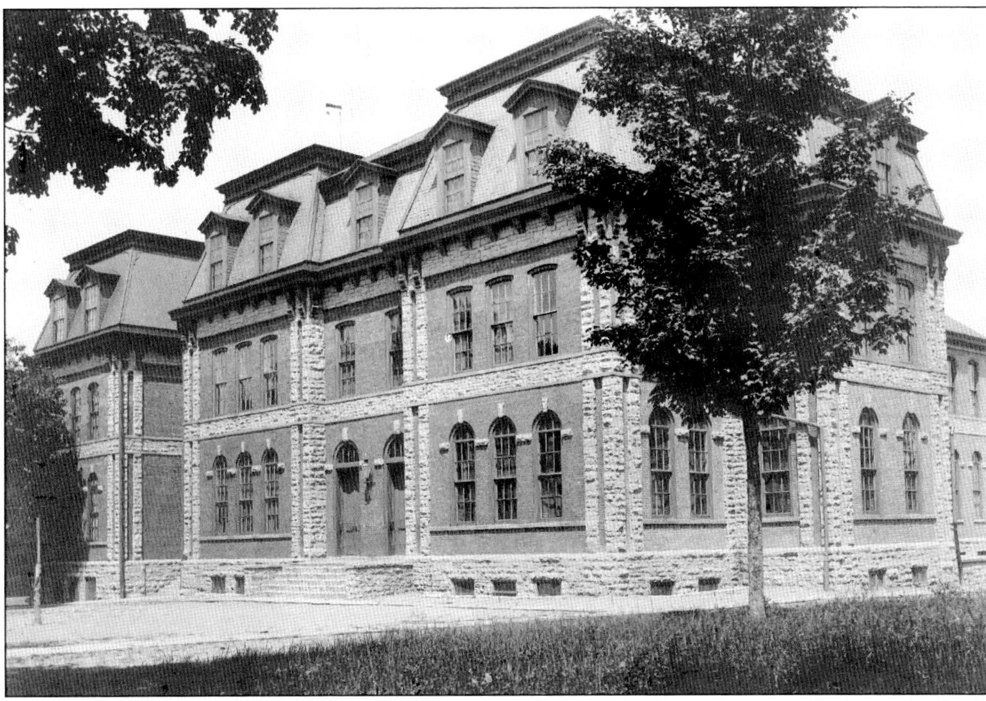

In 1867, the New Jersey Legislature enacted a public school law to provide state funds for public schools throughout the state. One result of this largess was that the Town of Newton commissioned architect J. Digby Daly to design a handsome new public school. The local contracting firm of Hoppaugh & Moore was engaged to oversee construction, and in 1869 ground was broken on a new site at the east end of Halsted Street. The school cost $26,500 to build, and an additional $6,500 was allocated for furnishings. The new building contained eight classrooms, including one room for a high school. It was dedicated on December 19, 1870, and approximately 400 students began attending classes. The building was enlarged over the years, and eventually demolished in 1962.

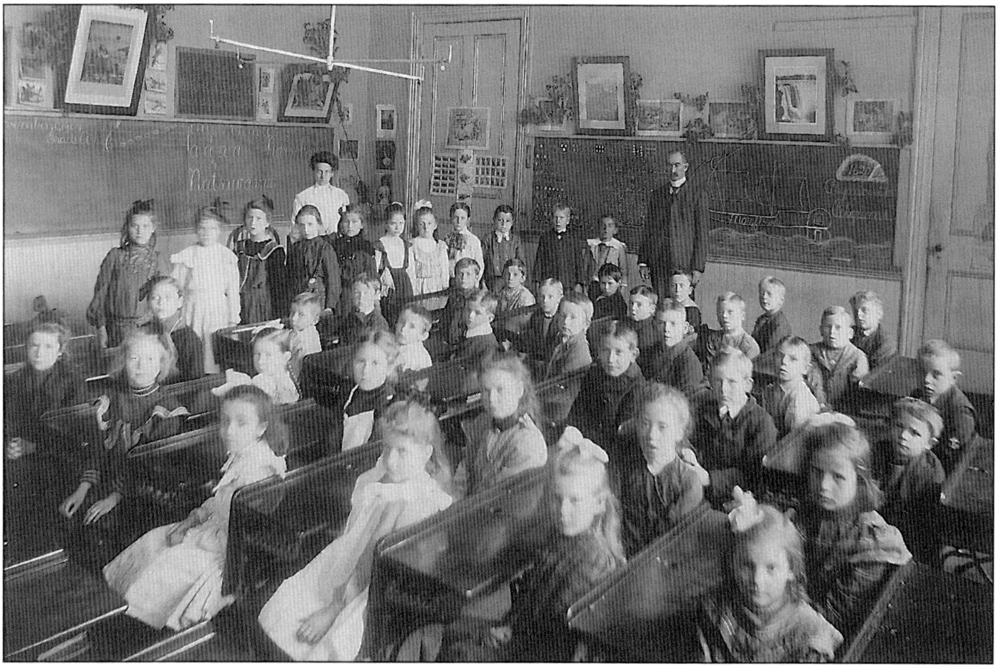

On November 4, 1904, Miss Kate Taylor and her 44 third-grade pupils were photographed in their classroom together with the school principal, Dr. Charles Marjory. Over the students' heads is a gas jet, used to illuminate the classroom before the building was electrified.

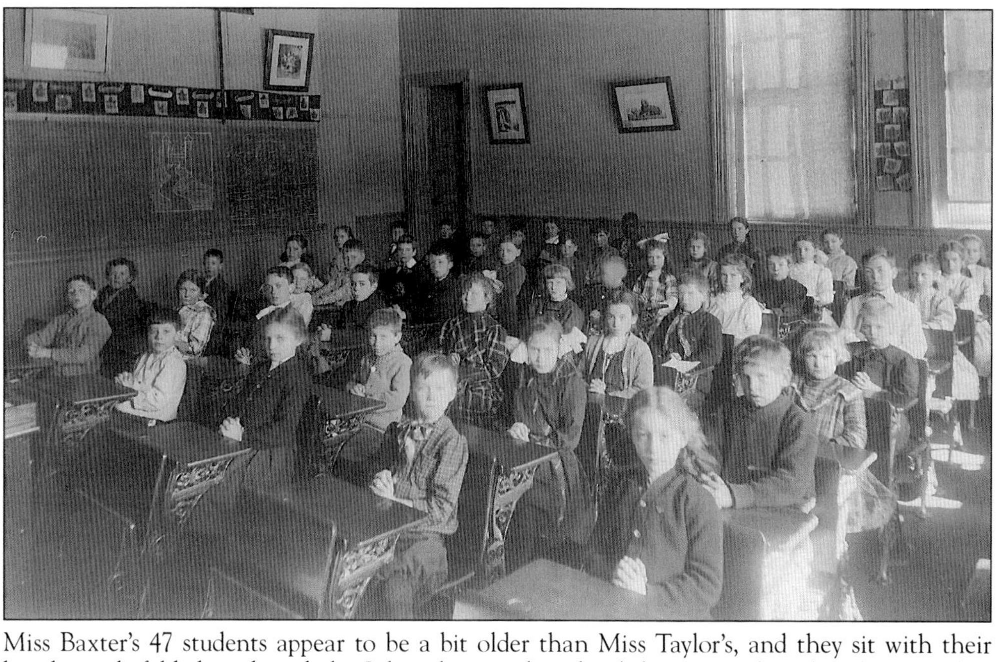

Miss Baxter's 47 students appear to be a bit older than Miss Taylor's, and they sit with their hands neatly folded on their desks. Like others in the school that November, this classroom has been decorated for Thanksgiving—a tradition which continues to this day.

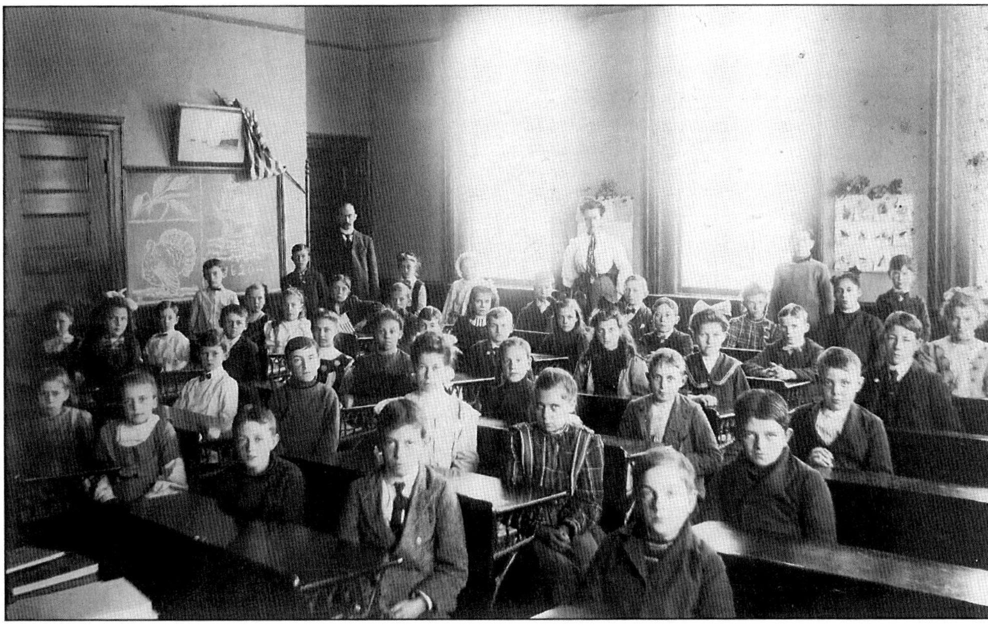

Once again, Dr. Charles Marjory oversees the class photography session on November 4, 1904. As the children get older, their clothing becomes more and more like that of adults. Notice that a few of the boys in this class are wearing coats and ties.

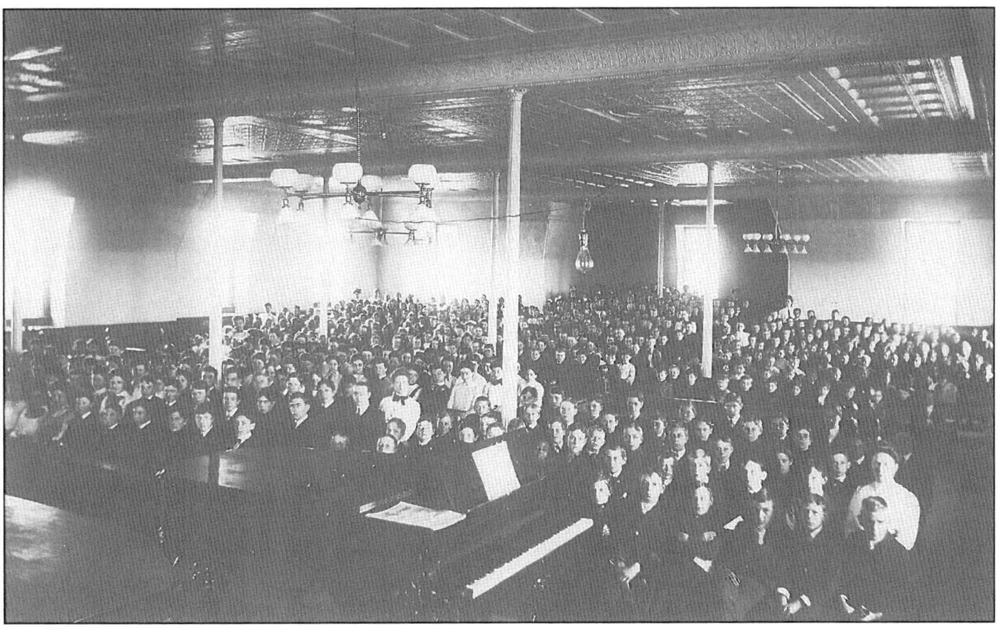

All 11 classes are assembled in the auditorium for a program—boys on the right, girls on the left. This third-floor auditorium could accommodate 500 people, and was probably near capacity when this photograph was taken in 1904 or 1905. Notice that the auditorium had electric lights, even though many of the classrooms were still illuminated by gas.

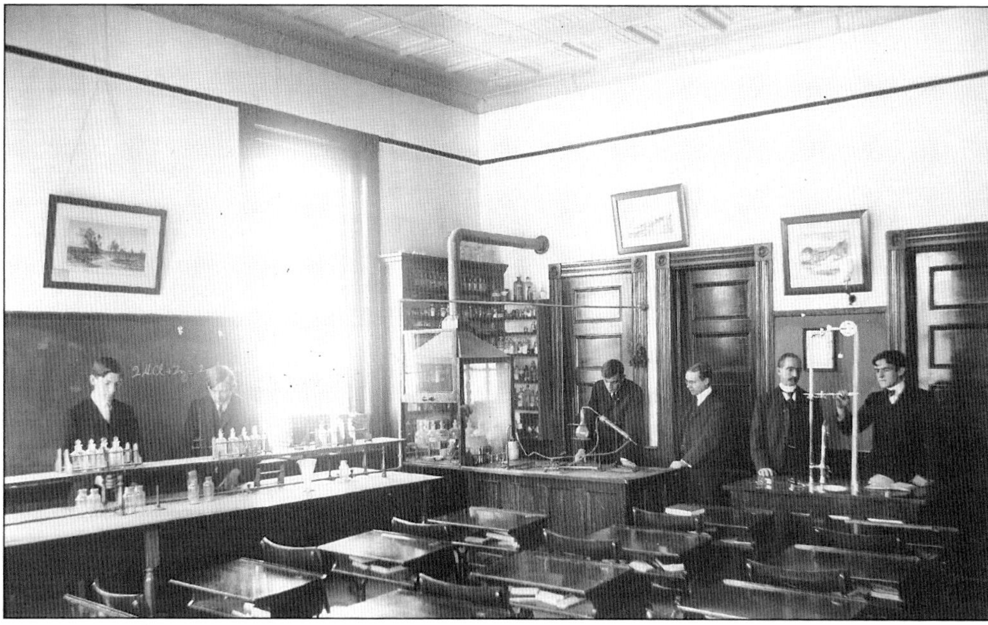

Milton Brundage, standing in front of the door facing left, taught the fourth year high school chemistry class. To his right is Dr. Marjory, the principal, and they are each supervising a student. The vented glass case on the counter near the window was used to store and mix some of the more hazardous chemicals used in the lab.

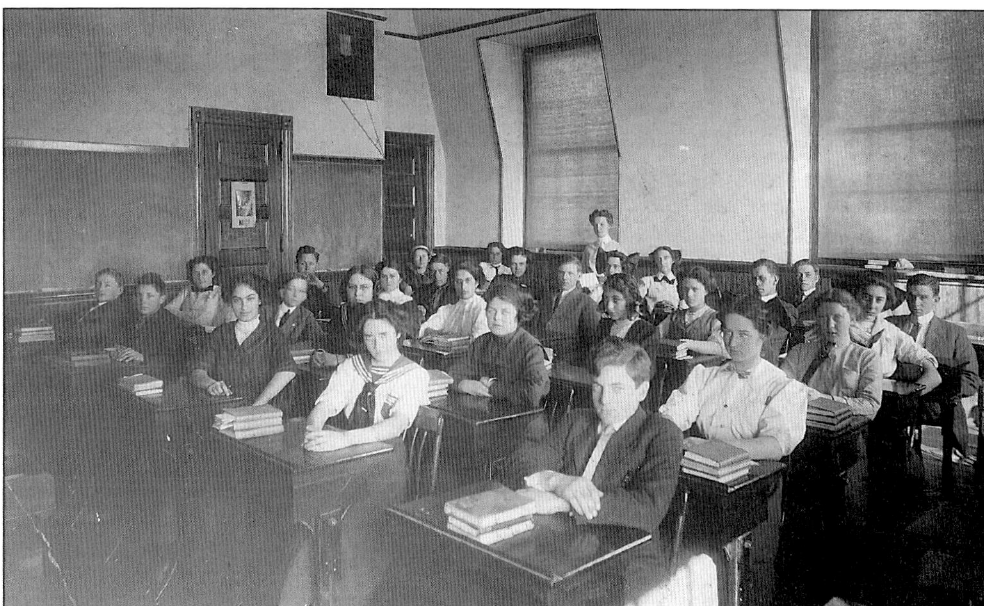

The high school algebra class was held in a room on the third floor of the school. This 1912 photograph includes 27 students, 11 boys and 16 girls.

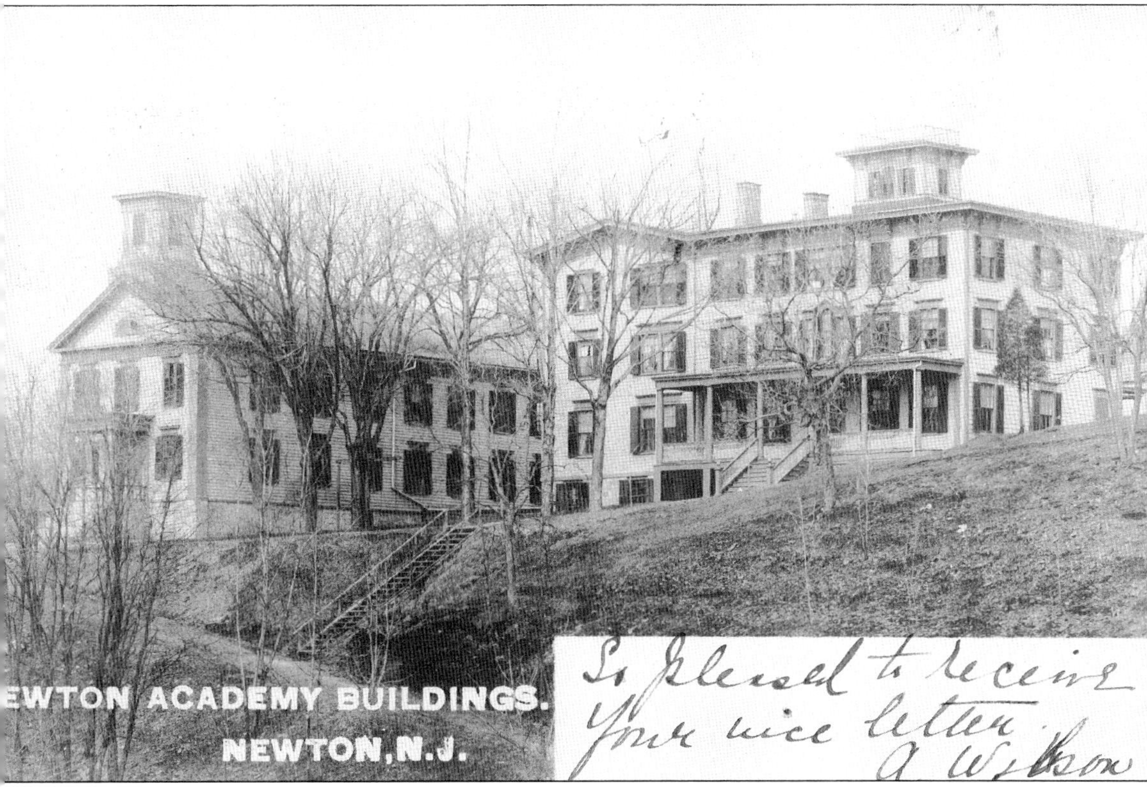

High on the hill overlooking the town stood the buildings of the Newton Academy, a private school for boys. When it first opened on Liberty Street, the school was known as Newton Presbyterian Academy. In 1853, the trustees moved the school to new buildings on Anderson Hill, later known as Academy Street, and in 1855 the name was changed to the Newton Collegiate Institute.

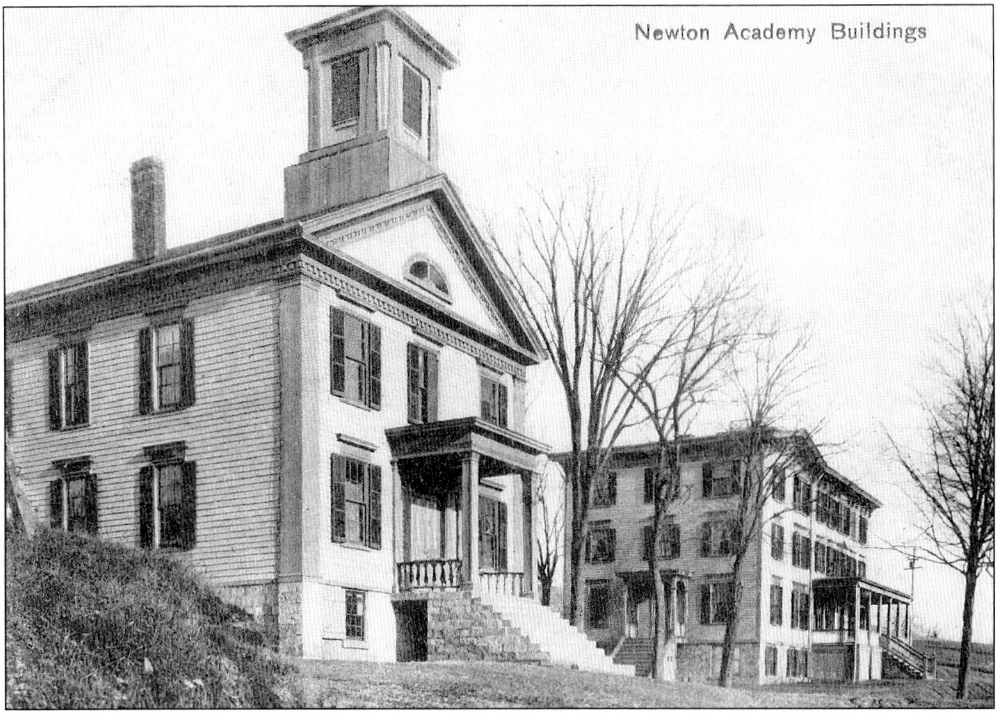

The 1853 teaching building (left) and the 1855 dormitory are seen in this c. 1907 postcard view of the Academy. An 1897 prospectus of the town boasted that the buildings were heated with steam, and that each division of the dormitory had its own bathroom. "Nothing that can promote health and comfort has been neglected," for any of the up to 50 boys who boarded at the school.

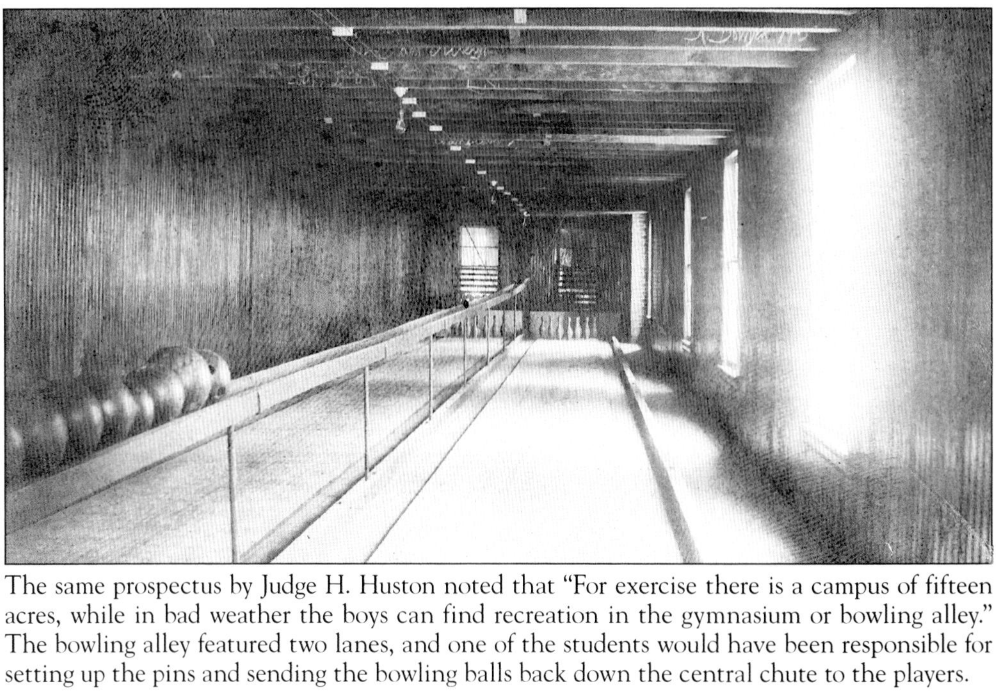

The same prospectus by Judge H. Huston noted that "For exercise there is a campus of fifteen acres, while in bad weather the boys can find recreation in the gymnasium or bowling alley." The bowling alley featured two lanes, and one of the students would have been responsible for setting up the pins and sending the bowling balls back down the central chute to the players.

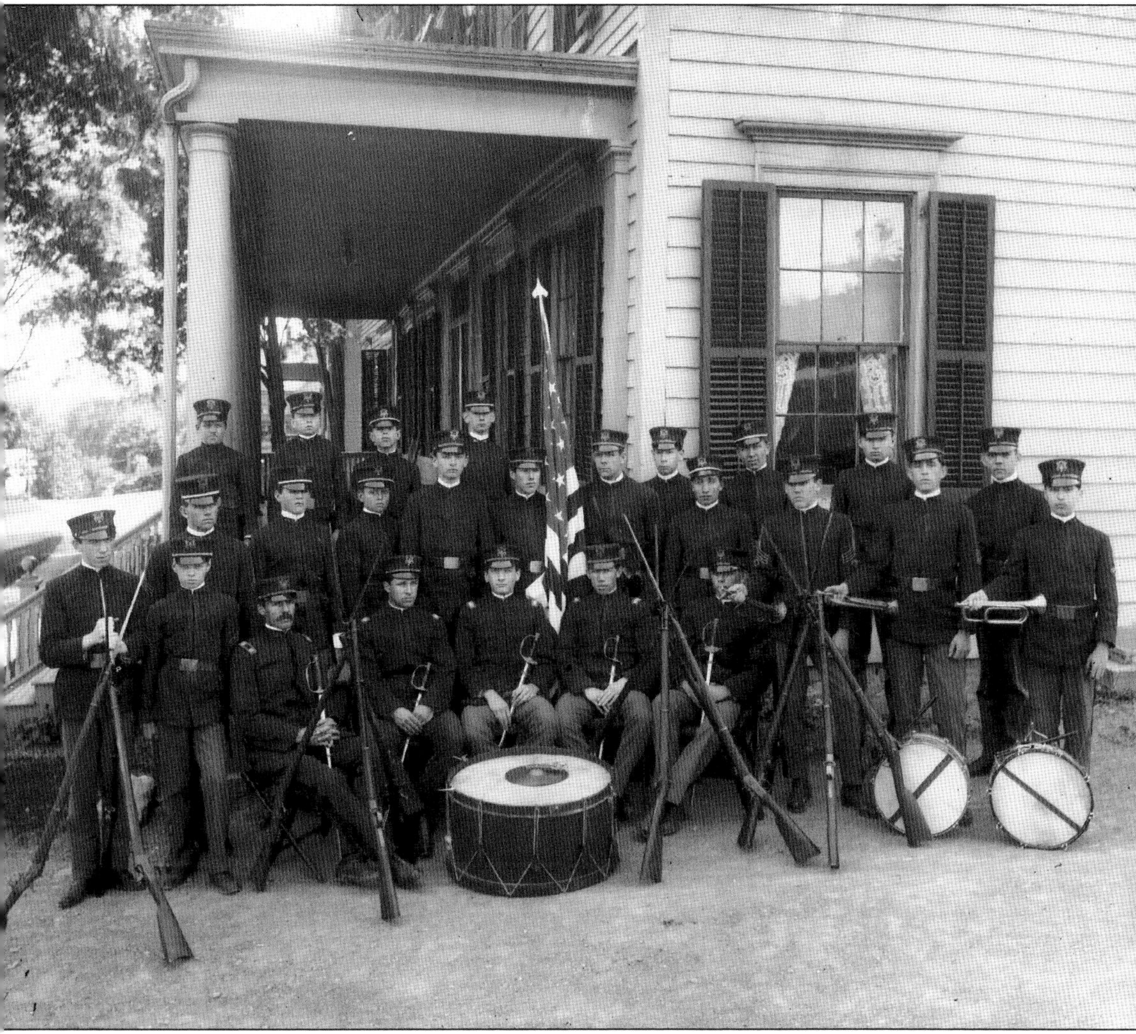

The young members of Newton Academy's cadet corps pose with their officers, arms and instruments at the north end of their dormitory porch in a photograph taken just before the turn of the century on a glass-plate negative. The Academy closed in the early 1930s, and the buildings were then purchased by the Anken Chemical and Film Corporation in 1947. They were ultimately demolished in the mid-1970s.

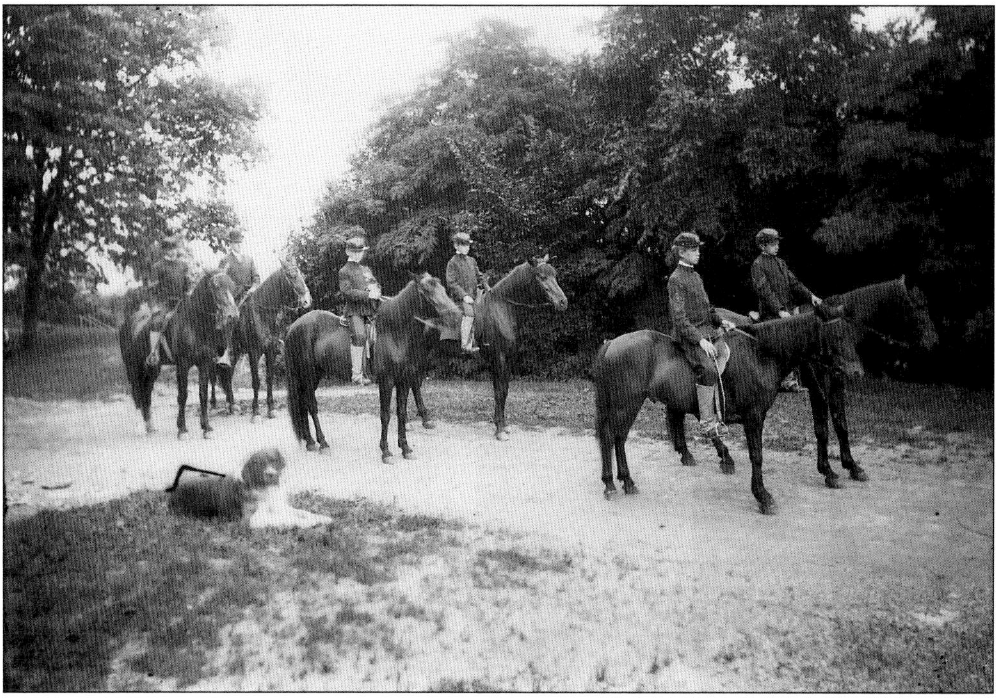

Five cadets, three of whom have been given the rank of non-commissioned officers, ride out with their bowler-hatted instructor in another turn-of-the century glass-negative photograph.

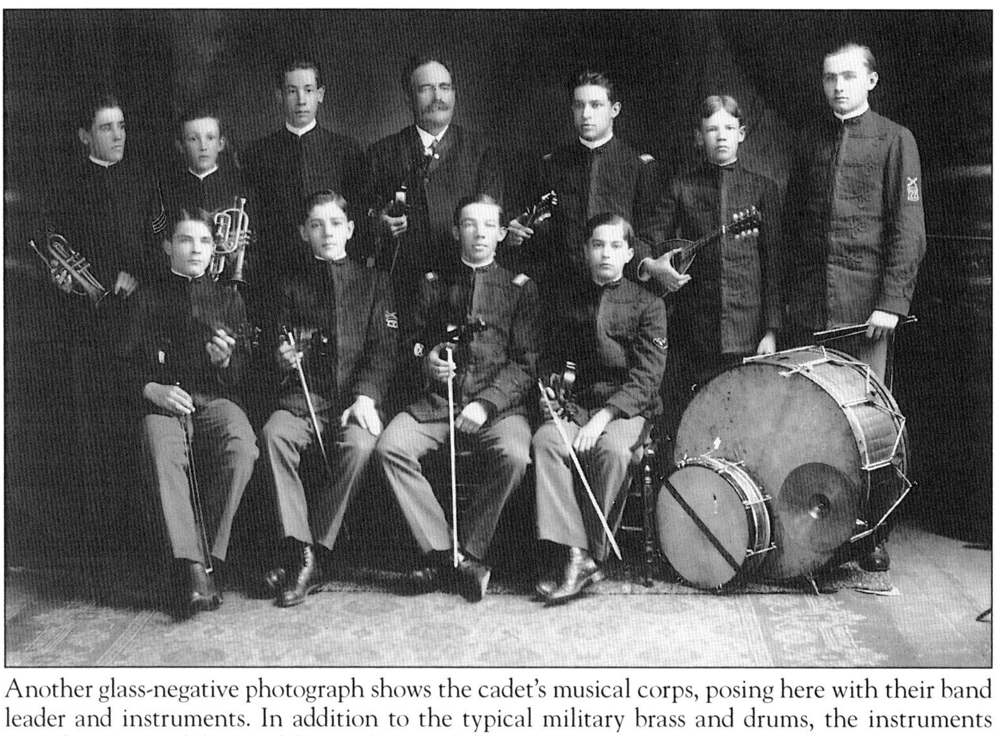

Another glass-negative photograph shows the cadet's musical corps, posing here with their band leader and instruments. In addition to the typical military brass and drums, the instruments include two mandolins and five violins, including the instructor's.

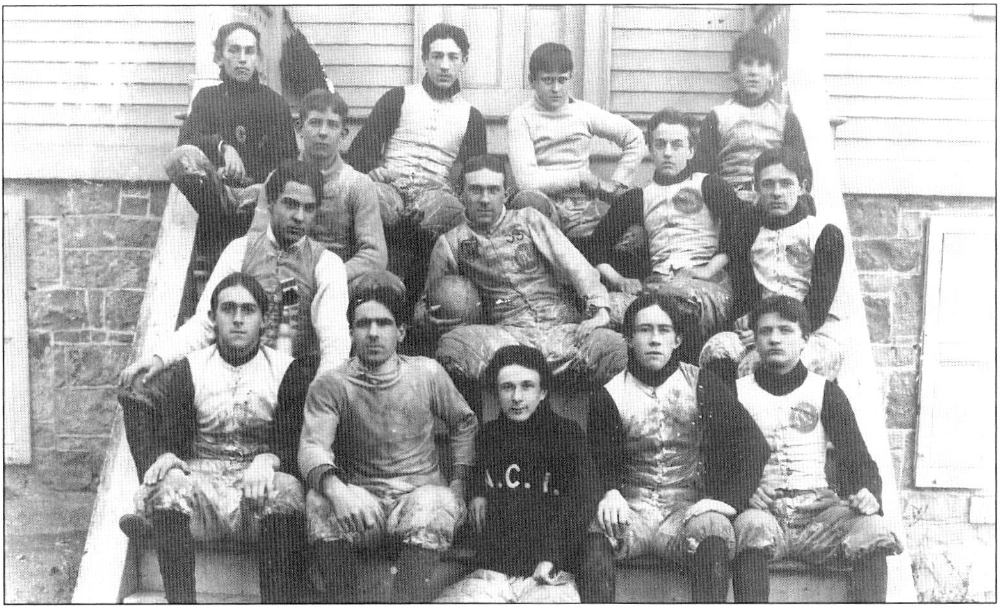

Here members of the Academy's football team pose on the steps on the south side of the dormitory. N.C.I. stands for Newton Collegiate Institute, even though the school was commonly referred to as the Newton Academy. The school prided itself on preparing boys for both college and business.

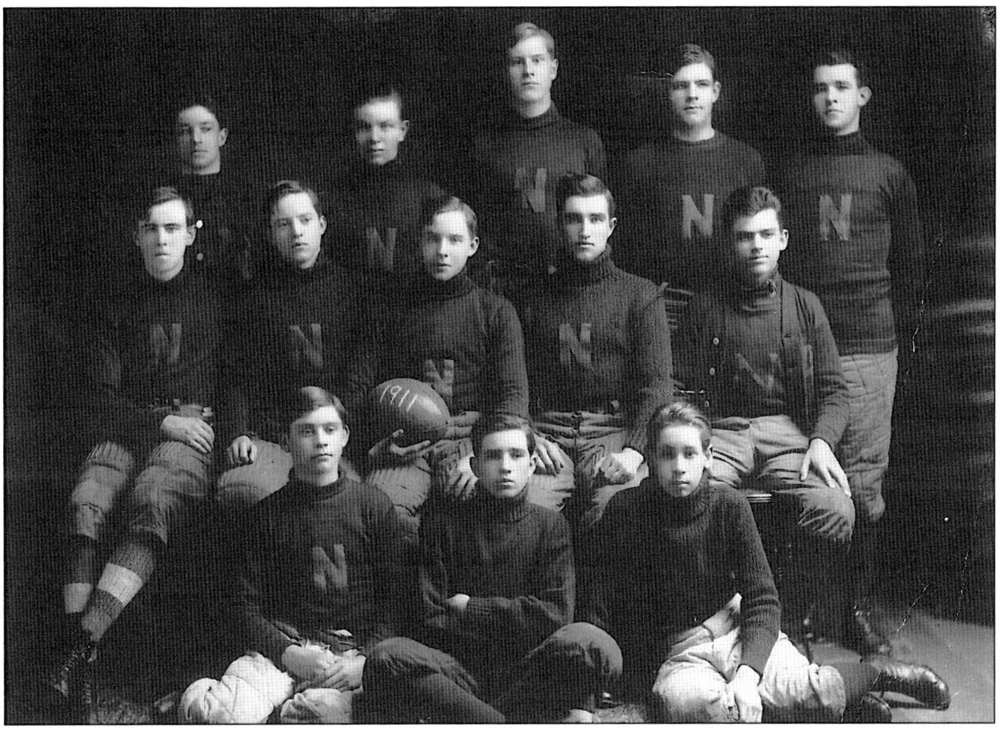

The Academy's 1911 football team posed for a formal portrait at the Townley Photographic Studio on Spring Street. The young man to the right of the boy holding the ball is Louis Budd Sr., one of the Academy's athletic instructors.

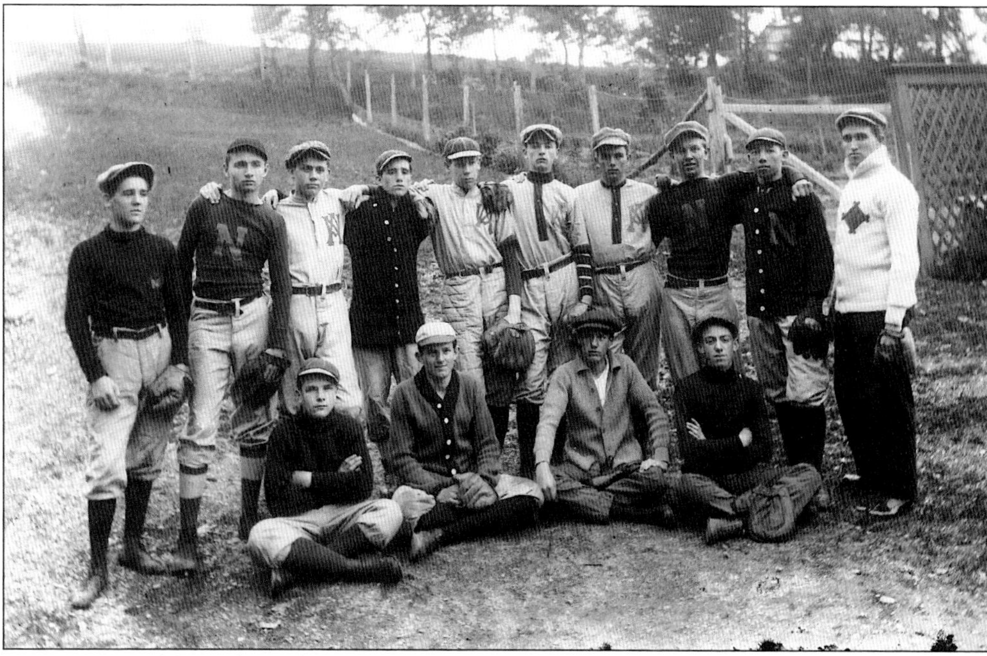

Here Louis Budd, on the right in the white jacket, poses with the Academy's baseball team in the spring of 1912.

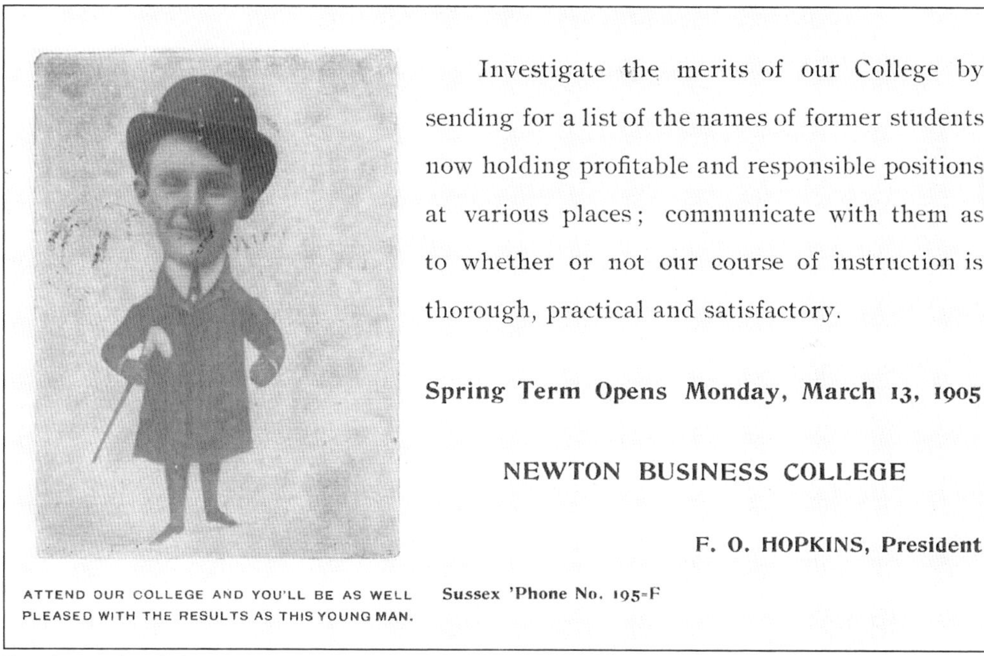

For those who did not want to pursue an academic career, there was always the Newton Business College, located in the Park Block building on Park Row. Here, according to Judge Huston's 1897 prospectus, courses were offered in bookkeeping, penmanship, stenography, typewriting, and "other branches necessary to make up a good business education." This postcard advertising the school was printed about 1905.

Seven

SPECIAL EVENTS

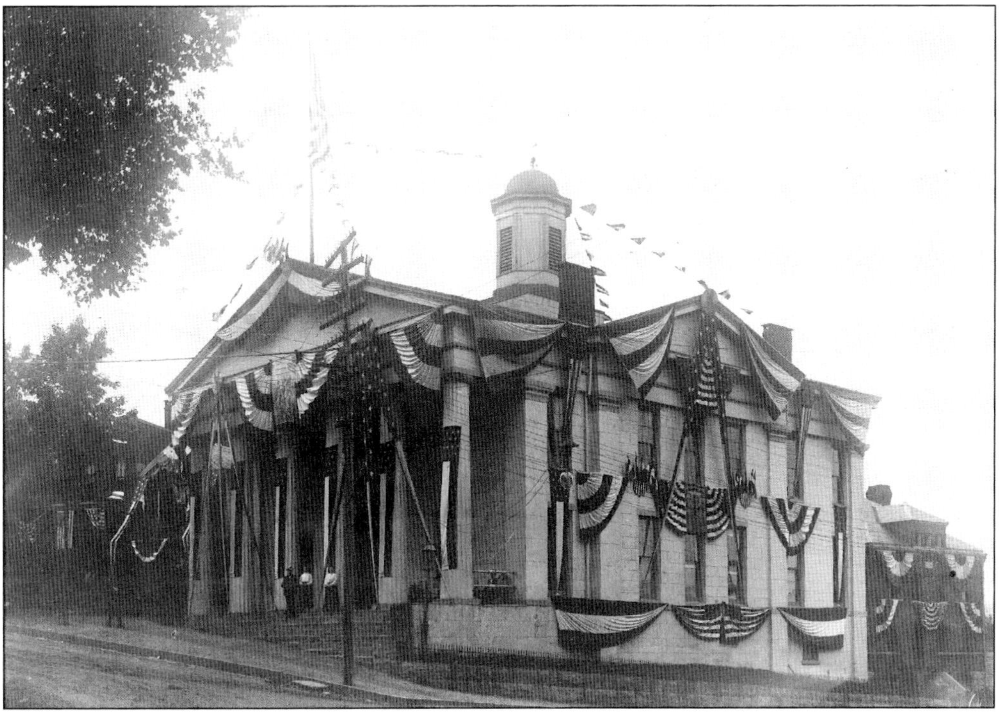

In 1903, the buildings in the center of Newton were exuberantly decked with flags and bunting to celebrate the sesquicentennial of the establishment of Sussex County on June 8, 1753. Here we see the county courthouse in all its patriotic glory. There is even a reproduction of the famous painting *The Spirit of '76* hanging above the entrance to the building. The following nine photographs of the decorations was taken by George Kintner's studio in Newton, and presented to Walter Pancoast, decorator, of Newark, New Jersey. Presumably Pancoast, or his firm, was in charge of designing and installing the bunting throughout the town.

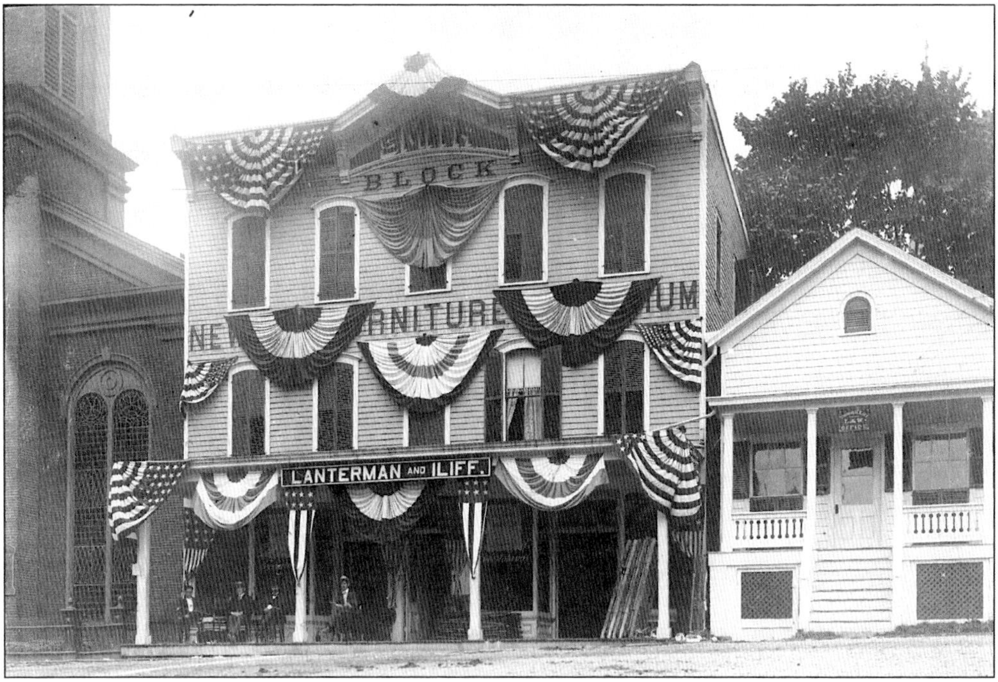

Lanterman and Iliff's furniture store and Thomas M. Kay's law office were the last surviving wood frame buildings on Park Row. They were demolished in 1929 to make way for the new County Hall of Records, which opened in July 1930.

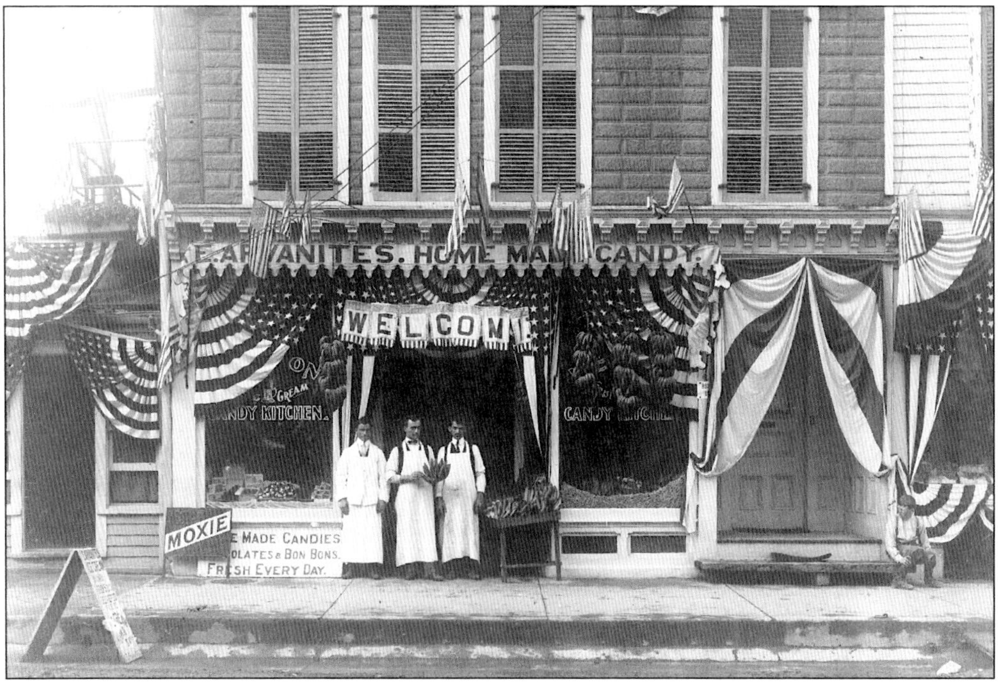

E. Arvanties or one of his employees proudly displayed a bunch of bananas when the candy store at 124 Spring Street was photographed. The little one-story building next to the store is gone. In its place is a driveway leading to the parking lot behind the fire museum.

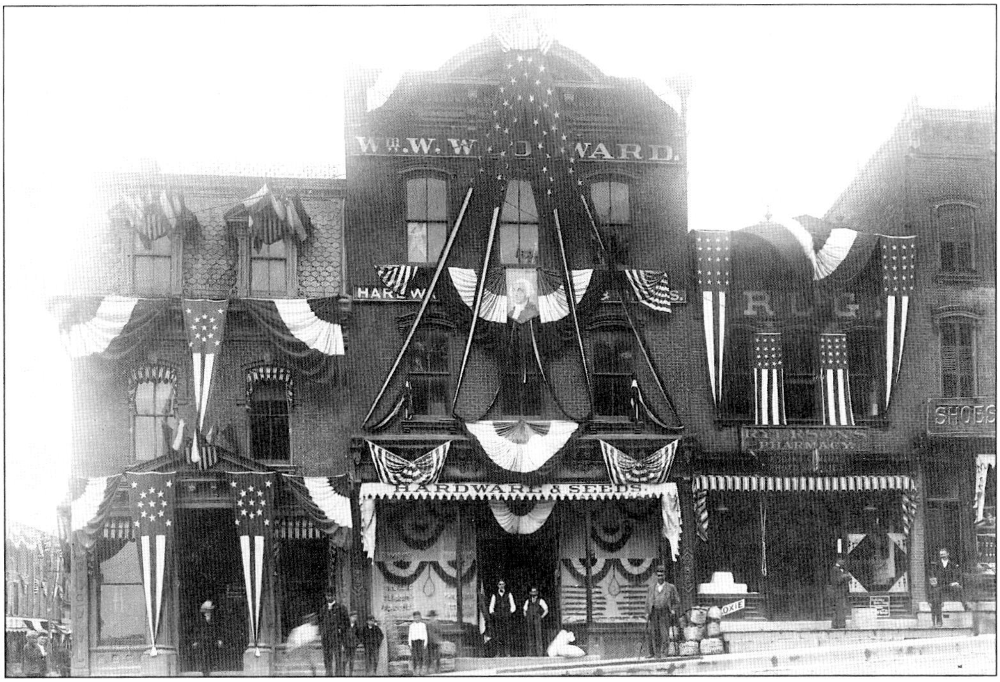

This photograph provides a very good view of the buildings at the corner of Main and Spring Streets, including the Sussex National Bank, Woodward's Hardware Store, and Ryerson's Pharmacy. They are all excellent examples of late 19th century commercial architecture. The bank building, with its Second Empire mansard roof, was built in 1871. Woodward's was extensively remodeled after a fire in 1873, and the pharmacy was built in 1881.

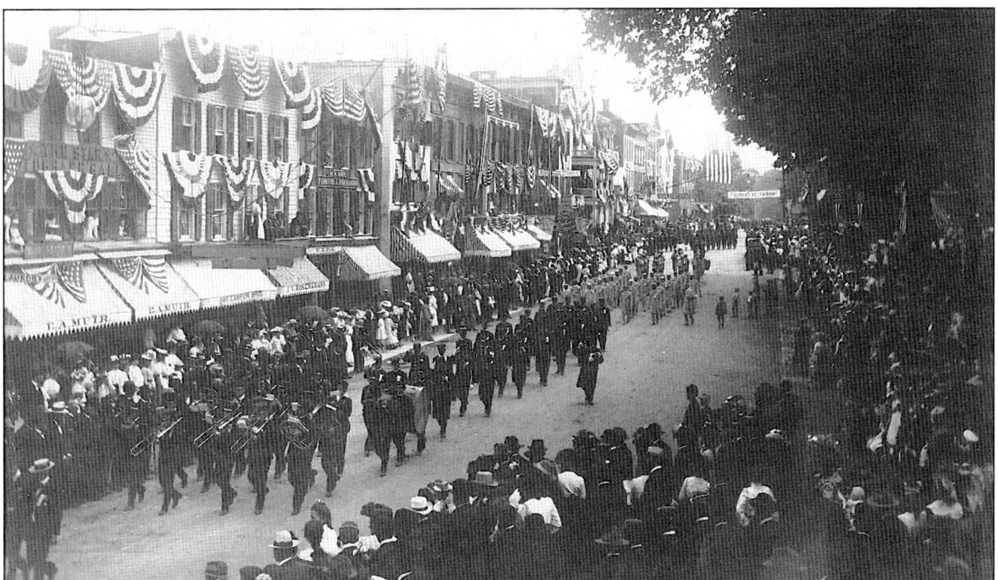

No celebration would be complete without a parade and speeches, and the sesquicentennial was no exception. Here we see a band coming down Spring Street in front of crowds filling the square and the street in front of the courthouse.

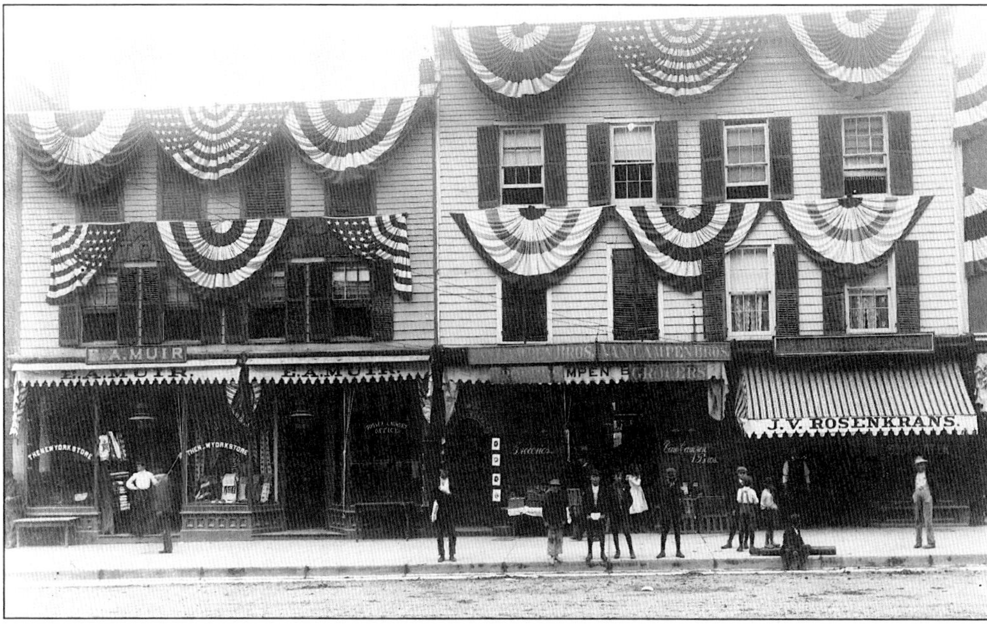

All of these buildings at the west end of Spring Street, near the courthouse, were demolished in the early 1970s as part of an urban renewal project. The site was further altered when the intersection of Spring, Water, and Mill Streets was reconfigured. E.A. Muir's establishment, "The New York Store," sold dry and fancy goods; the Van Campen Brothers sold groceries, and J.V. Rosenkrans ran a pharmacy.

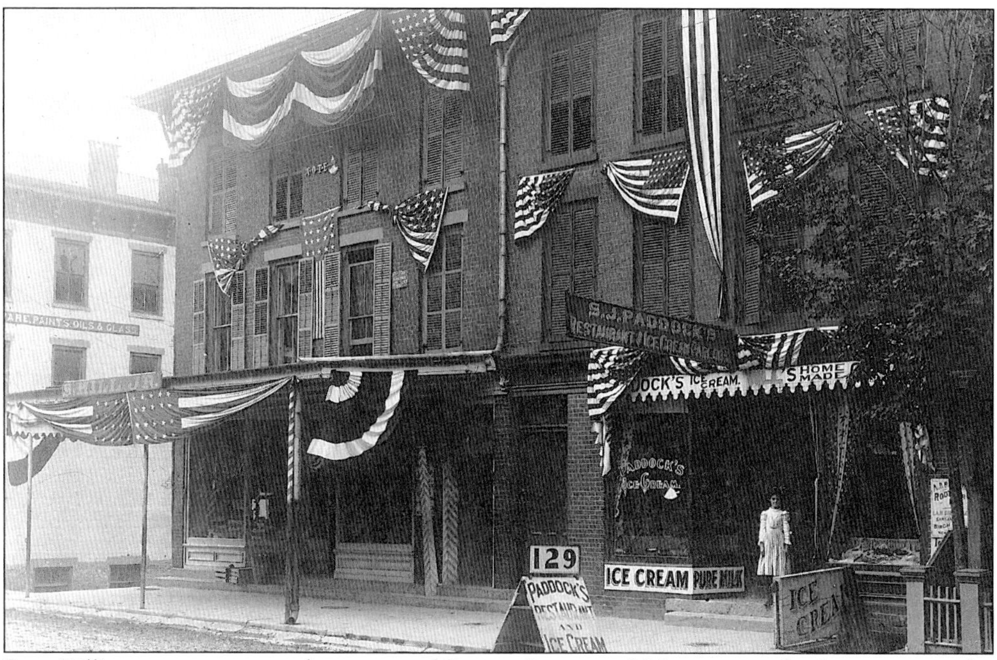

Sam Hill's grocery store, at the corner of Spring Street and Moran, was the last store on the street to maintain a covered shed over the sidewalk. In the mid-19th century virtually all of the stores on Spring Street had such sheds to protect shoppers from the sun and rain, but they were gradually abandoned in favor of canvas awnings.

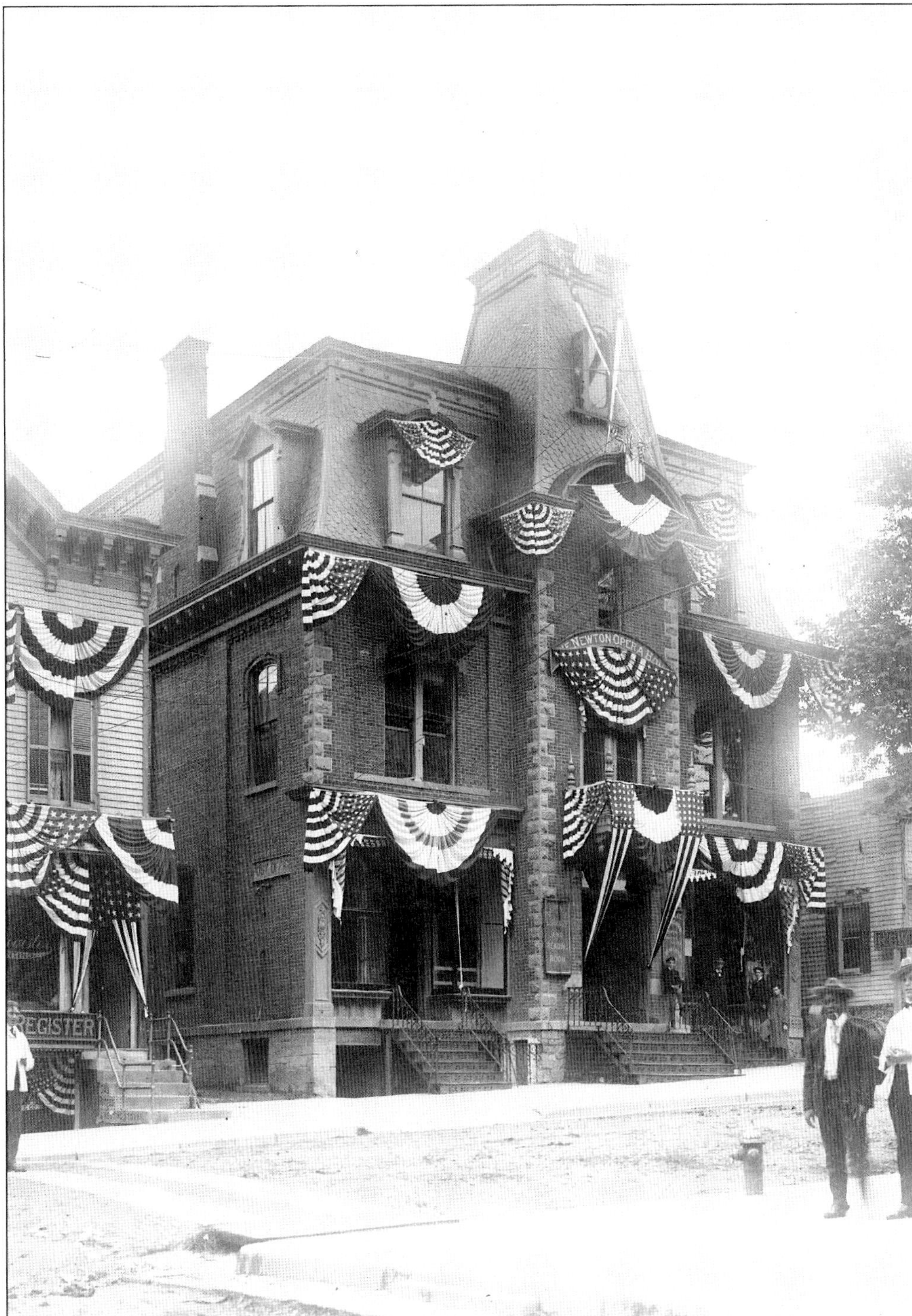

Not even bunting can lighten the somber facade of Library Hall. Built in 1871, this building housed the Dennis Library, the post office, and the Newton Opera House, as well as several businesses. It was demolished in 1958 to make way for the current post office.

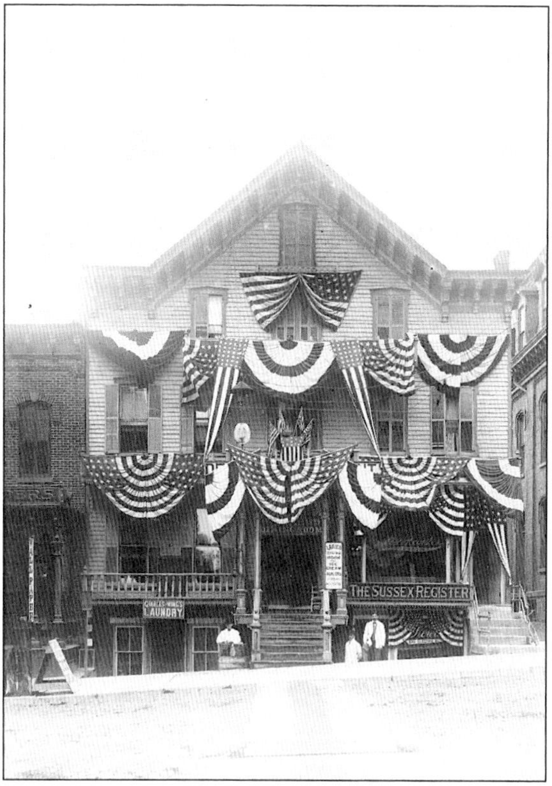

This handsome frame building stood on the site of the current post office driveway. It was home to the *Sussex Register*, one of Newton's two weekly newspapers. It also housed a Ladies' Dining Room and Ice Cream Parlor, owned by M.S. Devore, the offices of the Newton Gas and Electric Company, and Charles Wing's Laundry.

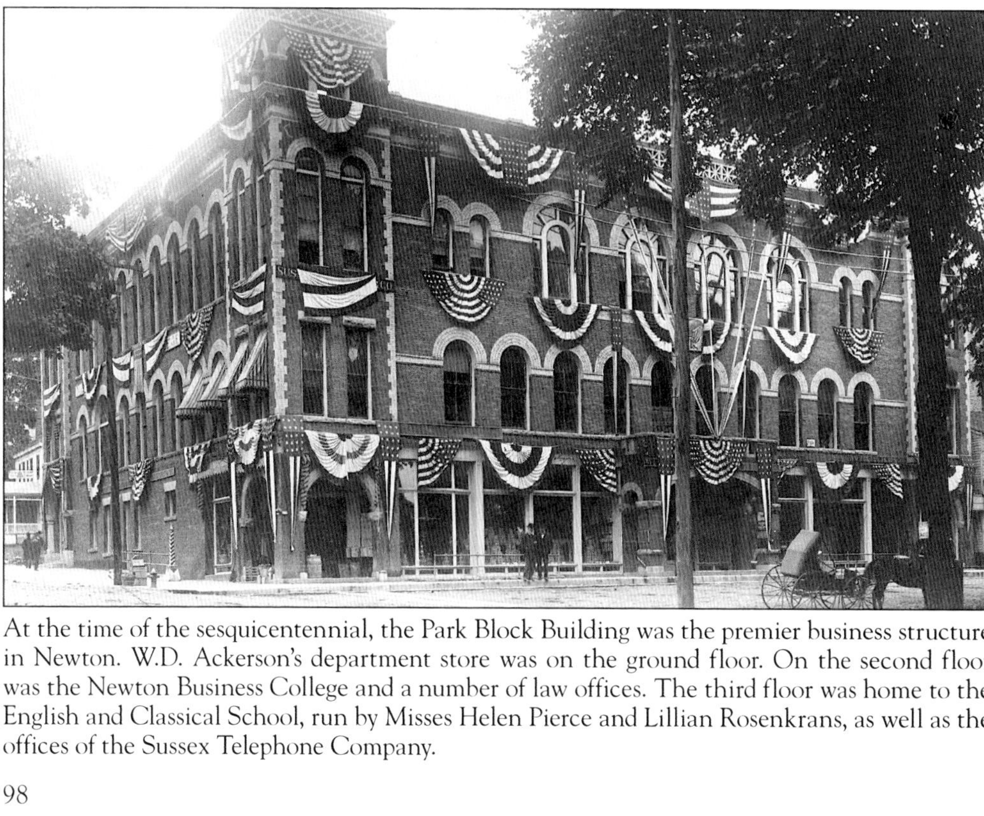

At the time of the sesquicentennial, the Park Block Building was the premier business structure in Newton. W.D. Ackerson's department store was on the ground floor. On the second floor was the Newton Business College and a number of law offices. The third floor was home to the English and Classical School, run by Misses Helen Pierce and Lillian Rosenkrans, as well as the offices of the Sussex Telephone Company.

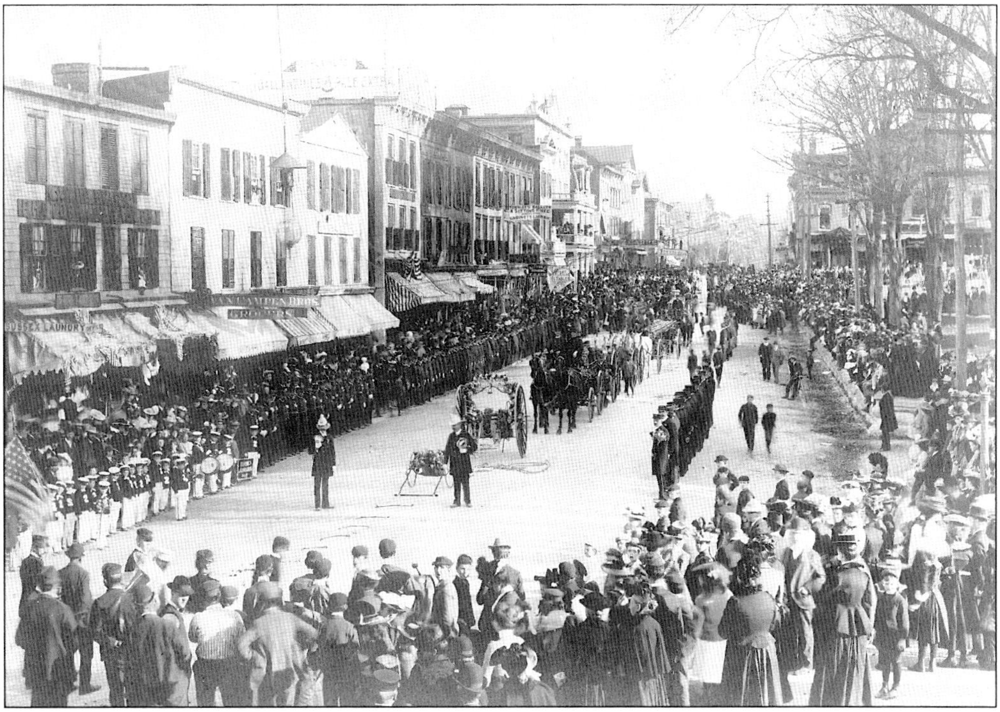

While the sesquicentennial was a one-time event, fire parades were held annually. The parades assembled at the railroad yard, and then marched up Spring Street to the courthouse—a tradition which continues to this day.

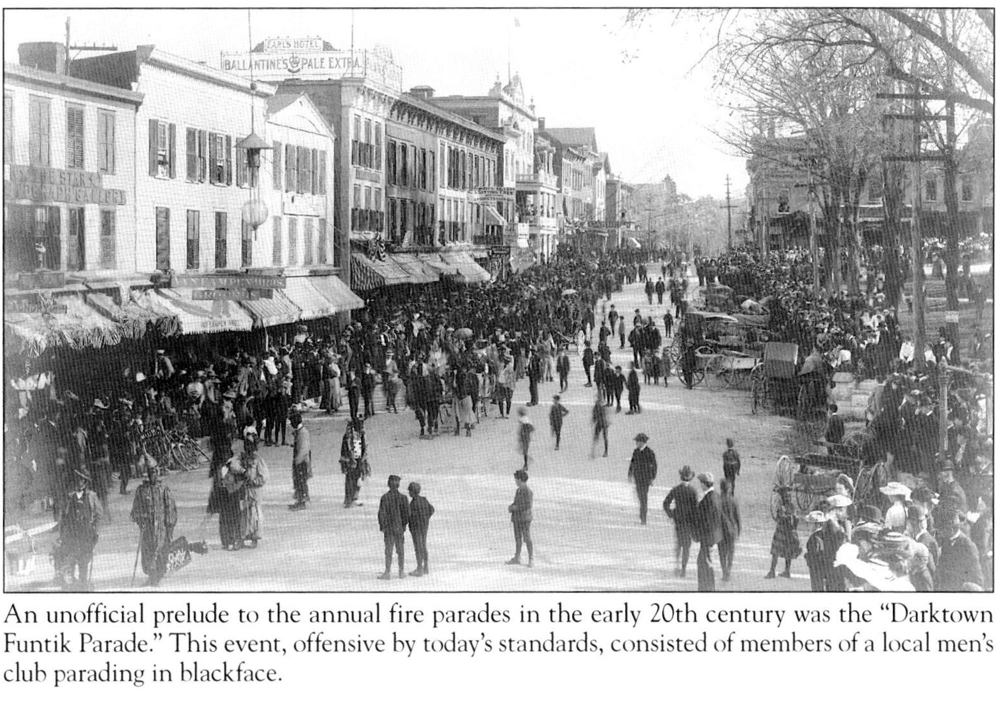

An unofficial prelude to the annual fire parades in the early 20th century was the "Darktown Funtik Parade." This event, offensive by today's standards, consisted of members of a local men's club parading in blackface.

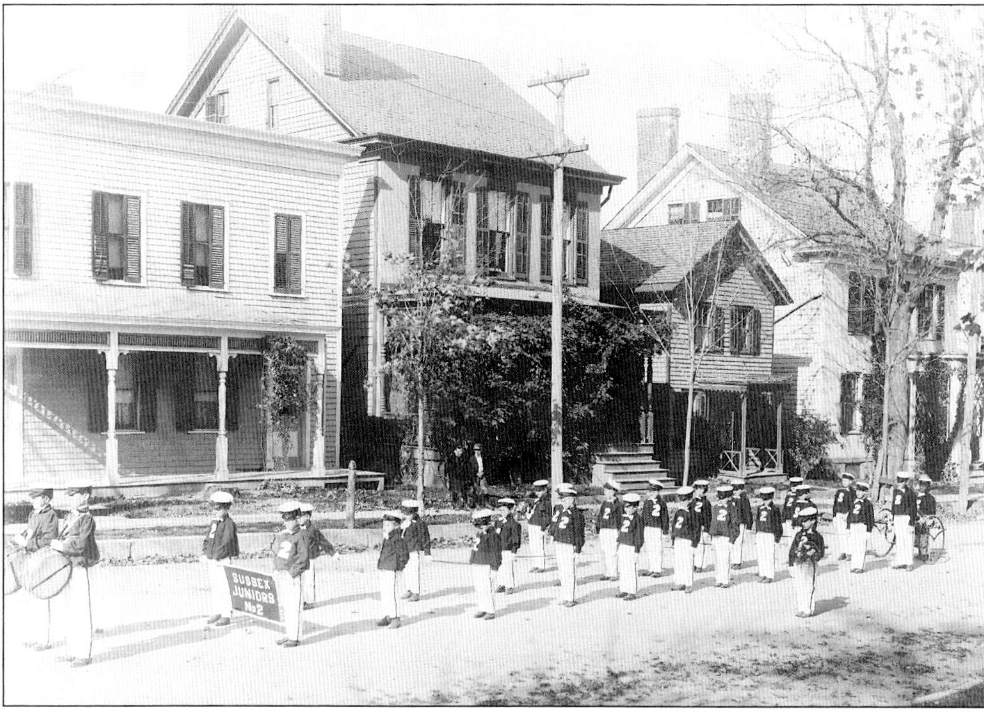

Newton's volunteer fire departments were family affairs. Here the boys of Sussex #2 Juniors pose on High Street in front of the Presbyterian church. Their firehouse is just behind them on the same side of the street as the church, where the hall of records parking lot is today. This photograph, taken about 1905, belongs to the same series of pictures as the two preceding ones.

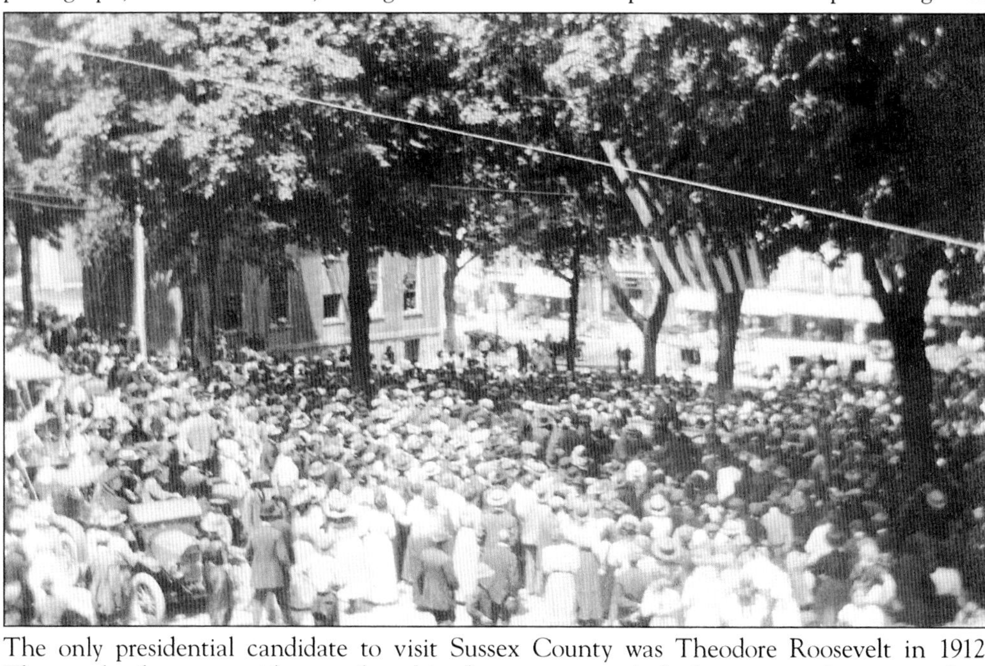

The only presidential candidate to visit Sussex County was Theodore Roosevelt in 1912. Thousands of county residents gathered in the square to wait for his motorcade to come from the railroad station to the speakers' platform set up on Park Place.

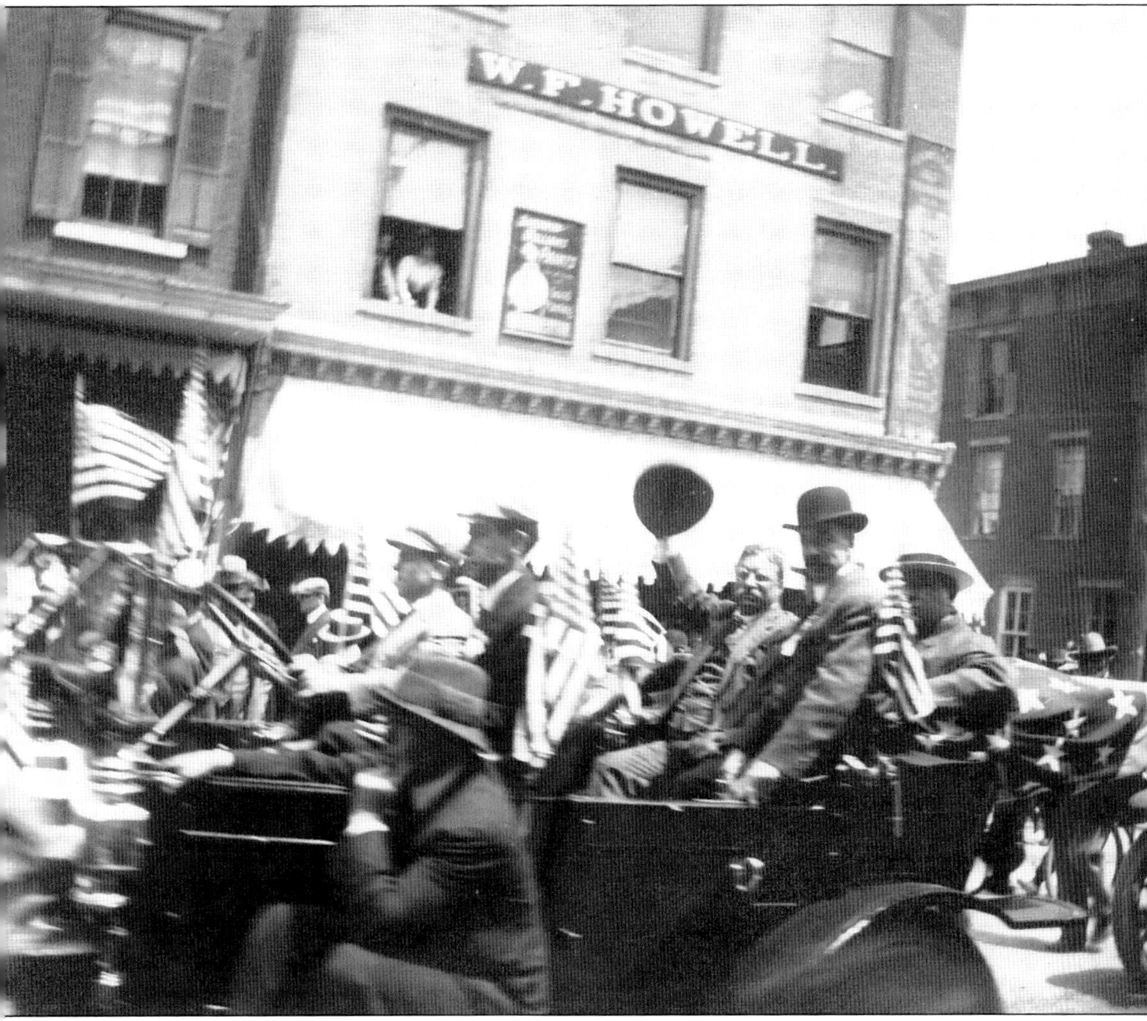

Theodore Roosevelt waves to the crowd from his car during his campaigning trip to Sussex County. Roosevelt first became president in 1901, upon the assassination of William McKinley. He was re-elected in 1904. In 1908, he was succeeded by his protégée, William Howard Taft. In 1912, he organized a third party, the "Bull Moose" ticket. Not only did he lose the election, his candidacy split the Republican party, putting Woodrow Wilson, a Democrat, into the Oval Office.

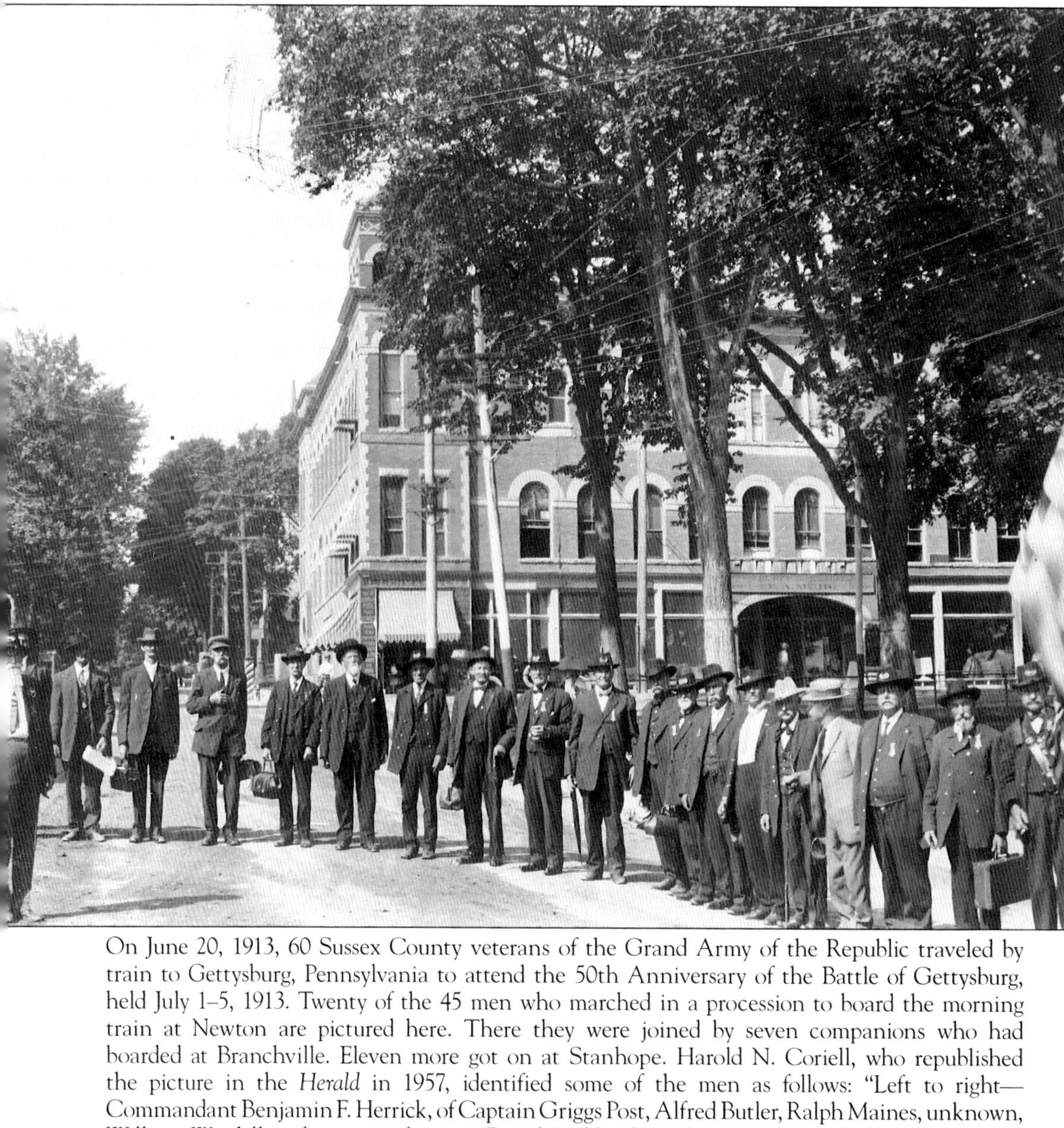

On June 20, 1913, 60 Sussex County veterans of the Grand Army of the Republic traveled by train to Gettysburg, Pennsylvania to attend the 50th Anniversary of the Battle of Gettysburg, held July 1–5, 1913. Twenty of the 45 men who marched in a procession to board the morning train at Newton are pictured here. There they were joined by seven companions who had boarded at Branchville. Eleven more got on at Stanhope. Harold N. Coriell, who republished the picture in the *Herald* in 1957, identified some of the men as follows: "Left to right—Commandant Benjamin F. Herrick, of Captain Griggs Post, Alfred Butler, Ralph Maines, unknown, William Wardell, unknown, unknown, David Webb of Franklin, unknown, William Howell of Branchville, unknown, J.B. Hendershot, the next four unknown, Horace Van Orden, John Emory, Michael Mohair, and John Calvin."

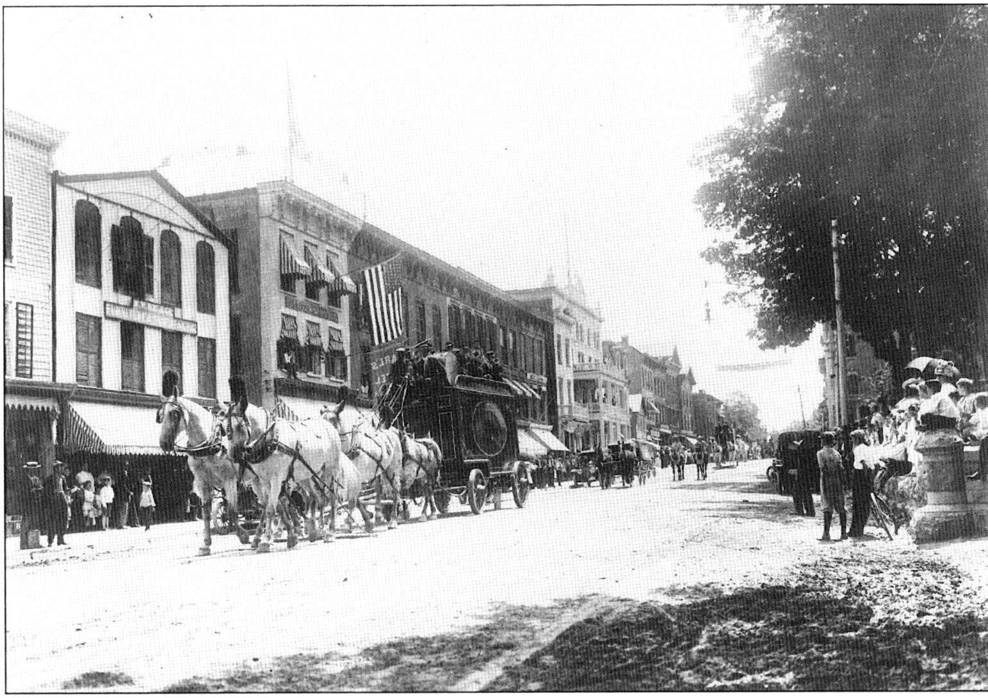

"The Circus is coming!" In Newton, as in many small towns across America, one of the highlights of summer was the Circus' annual visit. In this photograph, taken about 1910, the bandwagon is leading the Circus parade down Spring Street, followed by horseback riders, caged animals, and the omni-present and essential clowns.

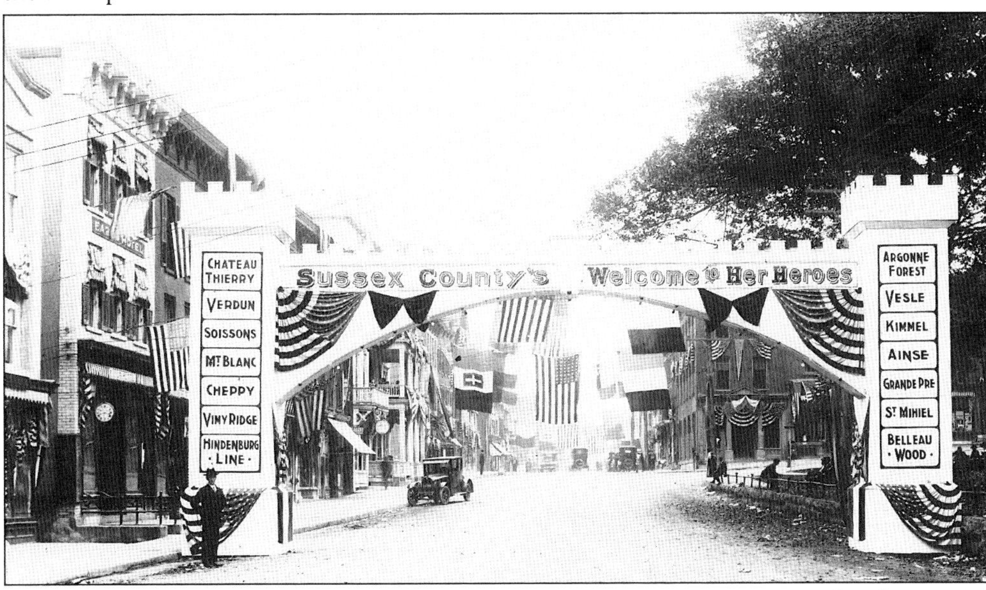

This wooden arch was erected by the Sussex County Hero's Day Committee on October 4, 1919, to honor returning WW I veterans. The day began with a parade, a free lunch, and speeches at Thompson's field, followed by a baseball game. Next came a "Retreat" at this Victory Arch. Then supper was served to all servicemen, veterans, firemen, and bands. A vaudeville show, concert, and fireworks concluded the evening.

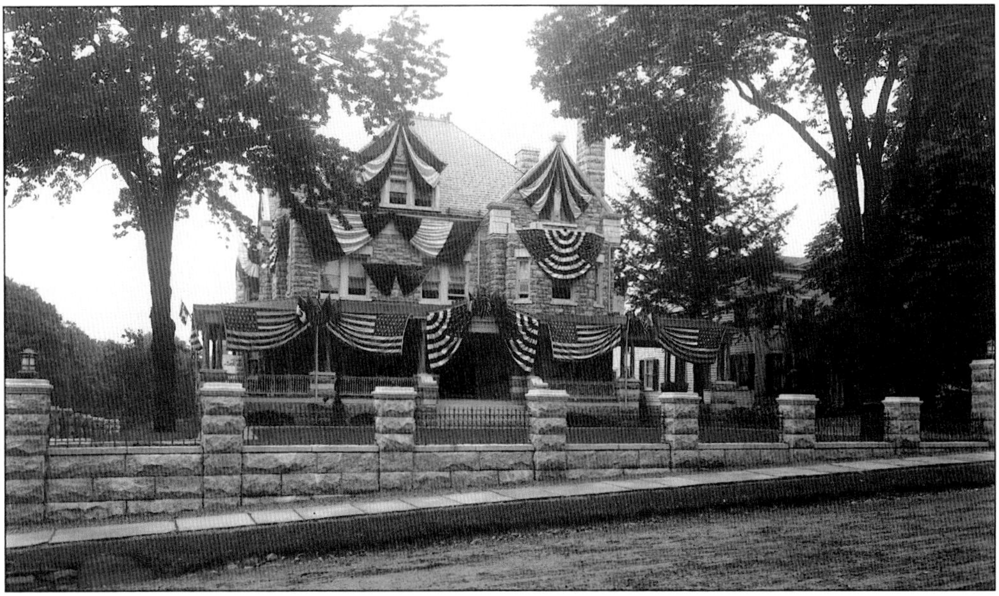

Here we see the Bentley mansion on Main Street decked with patriotic flags and bunting. The presence of British, French, and Swiss flags indicates that the decorations were probably in honor of Hero's Day on October 4, 1919. Notice that Main Street is still unpaved, even though slate sidewalks have been installed in front of the house.

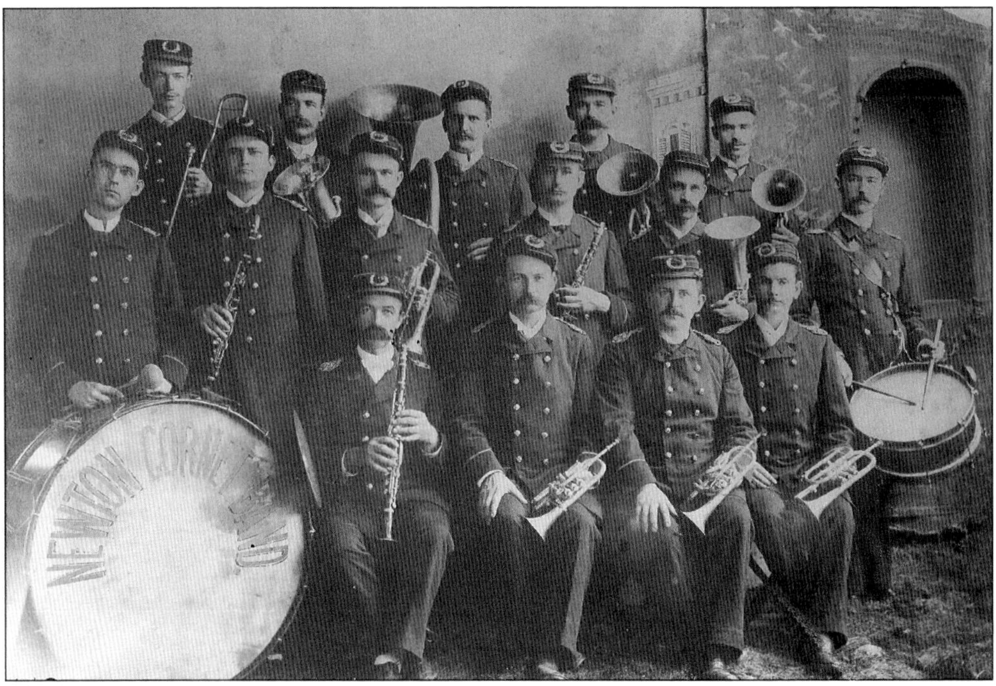

The Newton Cornet Band posed for a portrait in this 1880 photograph. They provided appropriate accompaniment to parades and local festivals. The members, from left to right, are: (front row) Tom Tinney, Andrew Brickner, James English, and Herb Smith; (middle row) Pete Burhard, Elmer Dutcher, John Bryant, Theo. Grinell, Al. Van Campen, and Marty Gilla; (back row) John Cosner, Amzi Cosner, Bill Hill, Tom Harty, and Ross McPeek.

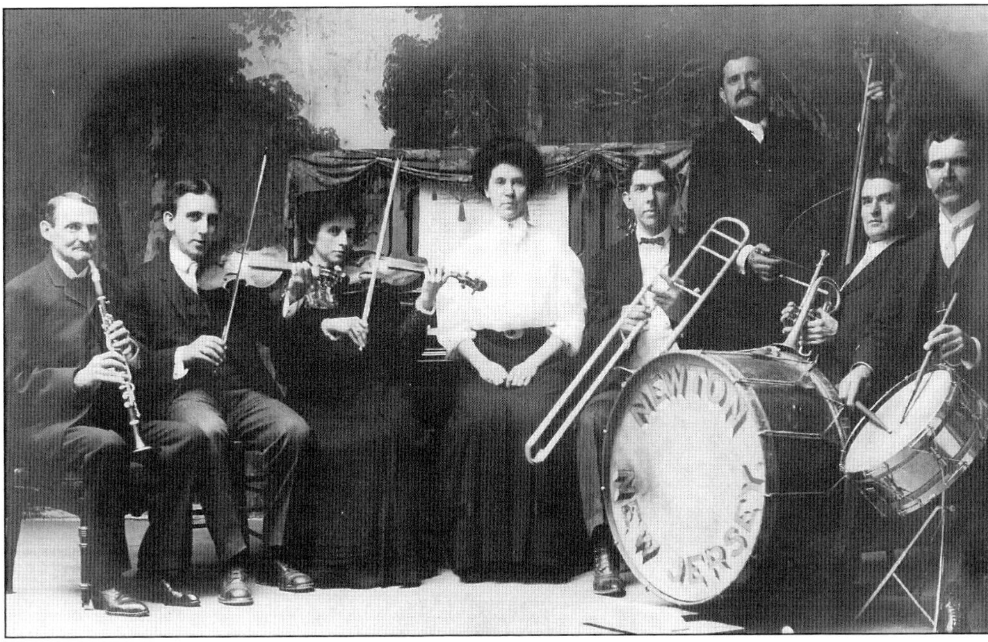

This musical ensemble, photographed about 1910, included both men and women, and may well have accompanied performances at the Opera House and the theater in the Park Block building.

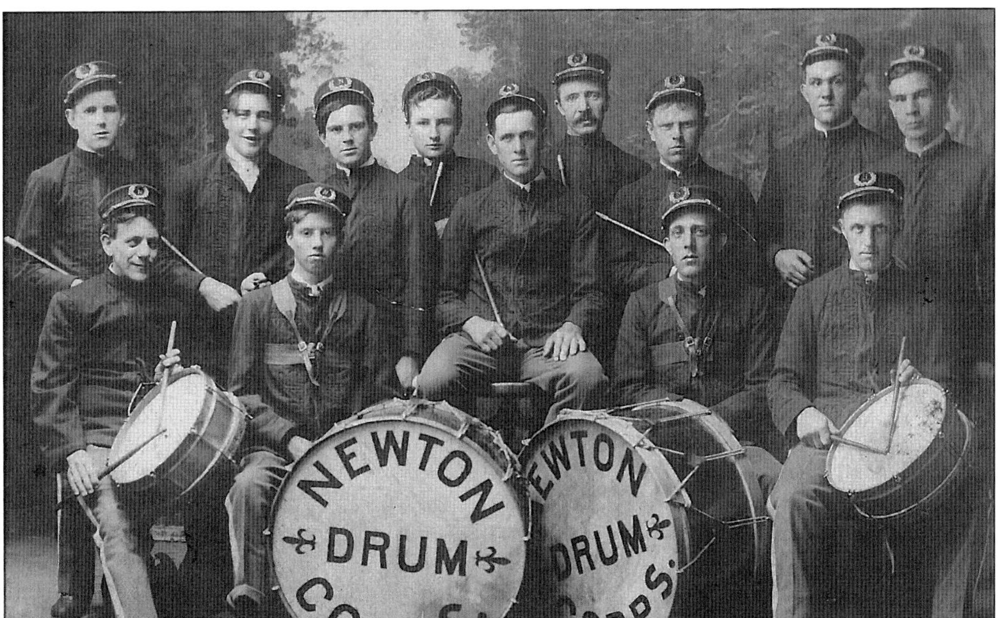

The Newton Drum Corps were an essential feature of parades and special events. Many of the members were also members of the local volunteer fire departments.

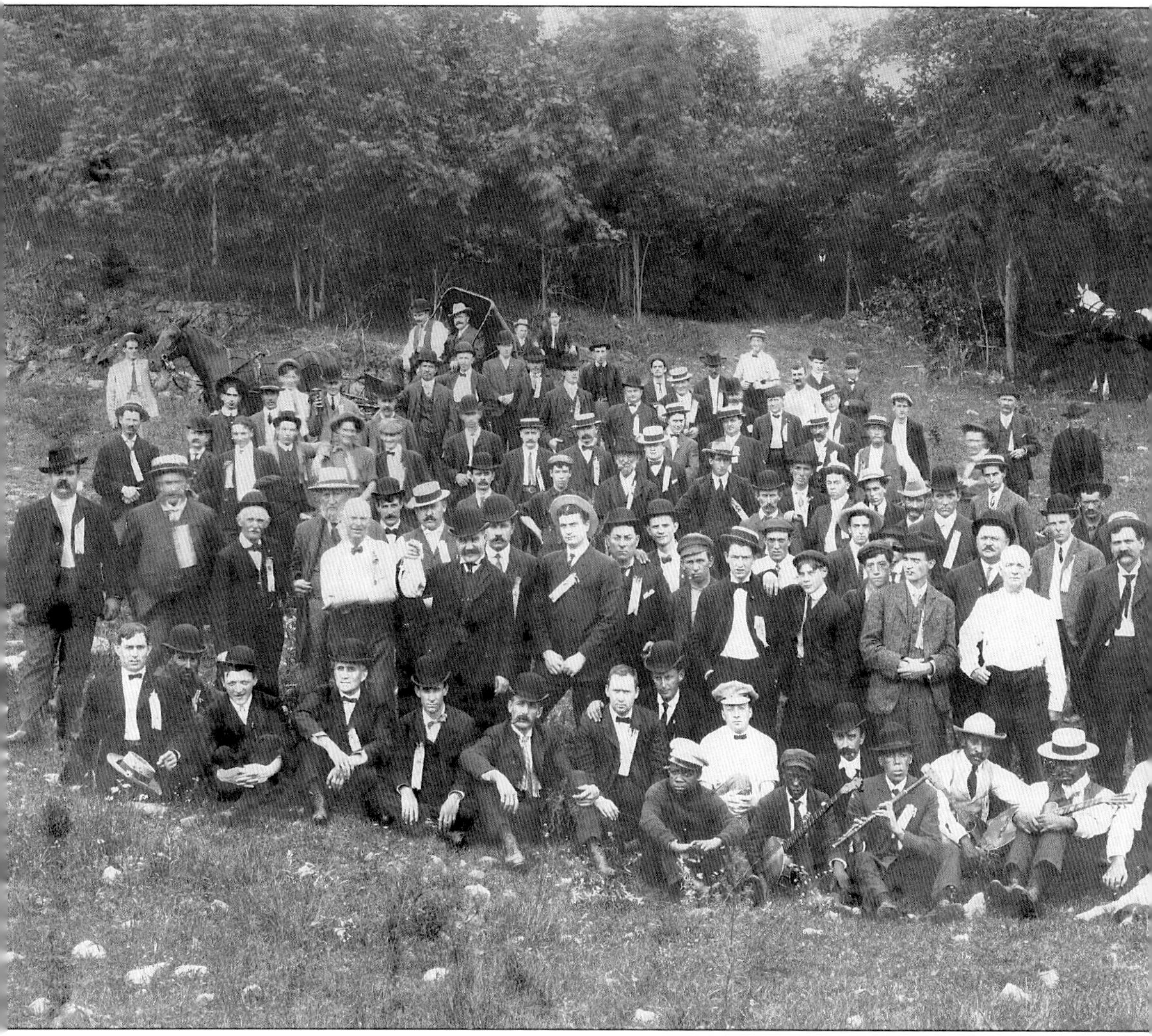

At the turn of the century, Newton's factory owners and the large social organizations often sponsored picnics and clambakes. This photograph shows the employees of the Merriam Shoe Company gathered for their annual clambake. Even at this festive event on a hot summer day, most of the men have retained their hats, coats, and ties—at least for the photograph.

Eight

FIRE COMPANIES

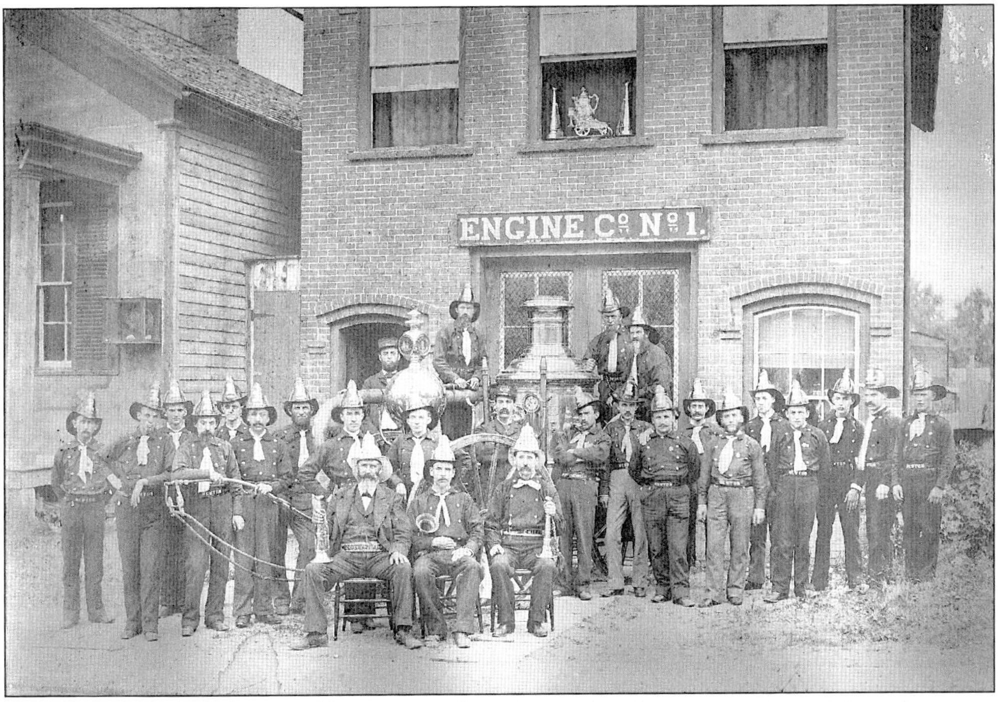

As Newton grew from a small country village into a bustling town, the residents began to feel the need for an organized firefighting service. The first fire company was formed in 1836, using a second-hand crank engine purchased by the town. Several companies were formed, and a firehouse was built on High Street in 1866. The following year the companies disbanded, abandoned their equipment, and left the town without organized protection. However, in 1873 a disastrous fire destroyed many buildings on Spring Street. A steamer from Hoboken responded to the call for aid. It so impressed the citizens that they immediately formed the Newton Steamer Company. In this picture, taken about 1875, the members of the Steamer Comapny pose with their equipment in front of the High Street firehouse. (Newton Fire Museum.)

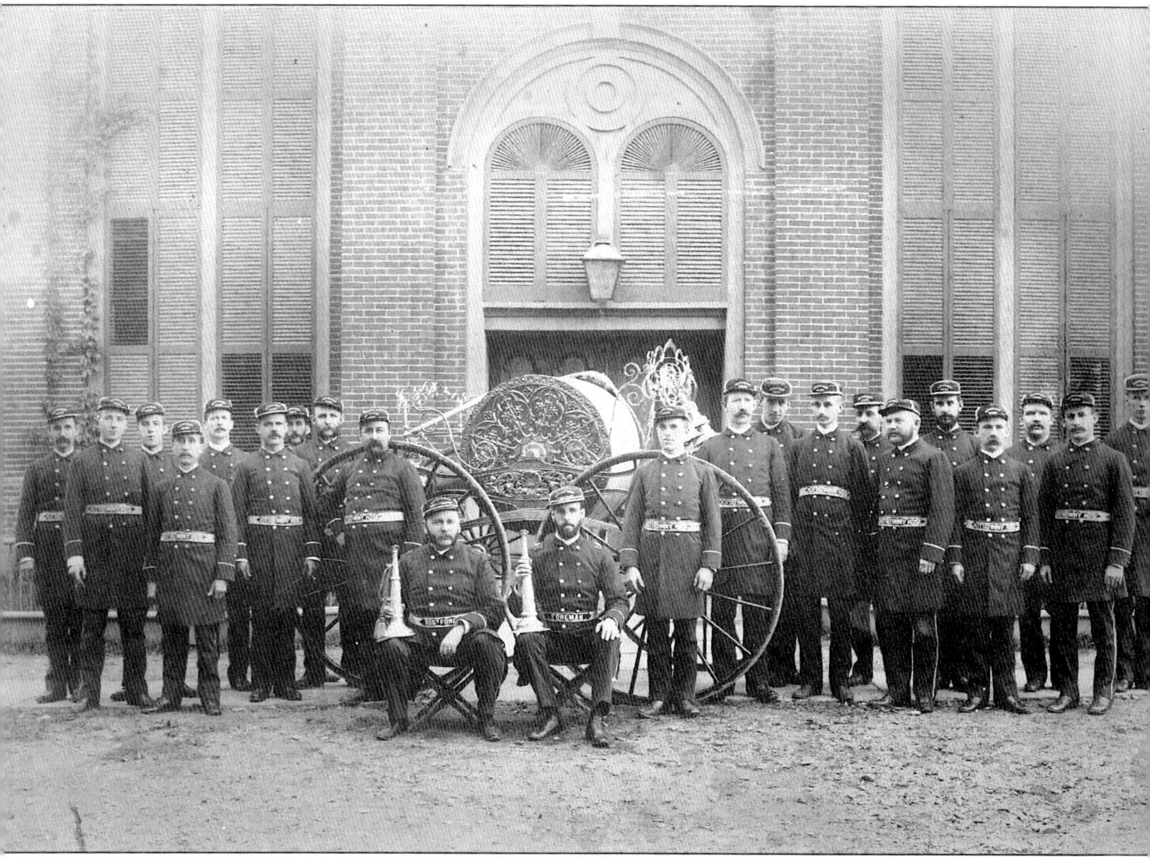

The Kittatinny Hose Company was founded as an offshoot of the Newton Steamer Company in 1879. Prior to that, the members had been "nozzle men" for the Steamer Company. In the 1880s the members of the Hose Company posed in front of the Methodist church on Park Place, just around the corner from the firehouse on High Street. The lacy brass ornamentation on the hose cart seems almost out of place in the tough and dirty context of firefighting.

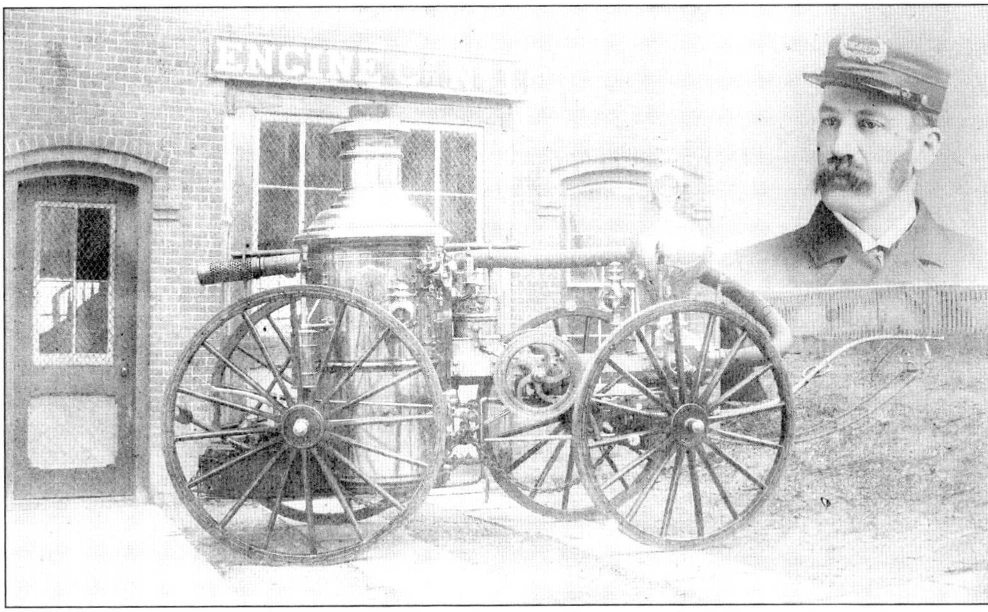

Charles Steele, the engineer of the Newton Steamer Company, had these cabinet photographs made of the company's engine with his own picture inserted into the upper corner. He was an influential member of the company and of Newton's business community for several decades.

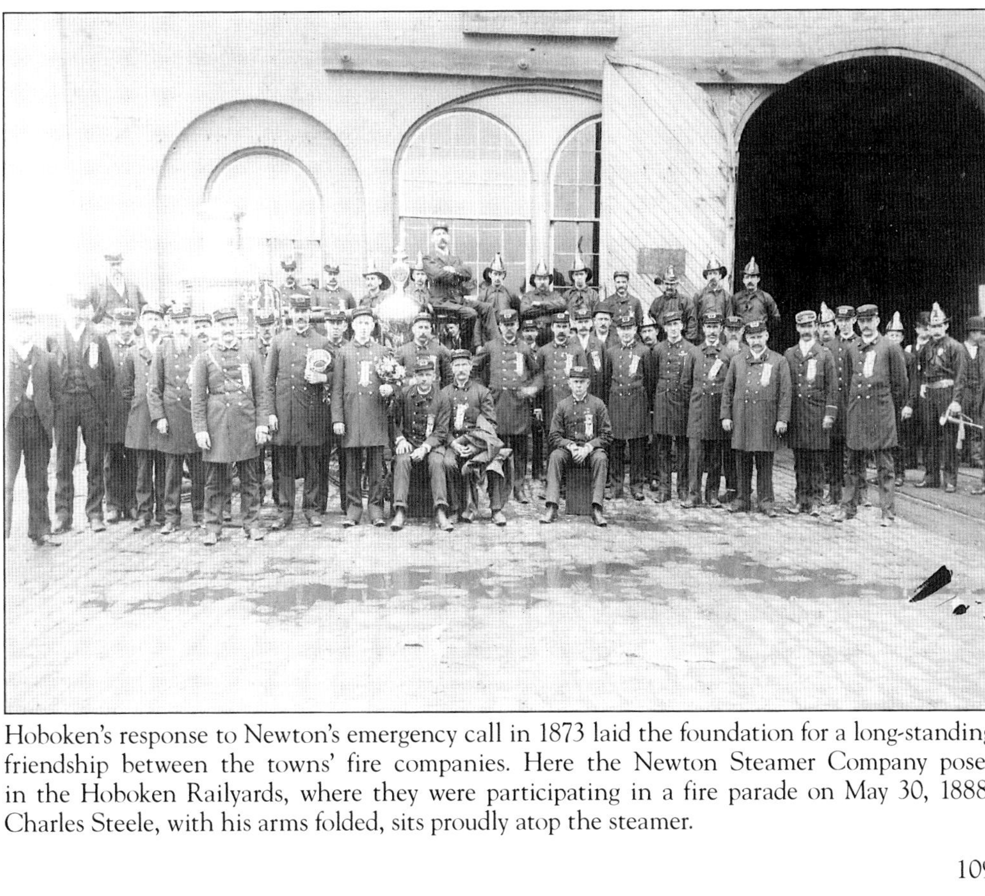

Hoboken's response to Newton's emergency call in 1873 laid the foundation for a long-standing friendship between the towns' fire companies. Here the Newton Steamer Company poses in the Hoboken Railyards, where they were participating in a fire parade on May 30, 1888. Charles Steele, with his arms folded, sits proudly atop the steamer.

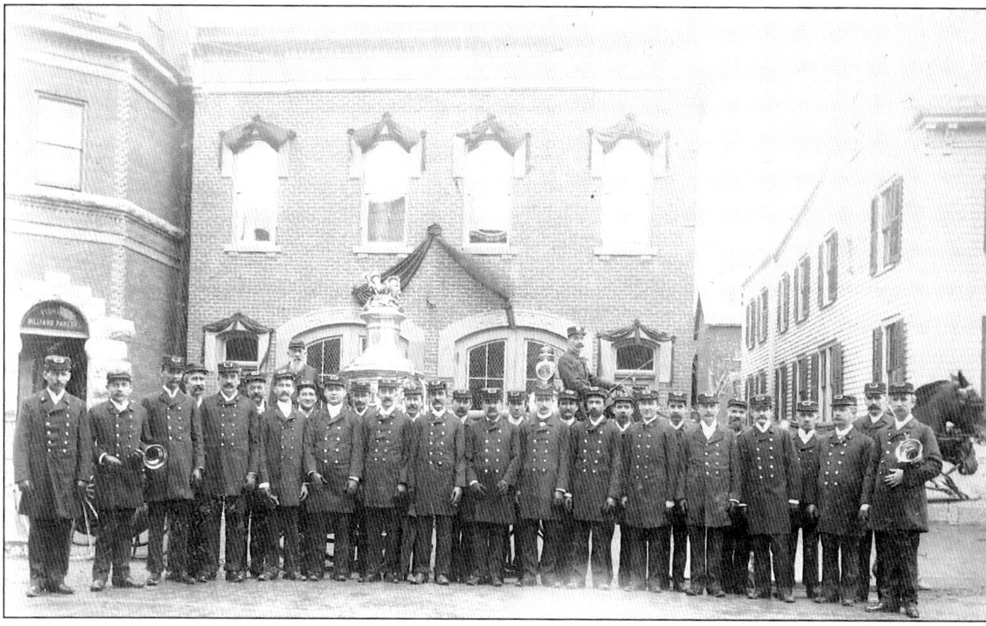

In 1891, the Town of Newton built a new firehouse on Spring Street for the steamer and hose companies. Here the members of the Newton Steamer Company pose in front of the new firehouse, which is draped in black to commemorate the death of a fireman. To the left of the firehouse is Dan Fisher's Billiard Parlor, located in the Cortelyou building. Dan Fisher was himself a fireman, and became chief of Hose Company 3 on Diller Avenue in 1903.

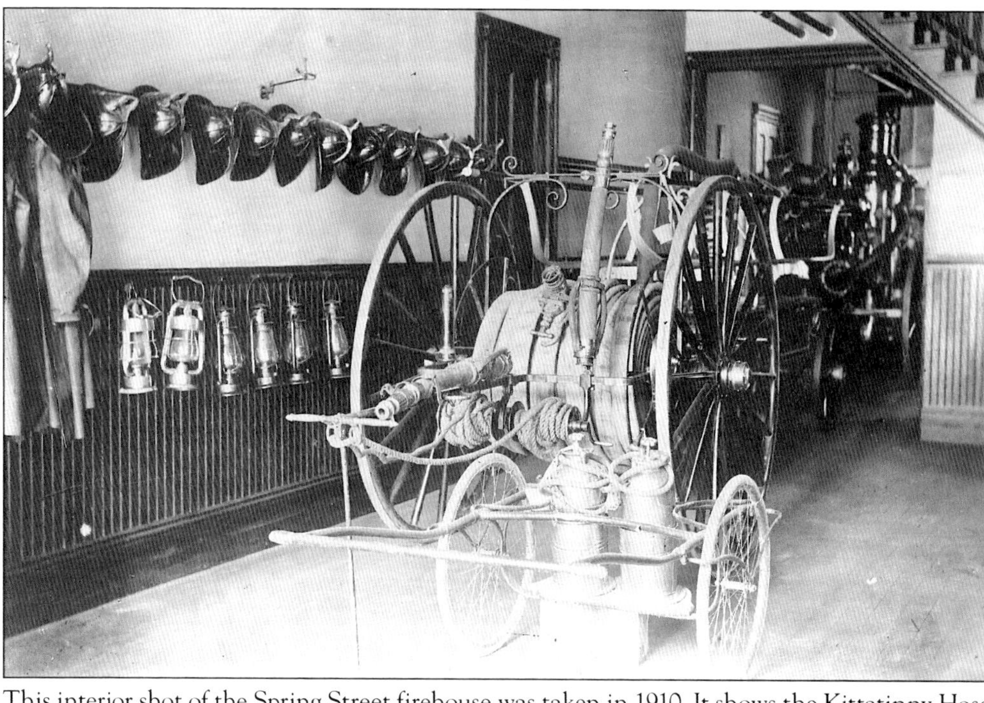

This interior shot of the Spring Street firehouse was taken in 1910. It shows the Kittatinny Hose Company's hose cart, with a little chemical jumper resting on a block in front of it. (Courtesy of the Newton Fire Museum.)

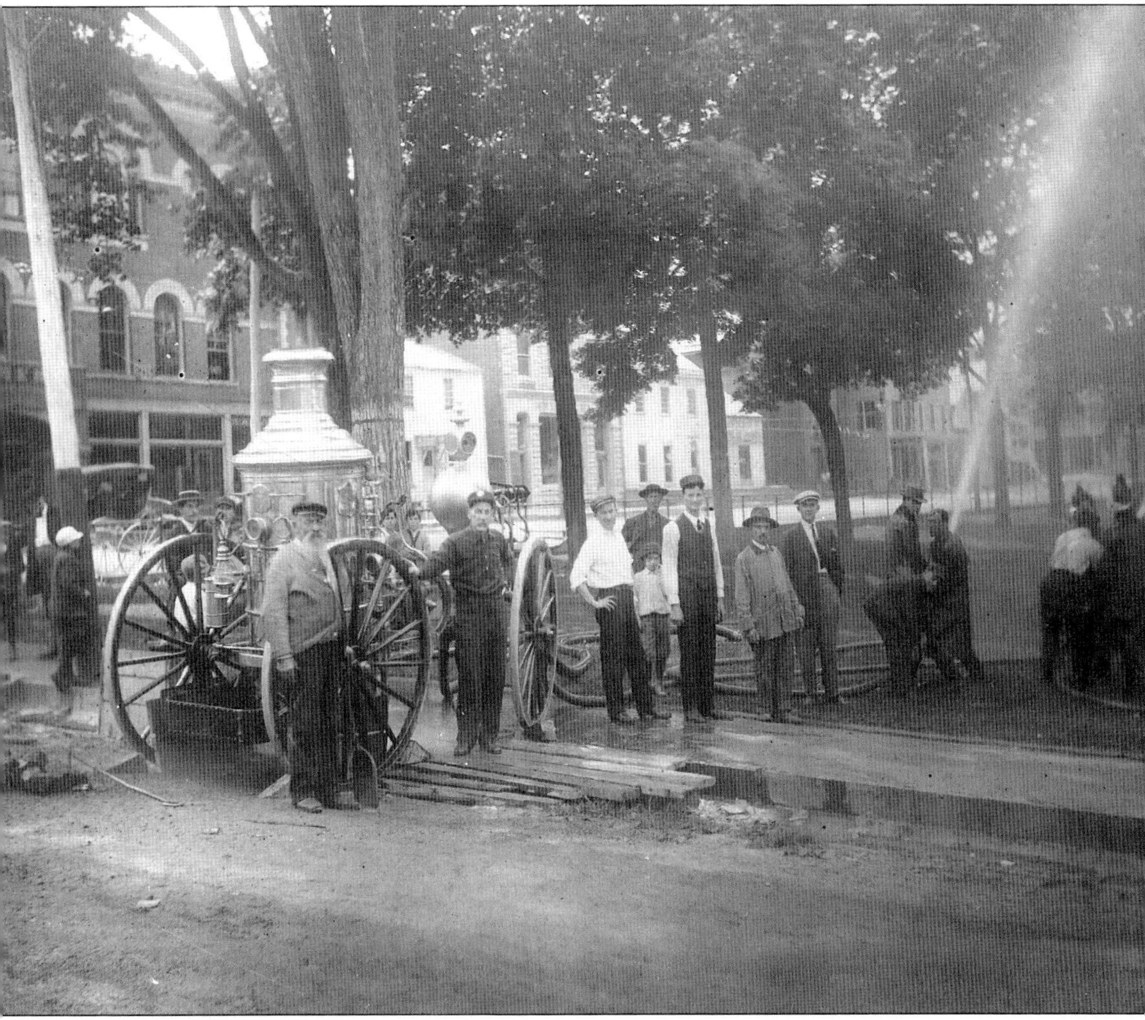

Members of the Newton Steamer Company demonstrate their equipment in the square in this 1910 photograph. The steamer is drawing water from one of two cisterns in the park that were fed by roof drains from nearby buildings and churches. Standing with his hand on the wheel of the steamer is Charles Steele, the chief engineer, who was prominent in local affairs for many years.

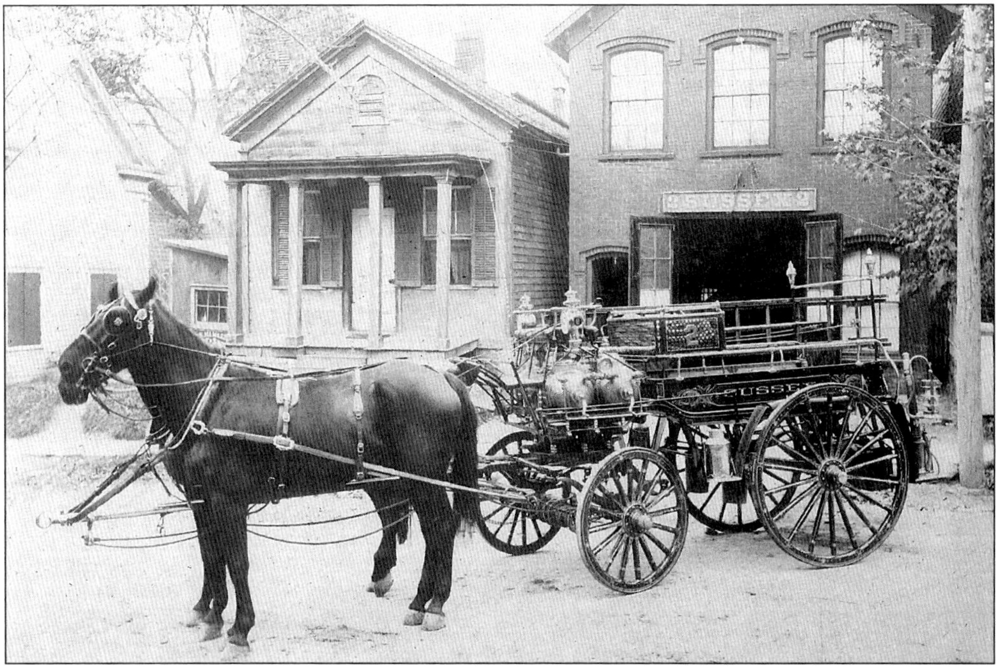

In 1892, the Sussex Engine Company No. 2 was formed, taking over the High Street firehouse recently vacated by the Newton Steamer Company (now No. 1) and the Kittatinny Hose Company. Rather than purchase new equipment, this company began by refurbishing a piano engine that had been abandoned in the firehouse in 1867 when an earlier fire company disbanded.

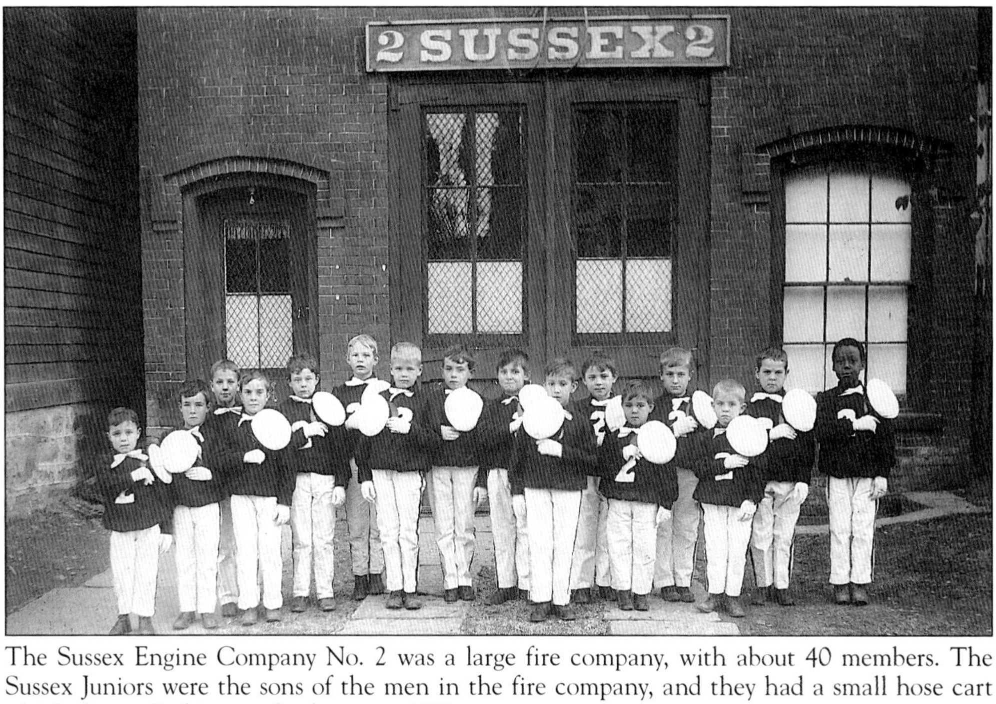

The Sussex Engine Company No. 2 was a large fire company, with about 40 members. The Sussex Juniors were the sons of the men in the fire company, and they had a small hose cart which they pulled in parades (see page 100).

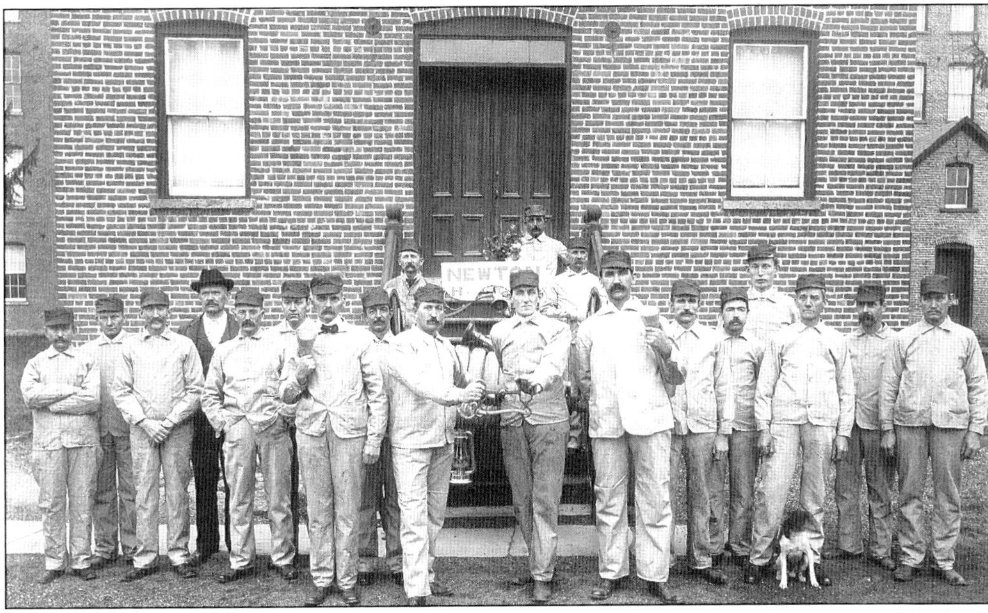

In 1900, men working at the Merriam Shoe Factory together with others in the neighborhood decided that the east side of town needed its own Fire Company, so they formed the Hose Company 3. The town provided them with a hose and hose carrier, and the Shoe Factory provided them with a building to house their equipment. Soon after the Company's founding, the members posed for this photograph.

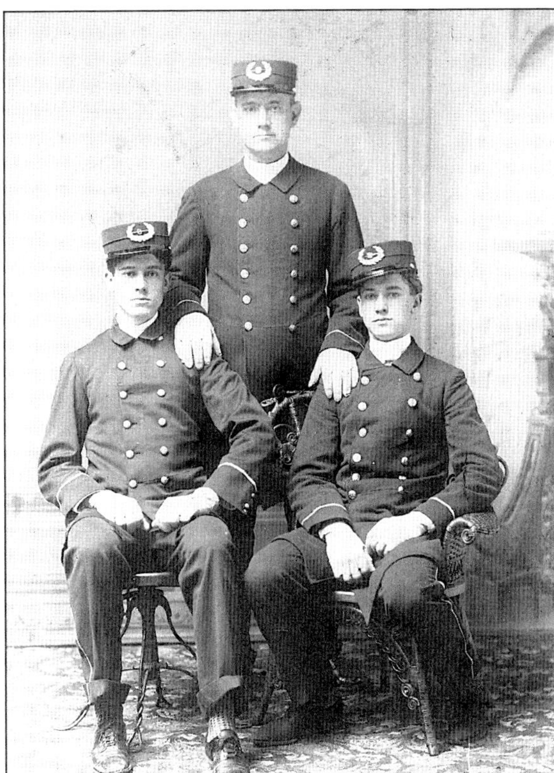

Nineteen-year-old Sanford Smith, his sixteen-year-old brother Raymond, and Robert Hamilton, all members of Hose Company No. 3, pose in their new uniforms. (Courtesy of the Newton Fire Museum.)

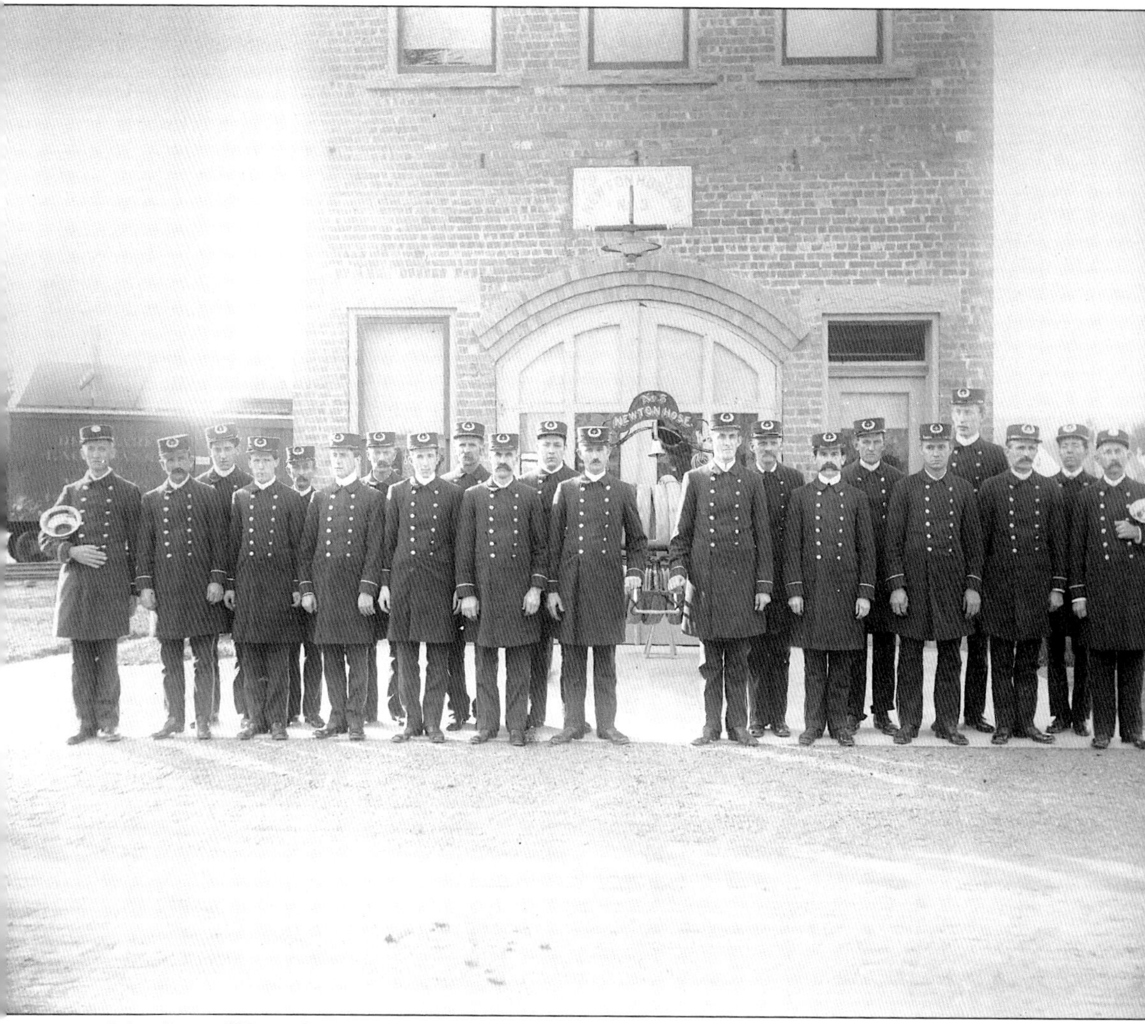

Members of Hose Company No. 3 pose proudly in front of their new firehouse on Diller Avenue. The firehouse was built in 1903. Just behind it, you can see boxcars standing on the main line of the Delaware & Lackawanna Railroad into Newton. (Courtesy of the Newton Fire Museum.)

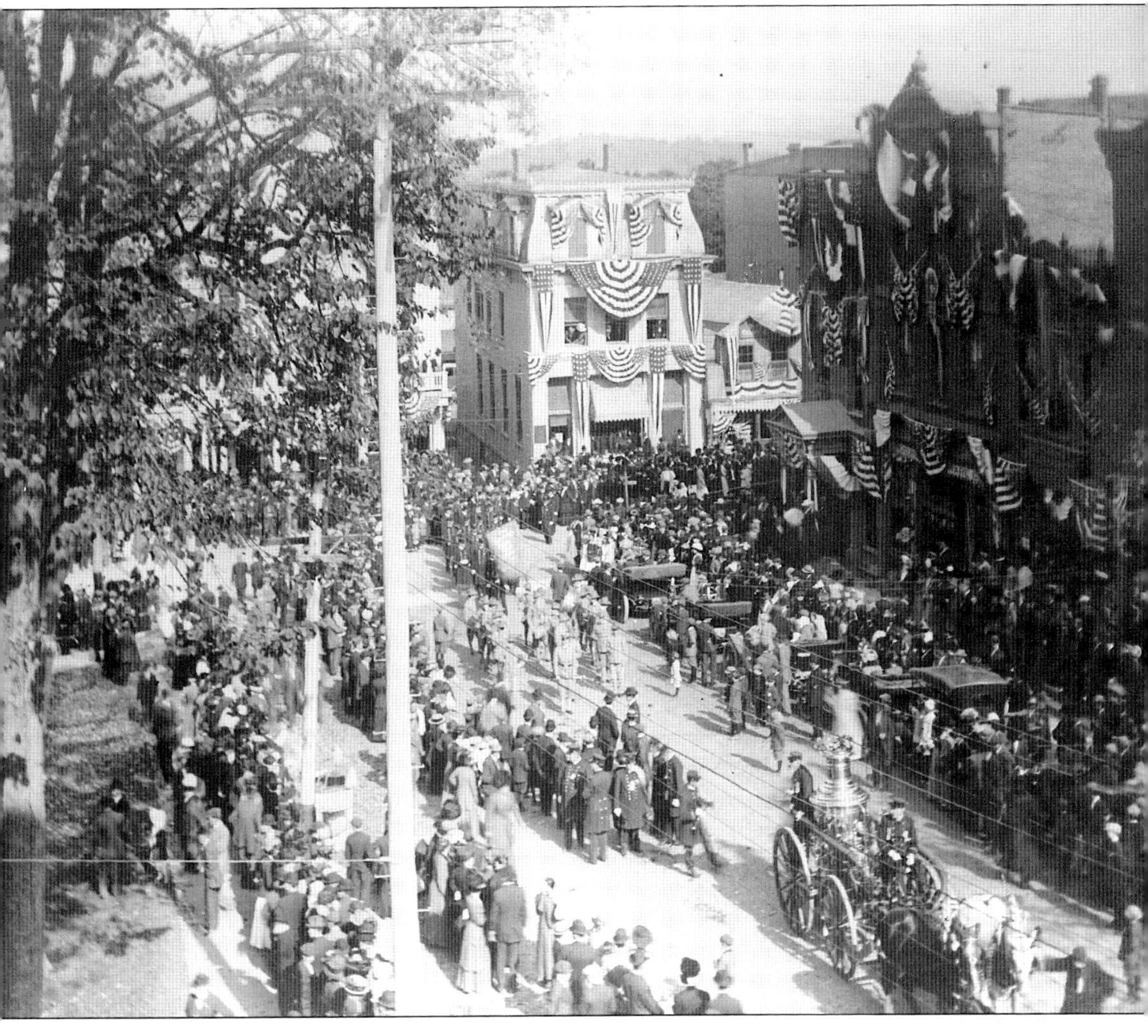

In addition to their essential work fighting fires, firemen and their equipment were (and still are) an indispensable feature of parades and civic festivities. Here Newton's firemen can be seen parading up Main Street, probably as part of the Hero's Day celebrations in 1919.

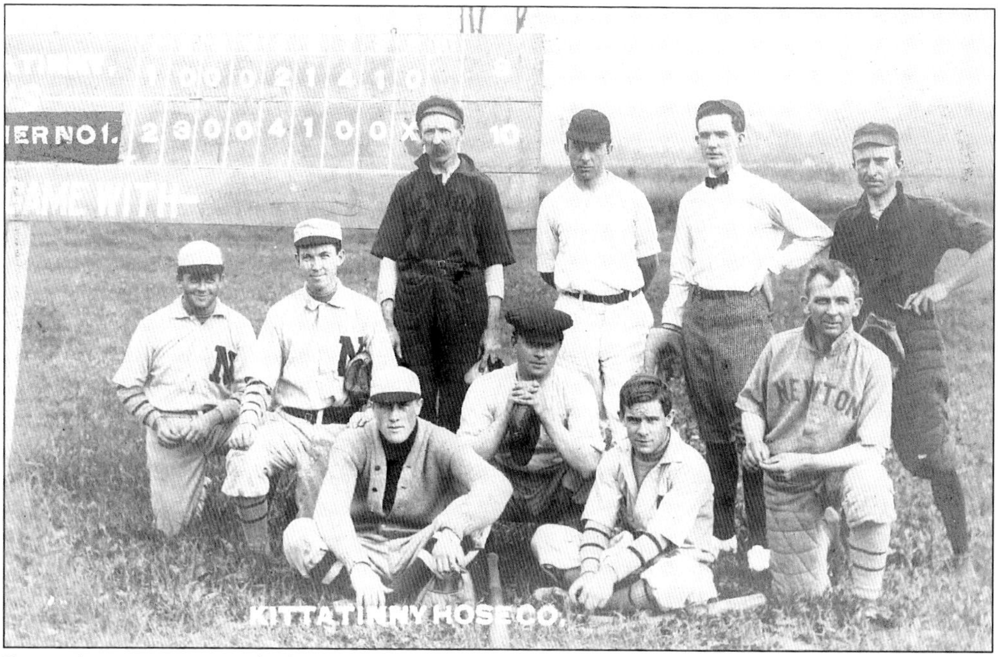

Esprit de corp was very high among the various fire companies. They even formed their own baseball teams in the Newton Branch of the Sussex County Baseball League and competed on a county-wide basis. This postcard commemorates a game between the Kittatinny Hose Company and the Newton Steamer Company No. 1 about 1910. The Steamers won with a score of 10 to 9.

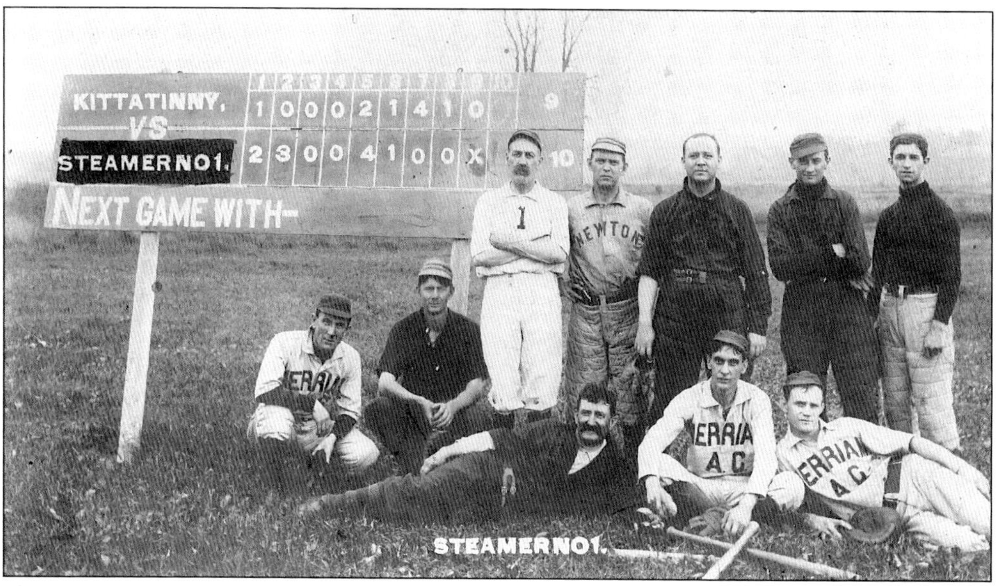

Shown here are the victorious Steamers. Pictured from left to right are: (front row) Jack McCluskey, Rube Shenkey, and Wm. Compton; (back row) Ed Hall, Cliff Lane, Charles Steele, Pete Burhardt, Harry Resh, Cliff Sutton, and Edward McLane.

Nine

PEOPLE

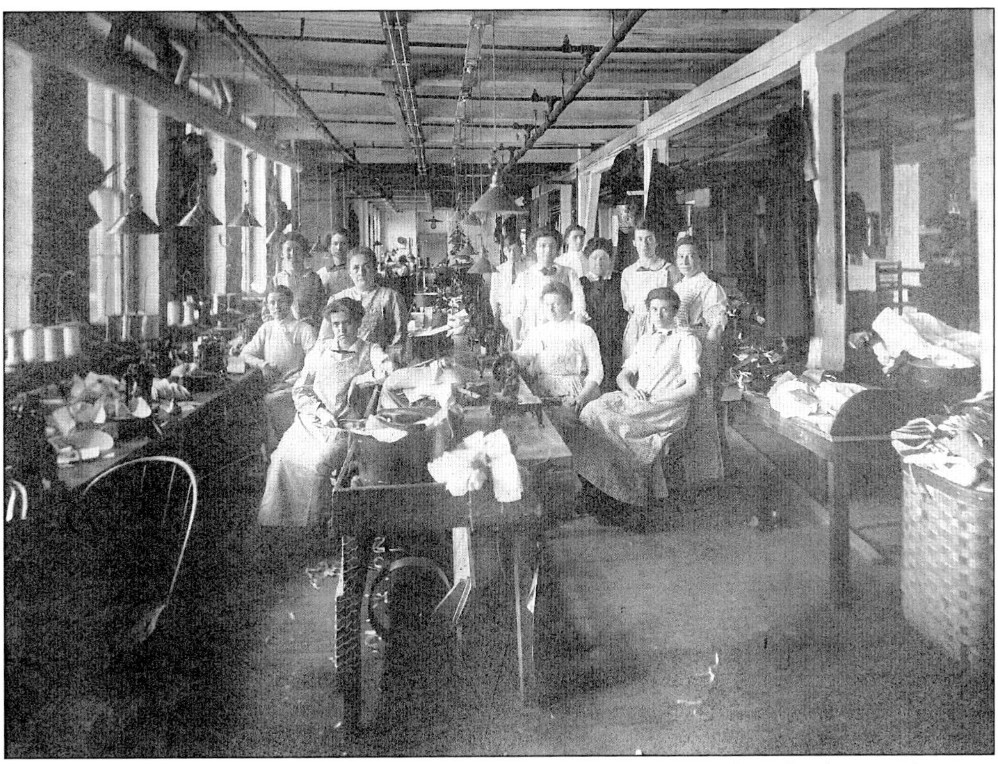

Without its people, the town of Newton would not be the place it is today. Shopkeepers, lawyers, factory workers, photographers, housewives, railroad men, farmers, doctors, and laborers all contributed to the unique character of the town. Here we see women working in one of Newton's many factories. They seem to be engaged in producing linings for shoes in one of the town's two shoe factories. (Courtesy of the Newton Fire Museum.)

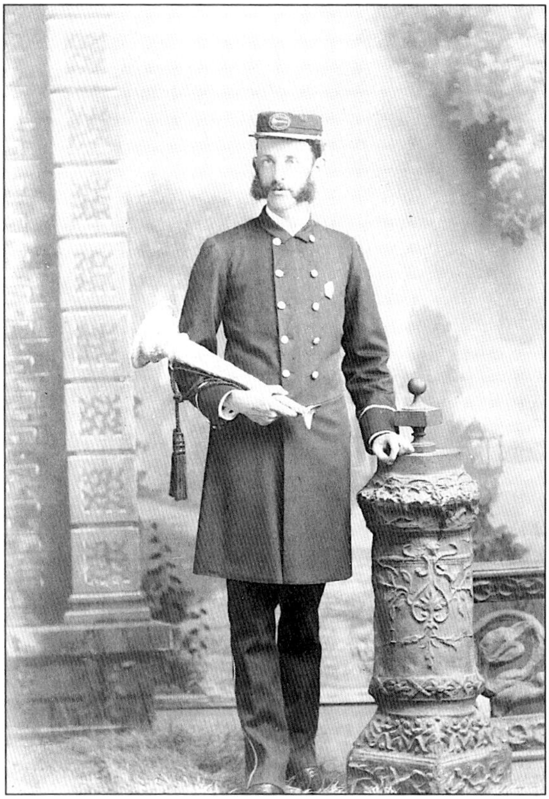

Lewis Morford, photographed in the 1880s wearing the uniform of the Kittatinny Hose Company, was an officer of the Sussex National Bank.

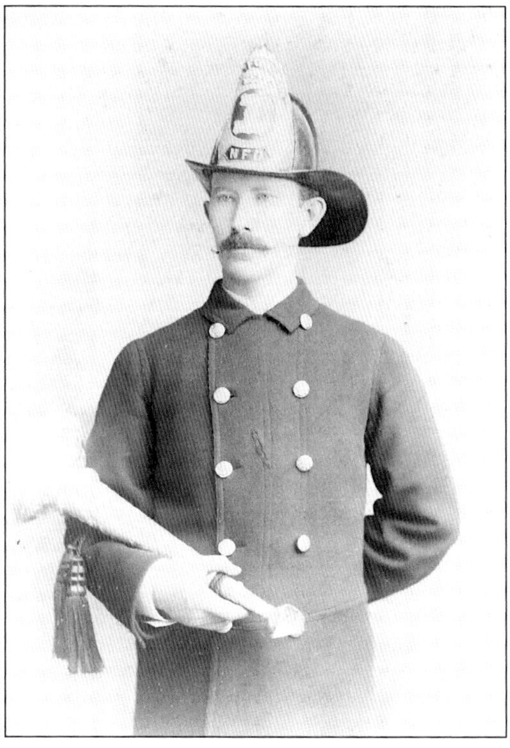

William Earl was the assistant foreman of the Hose Company, prior to its separation from the Newton Steamer Company. He was also the proprietor of Earl's Hotel on Spring Street and operated a soda bottling firm.

Charles Steele, who appears in so many photographs of the Newton Steamer Company, was in private life the chief cashier of the Sussex National Bank. In fact, he can be seen behind the teller's cage on page 31. He also served on many town committees.

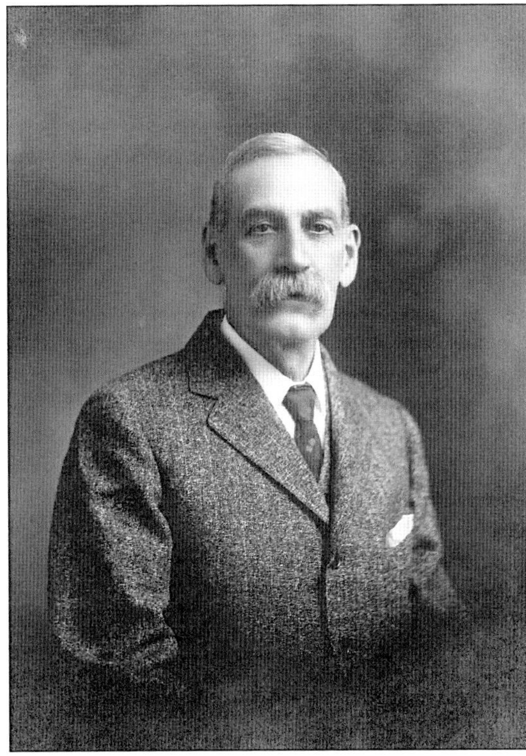

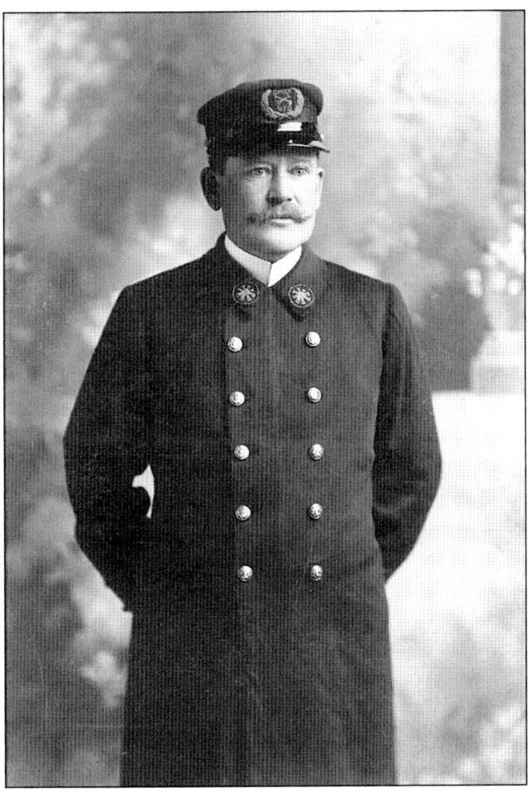

James Baldwin, chief of the Sussex Engine Company No. 2, was actually Newton's postmaster at the turn of the century.

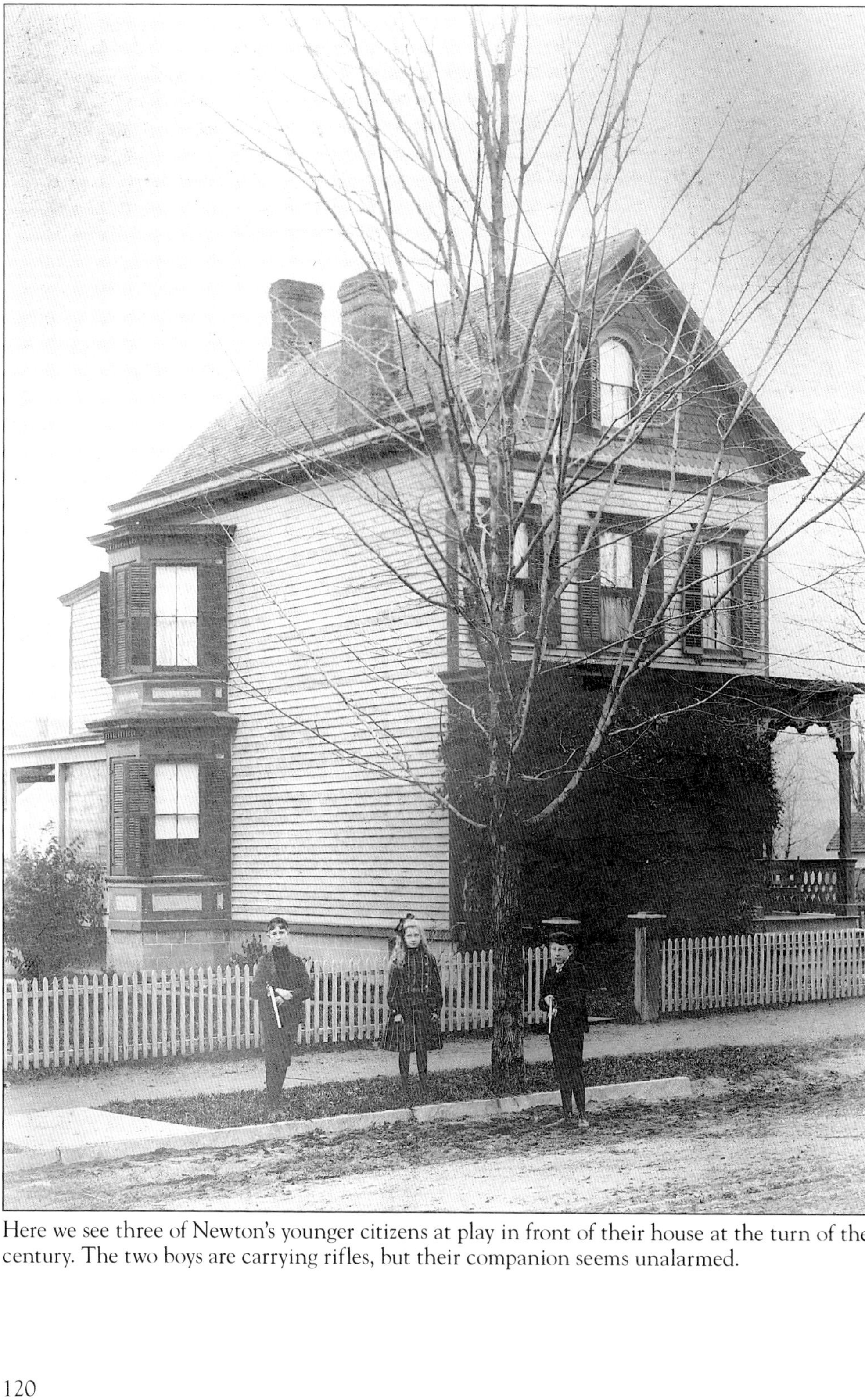

Here we see three of Newton's younger citizens at play in front of their house at the turn of the century. The two boys are carrying rifles, but their companion seems unalarmed.

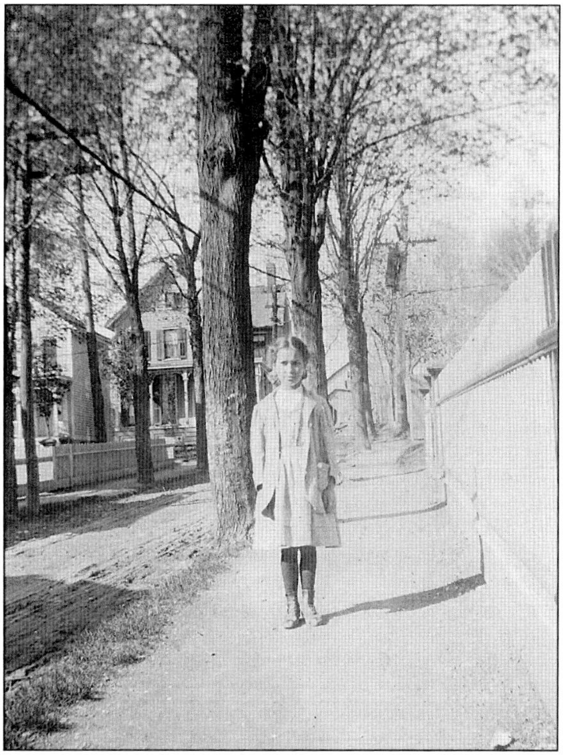

Eight-year-old Elsa Armstrong stands on the sidewalk on one of Newton's quiet residential streets.

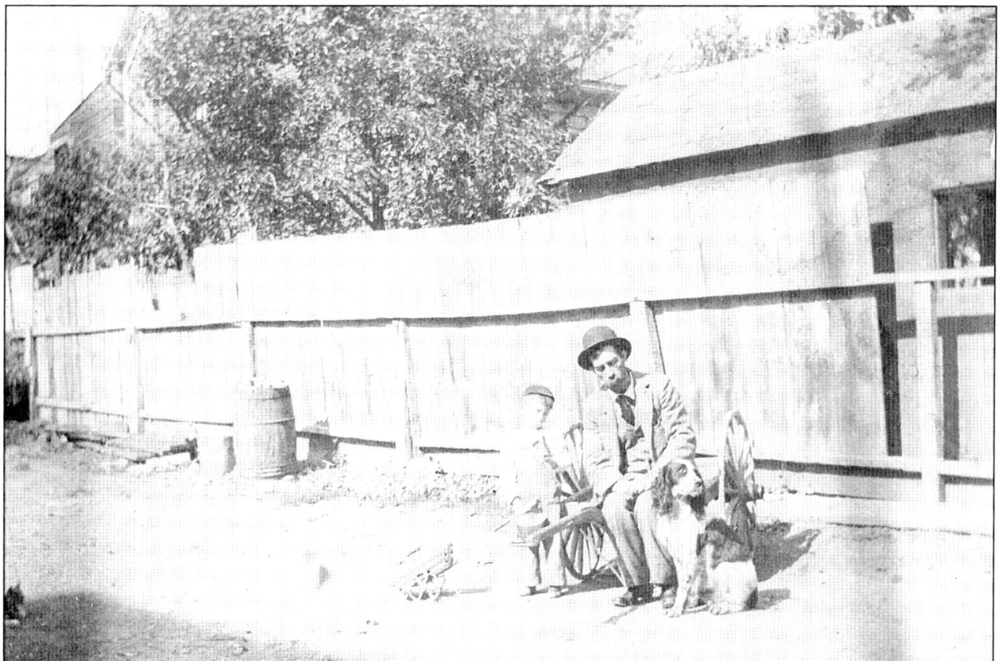

A man, a boy, and a dog rest in one of Newton's back alleys on a lazy summer afternoon. Most of Newton's alleys are gone, either widened into streets or incorporated into the backyards of the surrounding properties.

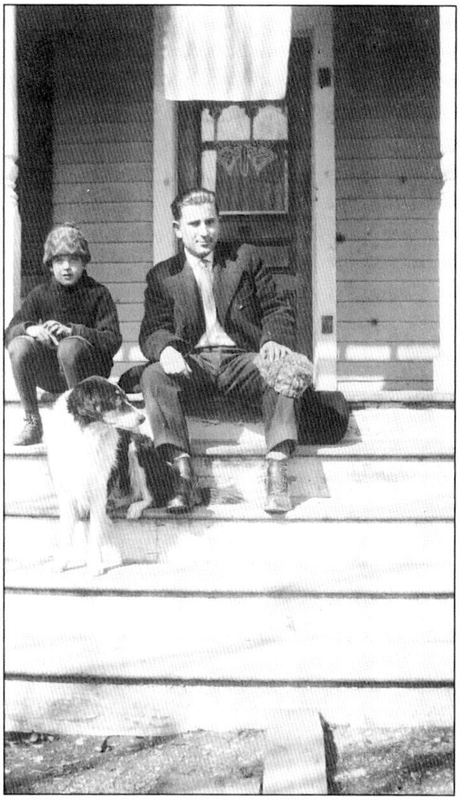

Charles Amn and Joseph Savonia pose on the front porch of their Sparta Avenue home in February 1918.

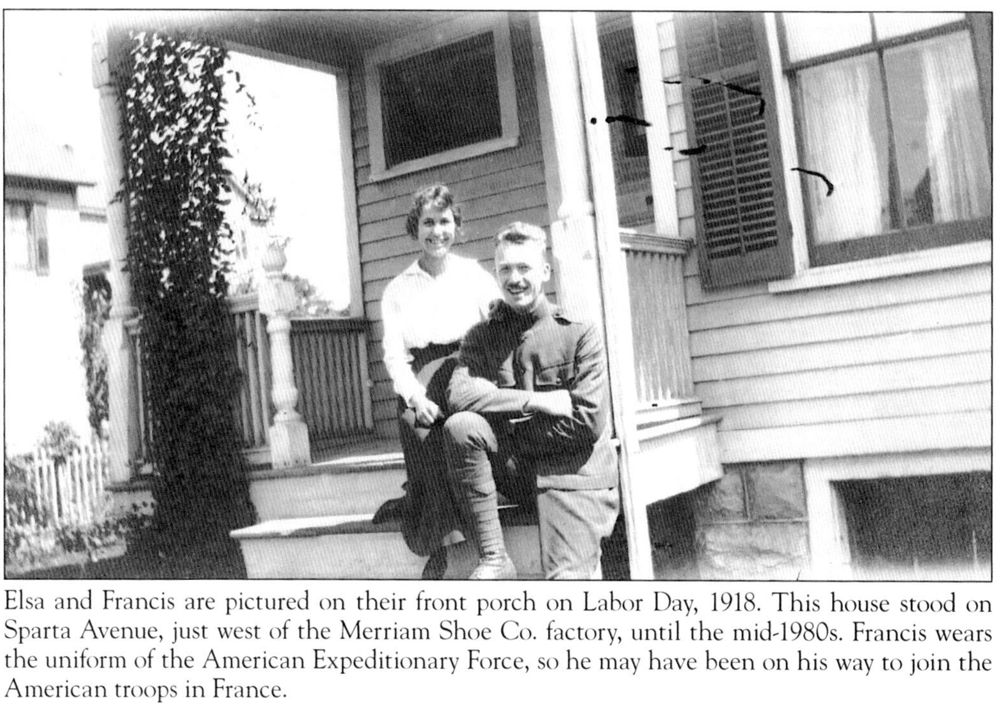

Elsa and Francis are pictured on their front porch on Labor Day, 1918. This house stood on Sparta Avenue, just west of the Merriam Shoe Co. factory, until the mid-1980s. Francis wears the uniform of the American Expeditionary Force, so he may have been on his way to join the American troops in France.

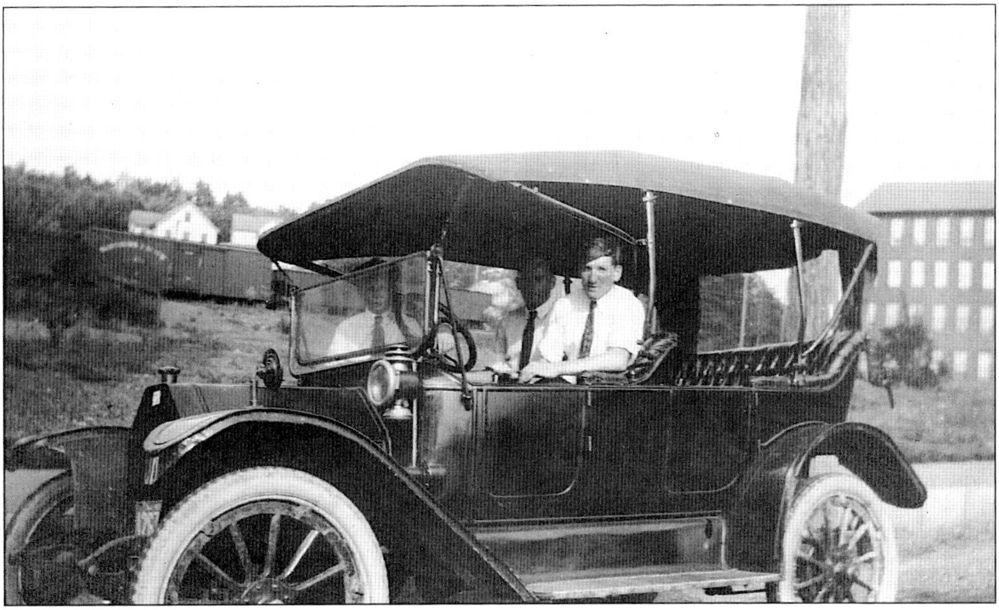

Robert Paterson, Mr. Easton, and Mr. Brown are photographed in their automobile near the Merriam Shoe Co. factory in July 1919.

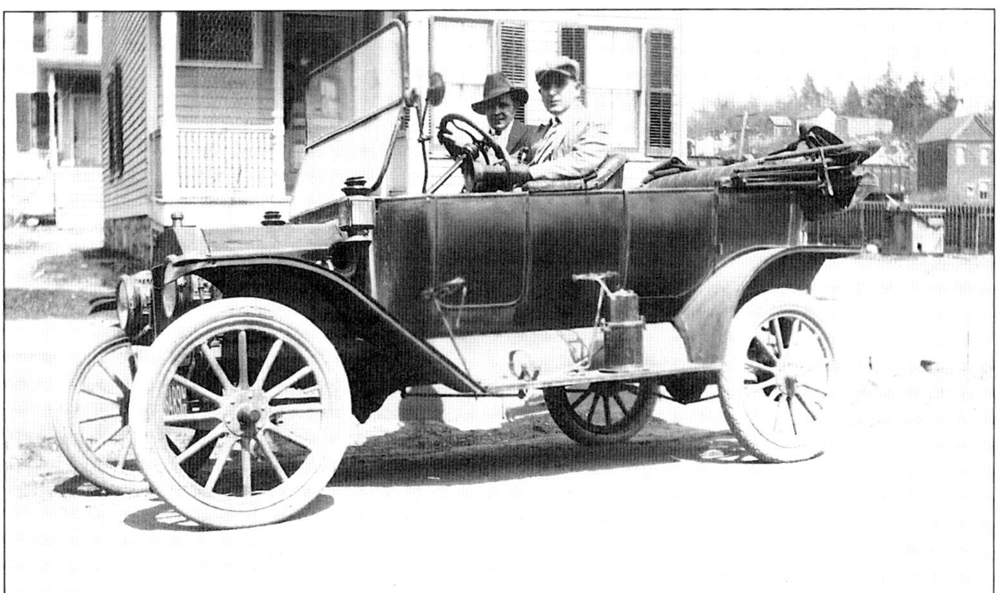

The back of this picture was inscribed "showing off the new set of wheels on Sparta Avenue in 1917." It was at this time that cars began to be available to the average American.

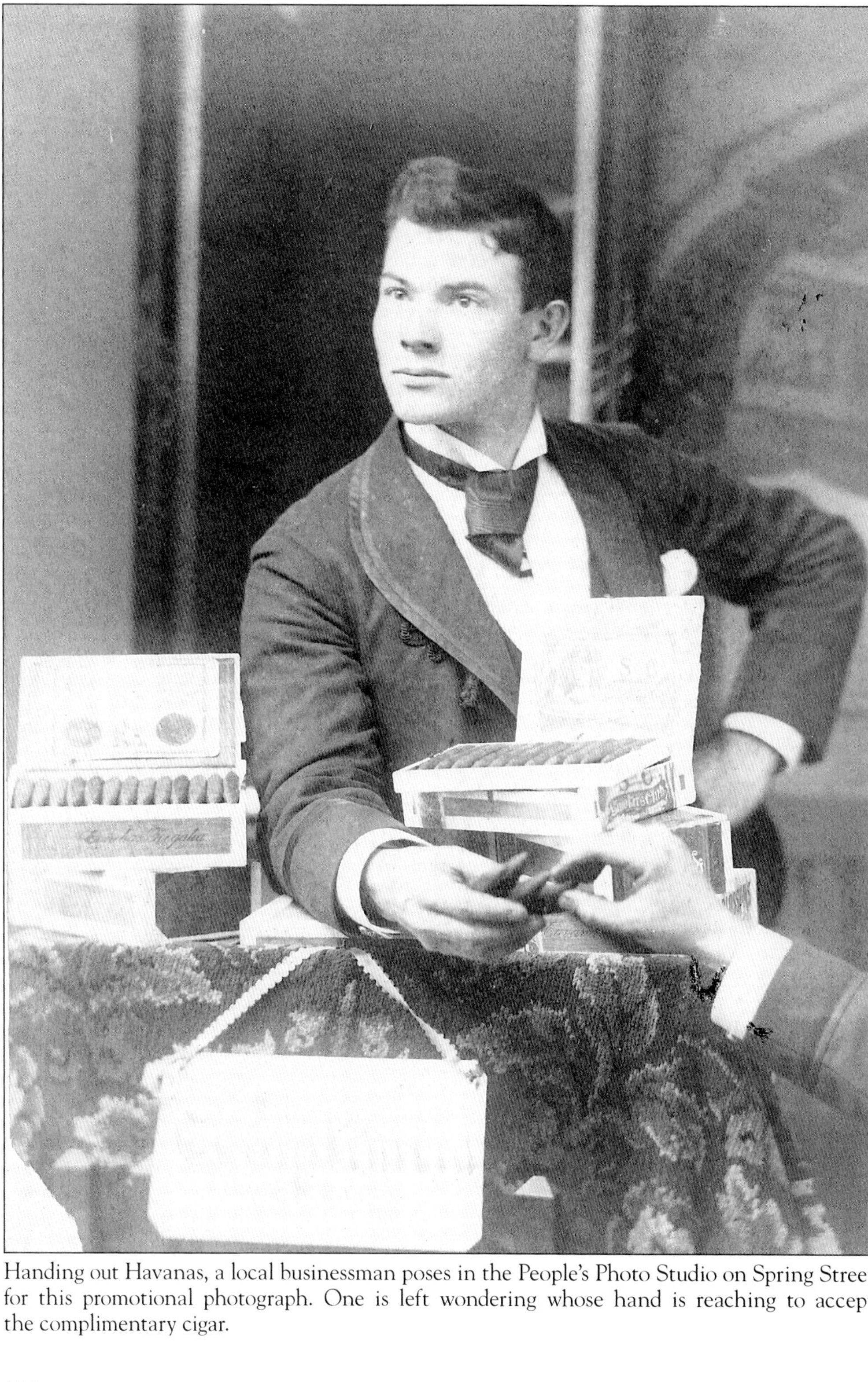

Handing out Havanas, a local businessman poses in the People's Photo Studio on Spring Street for this promotional photograph. One is left wondering whose hand is reaching to accept the complimentary cigar.

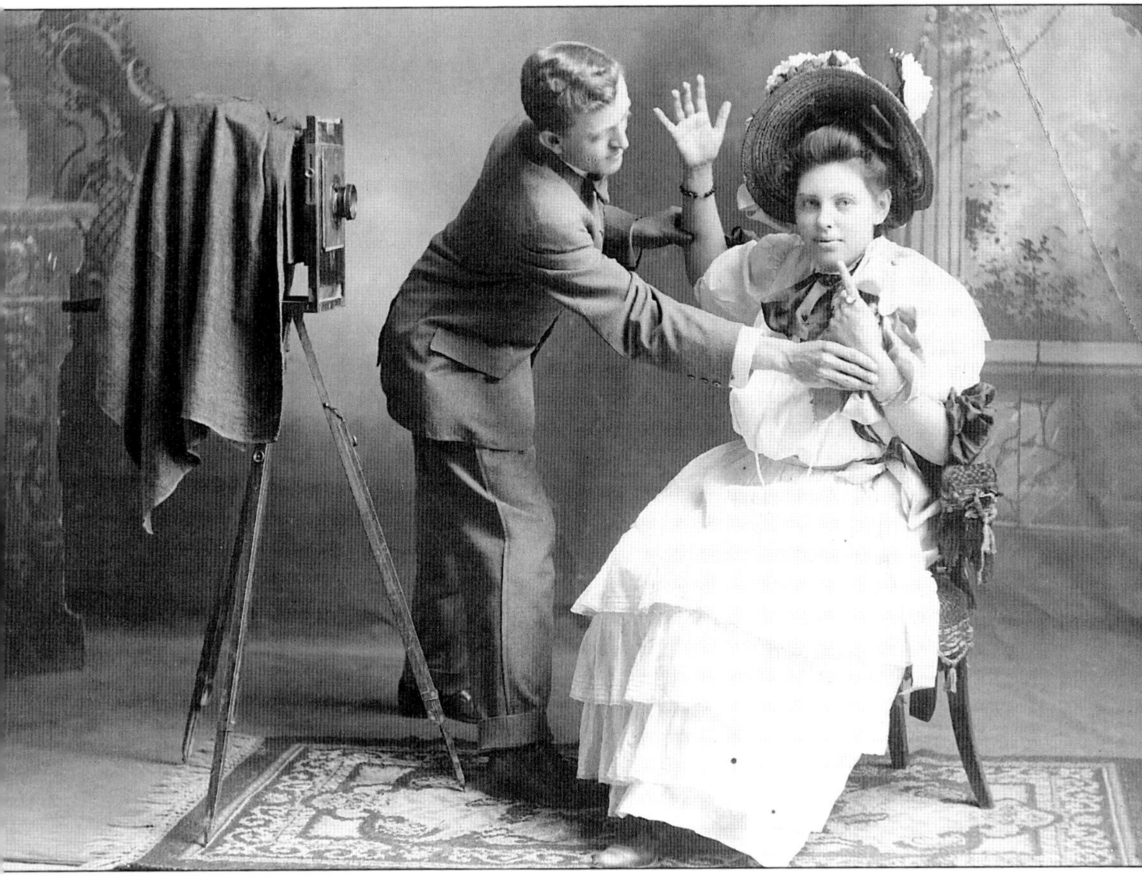

Clowning before the camera, this young couple was photographed at J.T. Jackson's studio on Spring Street at the turn of the century.

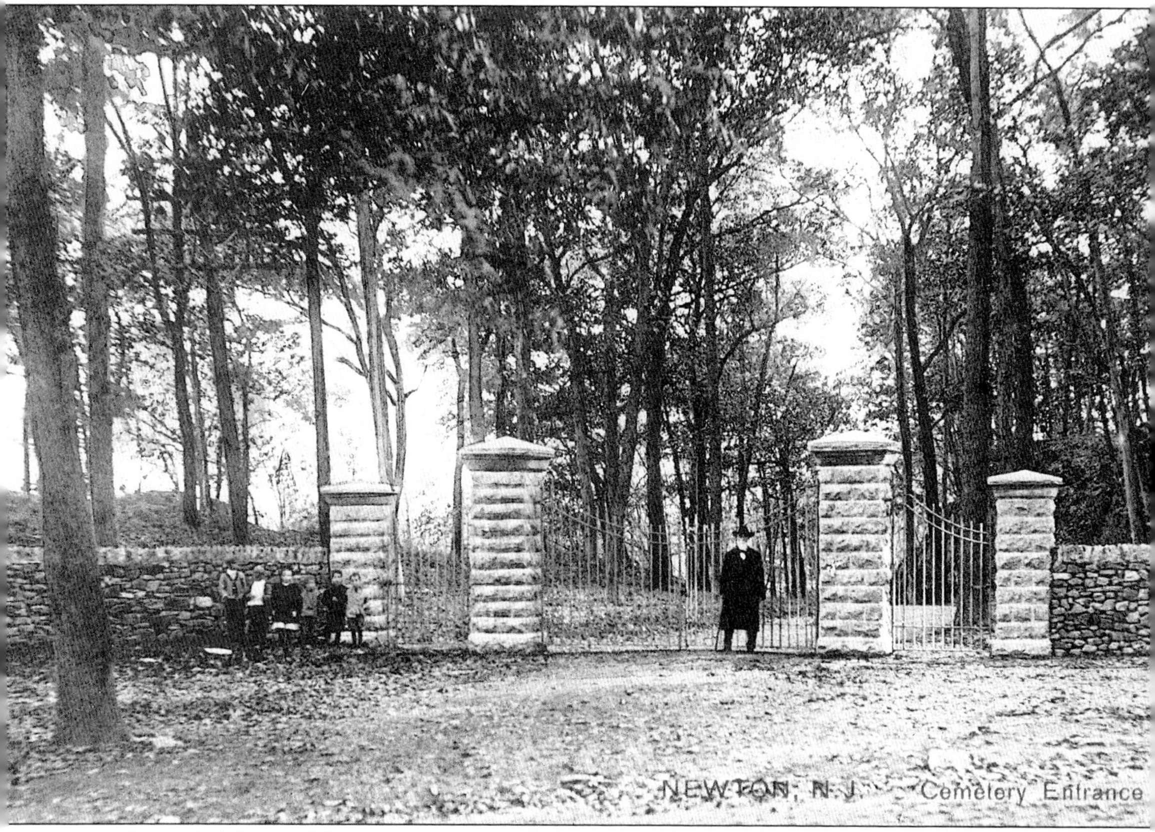

The end of the road for many residents of Newton was here at the gates to the Woodside Avenue Cemetery. This postcard shows the old formal gates on Halstead Street, at the top of the hill. This cemetery was established by the Newton Cemetery Association in 1865, because the old Newton Burial Ground behind Main Street was full.